# Teaching the Young Child with Motor Delays

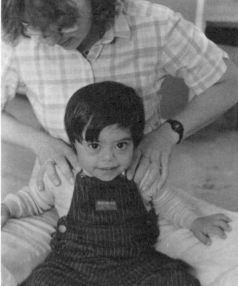

# Teaching

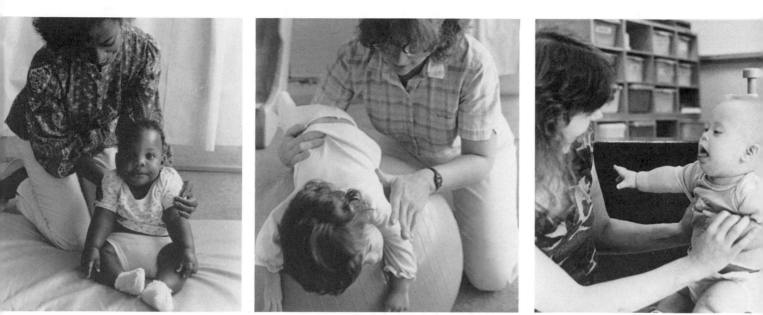

# the Young Child
# with Motor Delays

## A GUIDE FOR PARENTS AND PROFESSIONALS

**Marci J. Hanson, PhD**
Professor
Early Childhood Special Education
San Francisco State University

**Susan R. Harris, PhD, PT**
Associate Professor and Program Coordinator
Physical Therapy Educational Programs
University of Wisconsin–Madison

**pro-ed**
An International Publisher

8700 Shoal Creek Boulevard
Austin, Texas 78757

Printed in the United States of America

**Library of Congress Cataloging-in-Publication Data**
Hanson, Marci J.
   Teaching the young child with motor delays.

   Bibliography: p.
   1. Movement disorders in children.   2. Movement
disorders in children—Treatment.   I. Harris, Susan R.
II. Title.
RJ480.H36   1986   618.927406   85–25827
ISBN 0–936104–91–0

8700 Shoal Creek Boulevard
Austin, Texas 78757


6  7  8  9  10          97

# Contents

# Preface

*Teaching the Young Child with Motor Delays* is designed for parents of children with movement difficulties and for professionals who work with these children and their parents. The book is not meant to replace the more direct and intensive services of physical or occupational therapists or staff members of early intervention programs. Rather, it is designed to facilitate the communication between parents and professionals and to help parents obtain the services and training that enable them to meet the child's individual needs.

The book has two main purposes: (1) to answer basic questions about motor disabilities and suggest sources of additional information and assistance; and (2) to offer basic teaching and handling strategies that can be used in daily activities to help overcome a child's motor problems.

Part I provides general information for parents about delays in motor development and intervention approaches. Chapter 1 consists of the experiences of parents of young children with motor delays. These personal accounts discuss parenting a child with motor impairments and the rewards of taking an active role in the child's development. Chapter 2, written by Peter Blasco, MD, presents the medical aspects of the major types of motor disabilities—their causes, their characteristics, and the concerns often associated with these conditions. Chapter 3 illustrates the range of issues that families of children with motor disabilities encounter and the various types of early intervention services required by these children. Four case studies are presented, including the complete individualized education program for one child. Chapter 4 discusses the role of parent-infant interaction in the teaching and learning process. General teaching strategies and techniques are also included. Chapter 5 explains how to develop teaching goals and organize teaching activities that meet the child's individual needs. This approach forms the basis of the more specific activities described in Part II of the book. The chapter contains simple practice exercises to give parents more familiarity with this approach. Chapter 6 presents a system for observing and recording the child's progress in learning. A sample recording sheet and the developmental charts are included in this chapter.

Part II consists of specific teaching and therapy activities. Chapter 7 discusses preparatory activities and positioning and handling techniques that will make movement easier for the child with motor impairments. Adaptive equipment is also discussed. Chapter 8 contains detailed motor activities with specific, developmentally sequenced teaching objectives. These activities are grouped in three sections: gross motor activities, fine motor activities, and oral-motor activities. Chapter 9 suggests various social, cognitive, and communication activities to facilitate the child's development in these important areas. Many of the activities in Part II are very detailed; you may want to skim these chapters the first time through the book. Don't let yourself become overwhelmed at this point. The activities will be easy to understand when you begin working through them one by one. Remember, you don't have to learn everything at once!

The remainder of the book is devoted to a glossary and four appendices and Baby's Record. The Glossary lists terms used in early intervention and therapy programs and by professionals who specialize in developmental disabilities. Appendix 1 provides charts of developmental milestones for children in the first 2 years. Appendix 2 lists commercial sources of adaptive equipment, books on motor development, and other resources for parents of a motor-impaired child. Appendix 3 lists books on child development, behavior management, learning activities, and other resources for parents. Appendix 4 lists parent and professional organizations of interest to families with a disabled member as well as advocacy groups and agencies that provide information or services to disabled persons. Finally, Baby's Record provides a place for recording personal information, developmental achievements, and other important notes about your child.

This book should not be used like a "cookbook" of programs for your child. Rather, it is a comprehensive reference source. Children with movement or motor difficulties should be seen regularly by a physician and a physical or occupational therapist so that specific diagnoses can be made and individual programs designed. This book is intended to help you understand some of these diagnoses and treatment approaches so that you can more effectively communicate with these professionals. It also provides guidelines for assessing your child's motor patterns as well as suggested teaching programs for helping your child develop more fully. Remember—*you* are the most important person in your child's life!

# Acknowledgments

The authors would like to express sincere appreciation to the following persons:

- To the parents and children who shared their experiences and photographs. Their contributions greatly enriched the quality of this book.

- To Philippa Campbell, PhD, OTR, who contributed her expertise in working with young children with motor delays by providing written materials and feedback on many portions of the book.

- To Peter Blasco, MD, for his participation by authoring a chapter on medical aspects of physical disability.

- To Arden Munkres for the graphic designs used to illustrate developmental milestones.

- To Janet Ball, Diane Beaty, and James Nance for their valuable assistance in the typing of the manuscript.

- To Marie Hanak, Marci Hanson, and Susan Sandall for photographs; Greg Owen for illustrations.

# PART I

# Developmental Issues

Many young children are at risk for developing movement or motor difficulties. Conditions associated with these difficulties include extreme prematurity, low birth weight, birth complications (such as cord injuries or intraventricular hemorrhaging), and lack of oxygen before or during birth. In addition, certain congenital syndromes, such as Down syndrome, may result in abnormal motor patterns. Because of the remarkable advances in medical technology and practices in hospital nurseries, the lives of many children who experience these traumas are being saved. These children may grow and develop normally, or they may experience delays in their development that range from mild difficulties to severe problems. Difficulties in the area of motor development are common in children who

are diagnosed as handicapped or at risk for developmental delay.

Because these children are identified in the early weeks and months as being at risk, most are carefully monitored through a newborn screening and follow-up program associated with a hospital or health care organization. Follow-up programs usually include periodic examinations by physicians as well as tests to assess the baby's overall development in areas such as hearing and vision and cognitive, social, and motor development. If delays in any of these areas are found, babies are often referred to intervention services. These services may range from private therapy provided by a physical or occupational therapist with pediatric training to an exten-

sive early intervention program.

For parents these early months can be particularly trying. Often a diagnosis is impossible. Furthermore, professionals are often unable to determine whether the condition is relatively temporary or likely to be persistent. Parents may feel that they are "getting the run-around" or may be confused by the many professionals and types of services that they must seek. All this comes at a time when they were expecting to bring their babies home and welcome them into the family.

It is the purpose of this book to provide basic information on common motor difficulties and present teaching strategies that you, as parents, can use to help your infants develop more fully. Strategies are presented for children from birth to approximately two years of age.

1

# Where to Go for Help

If you have any concerns about your baby's development, consult your child's pediatrician or primary-care physician. Parents are often the first to spot a difficulty. You may notice that the baby is stiff when picked up, that the baby fails to mold to your body when cuddled, or that the baby is extremely floppy. If you identify any of these characteristics, bring them to the attention of the physician.

Your physician may determine that there is no problem, or the physician may wish to continue to follow the baby and observe the baby more fully over a given period of time. At this point babies are often referred for physical therapy. This does not mean that the baby will be handicapped. Often these therapeutic services are recommended to prevent problems or alleviate the motor difficulties that do exist. When working with a therapist for the child's motor problems, you should choose a certified or licensed physical or occupational therapist who has been trained in pediatrics (the specialty that deals with young children). Your physician or local parent groups or local agencies serving persons with developmental disabilities can help you find an appropriate therapist.

Several major theoretical approaches to developmental intervention for motor problems predominate in the United States. One approach, neurodevelopmental treatment (NDT), is frequently utilized with young children with motor problems (Bobath & Bobath, 1972; Harris, 1981). Another treatment approach used by many therapists is the sensorimotor approach to treatment, developed by Margaret Rood (Stockmeyer, 1972). Both of these approaches are oriented toward the treatment of young children with motor delay since they both focus on facilitating developmentally appropriate patterns of movement. The neurodevelopmental approach does this through facilitating normal muscle tone and normal balance reactions, whereas the sensorimotor approach emphasizes the use of specific types of sensory stimulation (i.e., brushing, vibration, tapping, icing).

The important rule to remember in selecting therapists is that they be licensed or certified by their professional society and that they have some experience in working with young children. These therapeutic services are not the same as routine baby exercises and should be performed only by a well-qualified professional. Another important characteristic to keep in mind is the therapist's willingness to work with you, the parent. You spend the majority of the time with your child and will be the child's best and most important teacher.

# What Is Early Intervention?

Some children will be referred for more comprehensive early intervention services. These programs are sometimes referred to as infant stimulation programs or infant development programs. The term *early intervention program* is preferred because it encompasses a broader range of services and assumes that the infant is an active learner, not just a passive receiver of stimulation.

Early intervention services may include a range of educational, health, and social services for young children with special needs and their families. They may include a variety of staff members such as teachers, physical and/or occupational therapists, speech and language specialists, nurses, social workers, and psychologists. Most programs do not have all of these professionals on staff, but they do employ specialists from various disciplines. These early intervention services may be provided in a school or clinic, in the home, or through a combined center and home-based approach. Again, the best way to select an appropriate service is to ask other parents with similar needs, consult your local hospital or health care facility or local school district, or ask for a referral from the local agency responsible for services to persons with developmental disabilities. Visit the programs and select a program where you and your child feel comfortable. Most early intervention programs provide, at the minimum, services in these three areas: (1) programs for children across areas of development, (2) assistance to parents and other family members to help them work with the child, and (3) support for families through contact with a range of professionals who specialize in this area as well as contact with other parents.

The effects of early intervention services have been studied extensively. In general, the research has concluded that early services which actively involve the child's parents can positively affect the child's development. In many cases the child's difficulties are kept from becoming more severe or in some cases remediated altogether. Furthermore, parents have reported that they have benefitted from the support they received in such programs. These programs have been shown to be cost-effective also. That is, children who received early and systematic services and follow-up generally required less intensive and expensive services when they grew older (Garland, Stone, Swanson, & Woodruff, 1981; Hanson, 1984).

# The Parent's Role

Movement is basic to everything we do: walking, reaching, speaking, approaching. The infant with movement or motor difficulties may need extra teaching and care in order to be able to interact with the world. The primary world for the young infant is the parents. In addition to the loving, consistent care that all infants need to grow and develop optimally, your infant will need some special care. You may need to learn to feed your infant or dress your infant in a special way. You may need to learn special ways to position or handle your infant because of motor problems. You may also need tips on strategies for helping your motor-delayed child learn.

# Getting Started

The earliest years of a child's life are the keystone to future development. During this period, the child's primary contact is with the parents, and no professional can replace the parent as the provider of a motivating and realistic environment to help the child reach her or his potential. It is the quality of parent-child interaction that can most positively affect the child's development. Here are several important guidelines that will assist you in developing your child's potential to the fullest:

1. **Each child is an individual.** Even though your child may be diagnosed as having a certain disability such as cerebral palsy, your child is different from any other child—with a unique personality and intellectual and physical characteristics that have little relationship to the diagnosis or motor impairment.

2. **All children can learn and continue to learn.** All children can learn, and we can expect that they will continue to learn their whole lives. Learning won't always occur at the same rate; sometimes it appears that the child is moving ahead in leaps and bounds, and other times the going is very slow. However, as long as children are motivated to learn and are given opportunities for learning, they will learn.

3. **Parents make a difference.** The interactions you have with your child and the experiences you provide for your child are important factors in your child's development. What you do makes a difference.

4. **The earlier you begin working with your child, the better.** While it is never too late to begin teaching, early intervention can prevent additional problems and can typically facilitate the child's development. Early intervention also helps parents and infants to establish positive relationships with each other early on. This can provide needed support.

5. **Teaching goals are both developmental and functional.** Goals are defined from a knowledge of normal child development and also from observation of the functional skills (such as reaching, talking, feeding, dressing) that the child will need to best interact in the world. Parents should be actively involved in deciding what their children need to learn.

6. **The time to teach is during natural interactions.** Each interaction that the parent and child have with one another is a time for teaching and a time for learning. This is true for parents of normally developing infants as well as for parents of infants with special needs.

7. **Seek assistance from other parents and professionals in your geographical area.** If possible, become involved in an early intervention program. If your child has sensory problems such as visual or hearing impairments, find specialists in these areas and get the help you need. Often you will have to be persistent and patient in making and keeping appointments. When choosing professional assistance, ask if the person has had experience in working with young children with special needs and with families.

Like all children, children with special needs must have active involvement with their parents. The more parents participate in planning and carrying out their babies' programs, the more effective early intervention services are likely to be.

# CHAPTER 1

# Experiences of Other Parents

**B**eing parents of a 14-week premature son has given us many opportunities to experience feelings of joy and frustration. One day your child does something new and you are on top of the world, feeling happy and reassured about his future; the next day, someone tells you he should be doing something else, and all the doubts and fears return. The hardest thing for us has been to get a clear understanding of just how delayed our son is and what his long-range potential is. Robbie is our first child, and as nonprofessionals we had no way to gauge his development. The only physical sign of any problem was his eye muscles, and this was corrected by surgery. We were told when he was very young that he had hypertonicity, or tightness in his lower extremities, and that a physical therapist might do him some good. We were not told until he was almost 2 years old that hypertonicity is a characteristic of cerebral palsy and there is a chance he may never walk.

**Robbie**

The best thing we did for both Robbie and ourselves was to get him into an infant development program. It's so easy to sit home and tell yourself that he is just a baby and there is plenty of time for school. There isn't. We were taught ways of playing with Robbie so as not to increase the stiffness in his limbs along with a physical therapy program of exercises. We learned how to assess his present developmental skills, how to set goals for future tasks (stacking blocks, throwing a ball, etc.), and how to encourage achievement of these milestones. Most important, we got to know our son and assumed some control of his development and future.

I'm not going to say that we're not still frustrated at times and that doing his "homework" is all fun and games; it isn't. In fact, it's a lot of work. We are always conscious of what Robbie is doing and how he is doing it. We don't like the fact that our child has problems—no one does—but working with Robbie and teaching him new things has helped relieve our feelings of inadequacy. And sharing our frustrations by talking with other parents in the program lets us know we are not alone.

My husband and I are now actively involved in helping high-risk infants and other handicapped persons get the stimulation and education they need. We realize that the education of parents in teaching and working for their child is that child's only hope. We see Robbie smile while playing with his trucks, and we want to share the joy.

**Laura Repke**

**Miles**

**B**orn at 29 weeks with a birth weight of only 2.1 pounds, Miles Christopher Reed won a difficult struggle to survive. Now, however, he faces another struggle—that of overcoming possible developmental delays.

Miles is definitely at risk for such delays, so we have enrolled him in an early intervention program for infants. After only 4 months with this program we are seeing some very positive results, particularly in the area of gross motor development. We are now aware of Miles's tendency toward hypertonicity and are utilizing suggestions by his teachers to correct this problem. We have been shown more effective ways to feed, dress, carry, and play with Miles, all of which facilitate proper motor development. We have spent many hours under the direction of the early intervention staff exercising Miles's body. We practice moving his arms, kicking his legs, and twisting and turning him. We are also working on developing his midline body orientation.

Of major benefit to all of us are the periodic home visits by early intervention teachers. They make suggestions to guide us in providing the type of environment needed for Miles that will ensure optimal enrichment and further enhance his motor development. He is given opportunities for movement in different ways under different circumstances; for example, on the floor, in his crib, or outdoors.

Miles has come a long way since those early days when we peered into his incubator and wondered what the future would hold for him. Now we have seen what a positive difference early intervention can make.

**Kathy Reed**

**A**s a parent of a handicapped child, I have learned that an infant program like the one my daughter Marisela is attending can help a child with a handicap learn and lead a near-normal life. Seeing my child crawl, roll over, walk, and feed herself is a big joy.

**Maria Ochoa**

**Gerry**

**M**y son Gerry was born with Down syndrome. This handicap and its accompanying heart condition (requiring two open-heart operations in one year) greatly delayed his acquisition of motor skills.

When he joined an infant program at the age of 13 months, he could not sit up alone or crawl. He was just beginning to roll over, a feat most infants master at a far earlier age.

Through the first months of this development program, I was taught to observe and chart the many intermediate stages a child must attain before mastering a new physical skill such as sitting alone. I was shown by Gerry's teacher and his therapist in the program how to gradually build up Gerry's ability at each stage with carefully measured props and consistent cues. Equally important was building his confidence and enthusiasm for the skill through praise and other positive reinforcements.

In the ensuing year, Gerry has made rapid progress. He has learned to sit up, crawl, assume a hands-and-knees position, pull himself up at furniture, and is beginning to take steps! I feel that this program of careful data-keeping and progress-checking has resulted in a great improvement in Gerry's motor skills.

**Heather Hart**

**A**n early intervention program has been the salvation for our motor-delayed and multihandicapped 2½-year-old son, André. It has helped us build a special world full of knowledge and education. We participate and work directly with André in achieving set programs and services geared for his motor development. André's programs have been individually designed to meet his needs with the help of trained teachers and therapists. All this planning has a special name, the individualized education program (IEP). This planning is so thorough that André has adapted and performed very well in the class sessions. One reason for this progress is that André's level of performance was tested and studied way before he started class. Together with the teachers and therapists involved we checked out his physical and intellectual capabilities such as the use of his head, torso, legs, arms, eyes, ears, speech, and social interaction with peers. Only after having a detailed description of him did we consider setting up annual goals or tasks in areas where he needed them most: for example, holding his head up straight, relaxing his arms and hands, holding toys or a spoon. Each goal is broken up in several steps, enabling our boy to proceed at his own pace.

It is so wonderful because we can step back for a moment or so and actually see our son work toward the goal. We don't push him; our function as parents (and that of other family members) is to be his teacher and his guide. All we do is set up the atmosphere for André. Only when André achieves one step of a particular task will we go on to the next step, until all the steps are completed and he reaches his goal.

We were so happy when André got accepted into the program because we knew this is what he just needed: the immense individualized concern placed on his motor-delayed abilities. The infant program is trying to develop André's potential to its fullest. He's been working hard and progressing very well, but we don't know how far he'll progress. We really don't know André's capacity for learning. No one does. But we shouldn't let that unanswered question stop us from teaching him.

We know the program is working for André, and thanks to this program and many other new programs like it, André and similar children will have the opportunity to become much happier and contented children with a thriving and hopeful future ahead of them.

**Leonora Mendoza**

**André**

**Mark**

**A** few nights ago, after we had put Mark to bed, we heard crying from his room. Since Mark, who happens to have Down syndrome, rarely cries unless something is wrong, we quickly dashed into his bedroom. To our happy surprise, there was Mark standing up in his bed, unable to get back down! Another milestone, another goal—additional proof that our little boy is progressing developmentally. Each milestone reaffirms our commitment to Mark's full development and strengthens our hope that one day he will be able to be mainstreamed into regular schools, into our everyday society.

The sense of joy he instills in us as he struggles through his allotted tasks, sometimes smiling, sometimes moaning, cannot adequately be put into words. Suffice it to say that we have rebuilt our world with little Mark. Each day there is a new awakening to the reality of this tiny individual, this little soul who needs constant help and guidance (and who of us doesn't?).

We also have a deep sense of contentment with our early intervention program, a feeling of trust and joy of working with Mark as he goes from goal to goal, climbing higher and higher on the musical scale of his little life. The program has helped us to look at not only Mark's life but our own lives. We have been trained to take life in smaller chords, day-by-day "notes," if you will (like recording Mark's daily progress on an evaluation sheet). The program focuses us on what Mark is right now, doing something a step at a time, not Mark's entire life. Life will be a series of these growing steps, little bits that we look at all day. Each step that we are concentrating on will lead to the final goal, certainly, but projecting too far into the future only overwhelms us. Our trust is to each small individualized program goal, which will eventually lead to an independent Mark Sullivan.

Mark has learned to roll over, sit up, pull himself up to stand, and cruise at the furniture, and soon the goal of walking will be met! Another task that he has finally accomplished is clapping his hands. Did we ever think he would do it? There was try after try, repeating it over and over. They the joyous moment came when he actually did it! The overwhelming pride of seeing him happily clapping his hands still remains with us. These are precious moments to remember.

As with everyone, our tendency is usually to focus on end results, not how to get there. The program helped us to zero in on the immediate work right now. We have restructured our life today and tomorrow for the future of Mark. The importance of the program lies in helping us focus on the present. These daily steps that Mark has to take enable him to become a complete person.

Once we got over the dismay and shock at the hospital, and picked up our shattered dreams and hopes, we began the slow process of reorienting and reorganizing those dreams and hopes into a different set of rules, a different lifestyle. No, maybe our little Down syndrome boy wouldn't be able to realize some of those high dreams we had composed before his birth, but with a little reshuffling (and a lot of hard work) he will be able to realize other dreams that we are composing day by day. So the song will have different words and a different melody, but will still be a masterpiece.

**Timothy and Marilyn Sullivan**

**H**aving a developmentally delayed child was not in our plans when our second daughter, Jennifer, was born. I had had a difficult first pregnancy and was looking forward to an easier time. But as it turned out, we were told our child was going to be slower in achieving the developmental milestones and could possibly be mentally retarded.

The doctors and other medical professionals were quite supportive in those early weeks when various tests were given to find a diagnosis. The main course of action that was advised, regardless of diagnosis, was physical therapy intervention, specifically NDT. Being a PT, I wholeheartedly agreed.

We were quite fortunate to be in an area with qualified NDT-trained therapists, and Jennifer started therapy on a regular basis two times weekly at 2 months of age. Prior to that time we had been instructed in various intervention techniques, which we began and have continued to do.

We realize that Jennifer's education through her childhood will be a constant, ongoing process that must include appropriate services if she is to reach whatever potential she has.

I find I have to guard against comparing her with a "normally" developing child and being in too much of a hurry for her to progress. It has been a thrill to see her develop at her own speed, and I'm sure her exposure to therapy has accelerated the process. She has been a delight to us, and our wish for her is to find as much happiness as possible.

**Gretchen Braun**

**O**ne in every 1,000 babies born in this country has some form of spina bifida, the most common disabler of newborns. Our son, Jodie, is one of them. The cause is unknown, and until as recently as the past 10 or 20 years many, if not most, of these babies spent a life plagued by severe medical complications. Medical science can now treat babies like Jodie early and effectively with early closure of the spine and shunts to control hydrocephalus (a complication developed by about 80% of babies with myelomeningocele, the most severe form of spina bifida).

We were fortunate that a routine ultrasound test when I was 27 weeks pregnant revealed that Jodie had myelomeningocele. Knowing this before he was born gave us a chance to prepare ourselves and to plan a safe delivery for him. We left the hospital only 5 days after his birth with a beautiful, healthy baby. Jodie's spine had been open in the lower part of his back with some spinal cord protruding. He had hip and knee movement, but none below that. In addition, some of the muscles in his hips and thighs are weak. With his potential medical problems well in hand the question now was: "How do we make sure Jodie's development isn't delayed by his motor deficit?" The answer was an infant early intervention program.

Jodie, who is now 11 months old, has been attending the infant program since he was 12 weeks old. The teacher and physical therapist monitor his development closely to identify areas of potential delay and help us intervene before something becomes a problem. For example, they noticed very early that Jodie stiffened his shoulders back in an effort to compensate for loss of

**Jodie**

lower body tone and balance. This made it difficult for him to perform the midline activities that are so important to developmental progression. We were shown how to position Jodie to give him the support he needed and how to encourage midline activities. Now that Jodie is becoming mobile, we're working on upper-body strength and balance—things that he'll need to walk.

Motor-delayed children are also at risk for cognitive delay (if you can't get there to get it, how can you learn about it?). So his teacher is an integral part of his program. She evaluates Jodie and gives us activities that enhance his social, cognitive, and language development. Jodie gets excellent health care from all of the many providers he sees, but the infant program gives it all focus and purpose. Every week, we're able to clearly see his progress, identify his strengths and weaknesses, and plan a program especially suited to Jodie's needs. All parents want to be able to make life better for their children, and it's reassuring to be able to do something now that may make all the difference later. I believe that early intervention is the key to providing the best chance for children like Jodie to have a normal childhood and happy, productive lives.

**Donna Edgerton Blaylock**

# CHAPTER 2

# Medical Aspects of Motor Disabilities

Peter A. Blasco, MD

Along with the usual joys and frustrations of parenting any child comes the prospect of dealing with medical problems and medical professionals. This interaction with the medical profession can be a very positive, comfortable experience or a very difficult and frustrating one, regardless of whether the child is in good health. It has long been my belief that the parent who is well-informed has a better and easier time dealing with an illness, especially a chronic condition like a physical handicap.

The intent of this chapter is to provide the parents of children with motor impairments some basic medical facts about motor disabilities. The subject is very complex when taken as a whole, but this is to be expected because the disabled child presents complex problems. Taken from his or her perspective, life experiences will be irrevocably altered by many factors: the nature of the disability (e.g., mental retardation, cerebral palsy, blindness, etc.), the timing of the diagnosis, the severity of the disability (very mild as opposed to very severe), and the number and extent of associated problems. The chapter also contains some general information on the approach to medical diagnosis, the rationale for intervention, and prognosis (what to expect for the future). After addressing clinical issues, the chapter will end with some personal comments on parental characteristics, another extremely important factor in the child's development.

Figure 2.1

# The Nature of the Disability

We are concerned here with *motor* impairment in childhood as opposed to intellectual or behavioral problems. Some children with motor impairments also have intellectual impairments, behavioral disorders, or even other medical conditions, but these issues will be addressed later in the chapter.

Motor impairments have a reason or cause (in medical jargon we say *etiology*), and finding the etiology depends on a skillful medical examination that often includes a variety of laboratory tests. By means of these examinations and investigations the physician will be able to classify a motor disability into one of four general categories: (1) static central nervous system anomalies or insults, (2) progressive diseases, (3) spinal cord and peripheral nerve injuries, and (4) structural defects.

**Static central nervous system anomalies** or **insults** indicate some type of non-progressive brain damage. This can happen prior to birth (during fetal brain development), in such a fashion that the brain was never directed to develop properly. Such an abnormality would be termed an anomaly of the brain. The anomaly could be the result of improper information in the genes of the fetus (as, for example in Down syndrome) or a very early and subtle chemical imbalance that permanently alters the development of the brain from that point. On the other hand, a normally developing brain can be altered or damaged before, during, or after birth by a variety of what we call insults. Examples would be infection (such as meningitis), lack of oxygen (this is a special concern in premature babies), trauma (a physical head injury), ischemia or lack of adequate blood flow (as might occur in dehydration or a stroke), poisons (such as lead intoxication), metabolic diseases (as with phenylketonuria, or PKU), and so forth.

True brain damage is always permanent because the brain does not repair itself like many other body organs do. However, the healthy areas of brain continue to develop during childhood so that functional improvements can continue to occur at least up to a certain point. Development of motor areas in the brain is largely finished by 7 or 8 years of age, though some minor changes will continue to take place through adolescence. When a motor impairment is due to an anomaly (which always occurs before birth) or to an insult that takes place before mid-adolescence (roughly 16 years of age), we refer to this medically as **cerebral palsy**. This group represents the largest number of children with motor impairments.

Approximately 1 out of every 200 children has cerebral palsy (CP). Because CP is so common among motor impairments, it is worth briefly going over the classification of CP. It is divided into two basic types—spastic (also called pyramidal) and extrapyramidal (or nonspastic). These distinctions are made on the basis of the neurological examination and the presence or absence of certain physical findings. The neurological examination includes tests of muscle tone (the resting tension of the muscles), strength, and various reflexes (muscle reactions to specific stimuli such as striking the knee with a soft hammer). The physician and therapist also observe carefully for unusual movements such as ataxia (poor coordination), chorea (jerky movements), athetosis (a type of twisting or writhing movement), and others.

Physical problems associated with CP are deformities of the bones and tendons, which result from the influence of excessively high or abnormally low tone. The type of CP implies which of the several motor control systems in the brain has been primarily damaged. Knowing the type of CP has some utility in prognosis and in treatment planning. In spastic or pyramidal CP the cases are further divided on the basis of which extremities are involved. For example, hemiplegia indicates one side of the body is involved (usually the arm more than the leg); quadriplegia means all four extremities are involved; diplegia involves both legs (although as a rule the arms are also *minimally* involved).

In nonspastic or extrapyramidal CP, there is usually involvement of all extremities as well as the neck and trunk. The subtypes are determined by the tone pattern of the muscles or by the extra movements observed. For example, choreoathetosis (a combination of chorea and athetosis) is commonly seen in extrapyramidal CP. This subtype is called choreoathetoid cerebral palsy. Hypotonic CP is the subtype applied to children whose examination is most notable for low muscle tone. Generally children with Down syndrome are diagnosed as being hypotonic or having hypotonia rather than having cerebral palsy. The finding of hypotonia is quite common in those disorders due to recognizable, abnormal patterns often referred to as *syndromes*.

**Progressive diseases** of the brain, the nerves, or the muscles produce motor impairment that as a rule gets worse with time. The diseases in this group are very numerous, but each individual disease is extremely rare. Therefore the fraction of all motor-impaired children with progressive diseases is quite small. Knowing the particular diagnosis is important because it can help to estimate the rate of the progression. Most of these conditions are untreatable, but a few can be halted or reversed with medical treatment. Most will eventually lead to a fatal outcome. Examples of the more serious ones would be Duchenne muscular dystrophy (an inherited muscle-wasting disease of unknown exact cause) or Werdnig-Hoffman disease (inherited deterioration of the spinal cord nerves that supply muscles). Children with Duchenne muscular dystrophy usually die in their early 20s whereas those with Werdnig-Hoffman disease rarely live beyond 2 or 3 years of age.

It is extremely important to diagnose diseases like these early—not only to help the child and parents make the best of a very tragic situation but also to provide the proper genetic counseling to help plan for future children. Brain tumors would also fall in this group because, as long as the tumor expands in the brain or spinal cord, the patient experiences progressive loss of neurologic function. However, if the tumor is cured either by removal or by some other treatment, then the individual may be left with a *static* motor impairment.

**Spinal cord and peripheral nerve injuries** are all static like cerebral palsy except for the rare instance of a growing spinal cord tumor. They differ in that future functional loss is much easier to predict and there are different types of associated problems. In this category the largest single group consists of children with spina bifida (or meningomyelocele). This condition is an anomaly of the spinal cord whereby the early closing over of the cord fails to take place properly (about 3 weeks after conception), leaving an incomplete cord below the level at which the closure fails. Since this can happen anywhere along the entire length of the spinal cord, the resulting loss of motor and sensory function will vary greatly from person to person. It usually occurs at the lower end of the spinal cord, but there is almost always another anomaly present at the upper end of the cord as well (known as the *brain stem*), which leads to *hydrocephalus* (excessive accumulation of fluid within the brain). No one knows what causes spina bifida, but we do know that there is an inherited susceptibility for it to happen. More will be presented on spina bifida in the section "Associated Problems."

**Structural defects** refer to situations in which something is missing (e.g., a limb) or in which some support structure for the nerves and muscles is inadequate (bone and joint deformities, connective tissue defects, etc.). These are usually the most straightforward to understand of all motor-impairing conditions. Some may be progressive and may be extremely complex to manage. As examples, osteogenesis imperfecta (brittle-bone disease) and the many varieties of childhood arthritis would fit in this category.

# Timing of the Diagnosis

The ability to make an early diagnosis depends, in large measure, on the type of disability. For example, with spina bifida or Down syndrome the diagnosis is apparent at birth. Right from the start we know there will be motor impairments as the child grows. These can be anticipated and in some ways treated even before they become extremely apparent. In the case of cerebral palsy, diagnosis is usually delayed until a problem with motor development is recognized and investigated. Therefore, a parent, a relative, a friend, or a physician may be the first to recognize the delay based on a knowledge of normal motor development. The child with severe impairments is likely to be identified earlier (usually before 12 months of life) than a child with very mild delays because the former will more obviously fail to achieve the developmental milestones.

Of course this issue of early identification depends greatly on the experience of the observers. Individual therapists, teachers, physicians, and others trained in child development often disagree on what should be considered a significant or meaningful amount of motor delay. There is no uniformly accepted method for determining this. One rule of thumb that often proves useful, especially when combined with other aspects of the child's neurological exam, is the calculation of a *developmental quotient*. In the young child this is easy. It requires comparing the child's motor age (i.e., motor skills converted to the age at which they appear in the average, normal child) against the child's chronological age. This ratio of motor age to chronological age is referred to as a developmental quotient (DQ) for motor function. If the DQ is less than 0.7 (or 70%), then there is reason for suspicion, and the child ought to be checked by a specialist. If it is greater than 0.8, everything is probably all right. This ratio is easiest to apply in children under 2 years of age and, of course, is not absolute, but it is still a reliable and easy screen.

In the case of some progressive diseases, there may be a long period of normal development, which obscures the fact that a slow disease process is going on. In Duchenne muscular dystrophy, for example, the diagnosis is usually not made until between 4 and 6 years of age, when the child is noted to be increasingly clumsy or to be having a harder time keeping up with peers. Every once in a while a child with motor impairments will be identified not because of the motor impairment or because of some obvious birth defect but because of another problem, such as the development of seizures.

# Severity of the Disability

As with any problem, motor impairments can range from very mild to very severe. For children with mild cerebral palsy diagnosed during infancy, the eventual outcome may be a clumsy child who is otherwise indistinguishable from peers and who may develop academic troubles related to a specific learning disability. The infant with very severe impairments, on the other hand, may be destined never to achieve walking or even sitting ability despite the best care and treatment. Sometimes parents of children with mild impairments have a more difficult time accepting their child's diagnosis than do parents of the more severely affected child. Though this may seem odd at first, it makes sense when you consider the great frustration of having an "almost" normal child. It is quite easy to wish for or imagine the few missing abilities or to deny mild delays in order to have one's expectations met. On the other hand, when the delays are severe, denial is more difficult and less likely to persist. Although acknowledging that the problem exists may be considerably easier, it certainly does not ease the anguish of "losing" the normal child one expected to have.

# Associated Problems

We defined cerebral palsy as a motor disability due to a nonprogressive central nervous system insult or anomaly that occurs before the brain has completed normal development. Children with cerebral palsy typically have other problems as well because the brain serves so many other important functions. More than half of them will have intellectual deficiencies in the form of mental retardation or specific learning disabilities. Seizures are also a common associated problem and, when present, place increased medical demands on the family for diagnostic testing (like the EEG, or brain-wave test), for administering medications, and for blood tests to monitor for drug levels and for drug side effects. Communication problems are frequent and in some cases may be due more to dysarthria (the inability to produce clear speech) than to intellectual deficits. In the child with a disability severe enough to preclude speech, alternate methods of communication need to be provided (e.g., sign language, a picture board, or an electronic device). Blindness and deafness occur much more commonly in children who have nonprogressive nervous system diseases. Growth may be impaired in children with brain damage either as a result of the brain dysfunction itself or due to nutritional problems brought about by feeding and swallowing difficulties. Swallowing problems and food regurgitation are mostly seen in children with severe impairments and may cause pneumonia and lung damage because of recurrent episodes of aspiration of food.

Behavioral problems deserve special attention because they are common and are easy to reinforce inadvertently. Children with disabilities are first of all children and, therefore, have all the usual behavioral idiosyncrasies characteristic of childhood. But in addition they are more likely to be frustrated because of their disabilities. For parents, professionals, and especially friends and relatives, there is a strong temptation to "do for" the "helpless" child who is disabled. Though well meant, this indulgence often backfires and affects behavior—the child becomes "spoiled." It is indeed hard to know where to draw the line between what really deserves a little extra indulgence and what does not.

In some conditions, a host of other related medical problems can be predicted and therefore anticipated. As noted earlier, children with spina bifida almost always develop hydrocephalus (excess fluid filling and expanding the normal fluid cisterns in the brain), which requires the placement of shunt devices to drain the fluid away. These shunts in turn are prone to plug up or become infected. Spina bifida and other types of spinal cord injury usually result in major problems with bowel and bladder control. With these problems come more serious medical problems, especially kidney and bladder infections, as well as social problems. Since all sensation is lost below the level at which the spinal cord is damaged, injuries are not felt. The result can be large and severe sores from unrecognized burns, repeated trauma, or constant pressure from sitting all day in a wheelchair.

These examples of associated problems should illustrate three very important points. First of all, knowing the cause of a disability is a great help in anticipating other problems before they develop or before they get out of hand. This allows professionals to help parents plan ahead for problems and is what we call *anticipatory guidance*. Secondly, the family really needs a single, reliable, and responsive medical resource and advocate to help approach these problems and to coordinate and direct what may be a large group of medical and other professional consultants. Lastly, professionals skilled in many different disciplines—for example, speech therapy, audiology, occupational therapy, nutrition, education, nursing, physical therapy, recreational therapy, and psychology—need to work together and *in concert with the parents* to provide care to the child with a motor impairment, especially one who has multiple problems. This philosophy of care is what is referred to as the interdisciplinary team approach.

## Interventions

The first and most important step in treatment is diagnosis—determining the nature and severity of the disorder in order to know what you are treating. Without this information, therapy efforts are likely to be incomplete or misdirected. Diagnosis will include not only the primary problem and its cause (if known) but all the associated problems as well. Even if the cause of a disability is never understood, the primary disability and the associated problems can still be identified. To begin a therapeutic program without completing or at least initiating an interdisciplinary evaluation is short-changing the disabled child and misleading the family.

Direct treatment for the child with a motor impairment falls into four categories: (1) hands-on therapy, (2) assistive devices, (3) medication, and (4) surgery.

**Hands-on therapy** falls in the realm primarily of occupational and physical therapy, though education, speech therapy, and recreational therapy are important supportive disciplines. In addition to providing the proper treatment methods directly to the child, these therapists are also educators. They teach the techniques in a limited but very practical way to patients, to parents, and sometimes to other individuals involved in the child's care so the treatment program can be carried out in the home and in school at prescribed times and in a consistent and competent manner. It is important to emphasize that, for children, *pediatric* therapists are essential. The techniques used and the subtle changes in a treatment program that need to be anticipated and made as the child develops are the special competency of the therapist trained and experienced with children. These skills are not commonly understood or appreciated by therapists trained only to treat adults.

**Assistive devices** consist of braces and splints, usually constructed by an orthotist or an occupational therapist, and adaptive equipment generally constructed by a carpenter or manufactured commercially. Examples of the latter would be a wooden seat insert to help provide support in sitting or a wheelchair for mobility. These are always used with an eye to function and are introduced for use only at the appropriate developmental level of the child. Therefore, since 6- to 8-month-olds are ready to be sitting and interacting with the world mostly from an upright vantage point (rather than lying down), supported sitting becomes a very real goal by that age for children with motor impairments. Mechanical and electronic communication devices become appropriate as soon as the child is able to understand their use and can manipulate them. Common toys often need to be adapted for use by children with limited fine motor ability.

Occasionally, **medication** may benefit a particular type of motor disability. For example, the child who is limited by elevated muscle tone (stiffness) may improve functionally with the help of a muscle relaxant medication like diazepam (commonly known as Valium). For the most part, however, medicines are used to manage associated problems; for example, antibiotics for bladder infections and anticonvulsants for seizures. The use of medication almost always brings with it the need for laboratory tests, for regular medical follow-up, and for careful adherence to prescribed treatment plans. A frequent concern raised by parents is the fear that a child will get "addicted" to a certain drug. There is some basis for this fear, but not to the extent commonly believed. The body builds up a tolerance to many medications (diazepam or phenobarbital are good examples), *not* so much in the sense that the dose needs to be increased for the drug to keep working (as seen in narcotic drug addiction) but rather in the sense that rapidly stopping the medication causes the body to react adversely. This is because the child's system becomes used to the drug and is thrown out of equilibrium when it is stopped suddenly. The logical, easy, and safe way to avoid this is, first of all, to use the medication exactly as prescribed and secondly, if the drug is to be stopped, to do so by slowly decreasing the dose over time. We refer to this as *tapering* a medication.

**Surgery** is generally viewed as a last resort to prevent or correct orthopedic deformities. Motor-impairing conditions often lead to bone deformities or tendon contractures which, in turn, interfere with function, sometimes cause pain, and sometimes lead to other deformities. If the situation cannot be controlled with hands-on therapy and bracing measures, then orthopedic surgery may become necessary. As is always true, anticipating surgical needs is a lot better than trying to correct a problem that is out of control or beyond correction. Surgery, like bracing, therapy, and medications, is mainly aimed at improving or maintaining function. Occasionally surgery is done, mainly for cosmetic reasons. Because of associated problems, other surgical subspecialists may be required for children with motor impairments, such as the neurosurgeon (to treat hydrocephalus), the ophthalmologist (to evaluate and treat eye problems), and others.

# Prognosis

What is going to happen? This is the issue of prognosis, and none of us has a crystal ball to predict the future. However, knowing the nature of the disability and gaining a feel for the severity of the disability will go a long way toward providing the groundwork for an accurate prognosis. At the simplest level the prognosis for almost all motor-impairing conditions is clear—they do not go away. How much motor progress children will make requires enough time to determine how well they respond to treatment. For example, with cerebral palsy we know that most children who sit by themselves by 2 years of age will eventually walk. A good developmentalist and a good therapist will make use of other clinical information to help judge if and when specific milestones may be met. There are two extremely important facts to appreciate about prognosis. First, there is always some degree of uncertainty. The more precision a parent seeks (or demands) in answer to questions, the greater the uncertainty is likely to be in the response. Second, regardless of what happens in the future, it is very useful to keep a solid grounding in the present by doing what is necessary to allow the child to achieve maximum potential. Even though you do not really know what that will be, you can still set your sights on obtaining the best possible outcome by participating in the appropriate therapeutic program right now.

# Medical Resources

In simple and practical terms the child with a disability and the child's family need to consider two types of medical resources. The first is the local physician, usually though not necessarily a pediatrician. He or she will manage all the usual well-child and minor-illness aspects of care, and in conjunction with specialist physicians can provide continuity of care for special medical problems. The primary physician can be a parent's and patient's best advocate in dealing with other agencies. In addition, the primary physician will be there over the course of the many years during which other professionals have come and gone; and the importance of maintaining this stable, supportive resource must not be underestimated. The second medical resource is a clinic designed for and committed to the total care (that is, initial assessment *and* long-term follow-up) of children with disabilities. Such a facility should have access to all of the necessary medical and nonmedical services. Ideally the clinic directors should be pediatricians trained in the care of children with disabilities. The clinic is the family's base for specialized care and expertise with problems common to disabled children. It is also a rich resource for practical and helpful ideas from other parents as well as from the various professionals.

Most of the following chapters in this book focus on the practical aspects of hands-on therapy for children with motor impairments. It is hard to prove in a scientific way the value of early intervention services for large numbers of children with varying types of disability. However, at the very least it is easy to see in a subjective sense the enormous value of the therapist-parent and teacher-parent interaction. The outcomes in terms of the physical and emotional well-being of the child and the psychological adjustment of the parent would appear to be so positively influenced that it easily justifies the reasonable amounts of time, expense, and effort devoted to treatment. The alternative—to do nothing—is defeatist, uninspired, and unfair.

## Parents and Coping

I often marvel at the manner in which some parents are able to cope with the enormous and heart-breaking troubles of their children. They have to cope with the disabled child and the child's disappointments. They have to cope with themselves, their jobs, their marital relationship, and their own disappointments. Finally, they have to cope with outsiders whether that be a stranger in the supermarket or a professional contact.

Since the physician is often identified as the leader of the interdisciplinary team, it generally falls to me to confront parents who are having problems coping. I have not yet found the perfect formula to do this successfully. However, one strategy that works is to help parents organize their thoughts in a framework useful for understanding the basic nature of the problems and the basic nature of their own responses to them. This strategy of stepping back to take a more objective and perhaps slightly detached look at the many complex issues involved is usually very helpful in solving, or at least addressing, some of the problems at hand. It seems to me that, although people differ in their coping styles, they all reason things out (usually at a subconscious level) at three distinct and different levels in response to stressful situations. First is the personal and emotional response—the "gut level" reaction. Second are highly practical considerations, and third is the level of philosophical and religious values. The priorities and emphases placed on these different levels will vary from family to family and even from person to person within a given family as much as the individual personalities, the nature of the practical concerns, or the particular beliefs differ. The loving mother who "just cannot bear" to exert discipline for a tantrum or ignore an attention-getting behavior from her young child with a disability is responding at the first level. Others may see it as irrational, but it is a legitimate coping response to the immediate situation. Recognizing the nature of the response in a formal way can only be helpful in working out a better approach to the problem. At the second level it may be the father who is overwhelmed by the extra financial burdens or by the drastic alterations in lifestyle that accompany the birth of a disabled infant. The child with a disability may be an extra burden in all sorts of practical ways—in financial terms, in terms of personal time and lifestyle, in terms of other family members, especially siblings. There is great value in acknowledging that fact rather than trying to deny it, then moving on to the next step of solving which burden is most troublesome and what can be done about it. Finally, people respond to difficult situations based on their personal philosophy of life. This may be very narrow and self-centered or very broad and universal in orientation. It may be strongly based in formal religious doctrine, in personal interpretation of the Bible, in humanistic philosophy, in the examples set by one's parents or by admired individuals, or whatever. Once again, the purpose of the exercise is to identify the fundamental nature of one's beliefs in order to have a basis for going further in finding the solutions to a problem with coping or even to better understand how one is already coping with a difficult situation. This insight can be quite helpful to a spouse, a relative, or a friend in a similar situation.

It is extremely important to recognize and believe that outsiders—even though they cannot "know" what a parent is experiencing—can still help. The psychologist, the teacher, the physical therapist, the family physician, the clergyman—whoever relates to or communicates with a parent or a patient well—can help with expressing and organizing one's thoughts. The advantage of an individual outside of the immediate family is that he or she can be concerned about the situation yet offer a less emotional, perhaps more objective view of it. All of the involved individuals (including the parents) are members of the treatment team, working together toward the goal of the child's, the family's, and indeed society's well-being.

# CHAPTER 3

# Early Intervention

**A**s parents of a motor-delayed child, you may be experiencing fear and frustration about your child's future. Concerns about whether or not your child will learn to walk and communicate with others are natural. Parents also often wonder whether their child will grow and learn like other children, go to a regular school like others, and be able to live as an independent adult. These concerns are coupled with the frustrations of locating appropriate educational and medical services for the child, being referred back and forth among many different agencies and professionals, and absorbing the tremendous financial costs of providing special services. You may find that you share these concerns and also have additional concerns of your own. It may be helpful to know that many other parents also share these fears and frustrations as well as the joys and rewards that competent and loving parenting of a child with special needs can bring.

This chapter will present four case studies about children with movement problems and motor delays. These case studies illustrate a range of problems and circumstances that families encounter. Issues such as severity of the child's problem, geographical location and availability of services, special family needs, and commitment to teaching the child may all influence the child's development. Case Study 1 describes the progress of twins, both of whom have movement problems. The study provides an example of children living in a rural area where only limited services are available. The psychological adjustments of a family with a child with severe handicaps are discussed in Case Study 2. Case Study 3 describes a 2-year-old girl with motor delays resulting from extremely low muscle tone and a rare genetic disorder. Finally, a boy with mild motor delays due to high muscle tone is the subject of Case Study 4. Following this case study are detailed assessments and charts of the boy's behavior changes, showing the gains that may be possible over a year's time in an early intervention program.

These case studies give concrete examples of the diverse needs of children who have motor

**Figure 3.1**

difficulties. Each description is based on a real child currently or formerly enrolled in an early intervention program. Though three of these children happen to be boys, it is important to note that physical difficulties may occur in girls and boys and are found across all ethnic or cultural groups and across racial and socioeconomic groups. Furthermore, the problems may be caused by traumas or infections that occurred prenatally (before birth), perinatally (at or around the time of birth), or postnatally (after the time of birth).

No one can predict the future for any of these children with certainty. However, evidence does exist to show that appropriate physical therapy and early educational services positively affect the development of children with these special needs. An important ingredient in this success is the active participation and care given by the children's parents.

These case studies demonstrate the important role of the children's parents in ensuring the children's optimal development. Parents are critical to any early intervention effort for many reasons. First, most of the child's time is spent with the parents in the home. Secondly, when working with developmentally delayed children one-to-one teaching is often needed. Parents are certainly ideal sources for providing this intensive teaching. Finally, parents are probably the most reinforcing people to their child in that the child will be more likely to perform for the parent than for a stranger and will be more rewarded by a parent's praise than by praise from someone else. The research on early intervention definitely shows that parents can be very effective teachers of their children. The case studies presented in this chapter indicate that parents and professionals working together can help children with special needs to grow and learn.

## Case Study 1: Bobby and Ronny

Bobby and Ronny were born prematurely with respiratory distress syndrome and congenital heart problems related to low birth weight. Both boys received needed care and surgical operations in a regional neonatal nursery about 60 miles away from home.

The twins went home 5 months after birth where they joined their family, including their 4-year-old sister, on a farm in a rural, isolated area. Both boys had feeding difficulties, but Ronny had a particularly hard time retaining food. This difficulty created additional problems with vomiting, regurgitation, and aspiration. Although the boys' parents were told that Bobby and Ronny might have some difficulties that could include mental retardation, the physicians examining the children could not provide a definite diagnosis.

The only services available then in that county were supplied by a home training educational specialist who visited the twins in their home weekly and a therapist who provided home-based consultation services approximately four times per year.

As early as 8 months of age, problems with movement could be observed with both boys. Difficulties were particularly apparent with Ronny, who had trouble raising his head and had low postural tone. Bobby performed most developmental milestone skills within normal age limits (when age was corrected for prematurity). However, postural tone appeared to be increasing, particularly in his legs, which caused him to achieve milestone skills with unusual patterns of movement organization. The consulting therapist arranged at this time for both children to participate in an infant therapy program twice a month at a center about 50 miles from their home. By 12 months of age, both boys were diagnosed as clearly having cerebral palsy; Ronny continued to show more severe problems than Bobby.

Many parents reading this case study probably recognize that the twins' mother could not have cared for three young children, two of whom were motor-impaired, without considerable support and help from the boys' father and other family members. Both sets of grandparents as well as other family members frequently came to the rescue by providing care for the children and by accompanying the boys and their mother on the long drives required to obtain therapy services. Care for the boys was frequently allocated across family members so that the 4-year-old sister did not lose attention due to the twins' needs. The boys' mother worked with each child daily on a therapy program and provided programming under the guidance of both the home trainer and the therapists at the infant program.

Bobby and Ronny continued to progress, and by the time they were 3 years of age, the local county school board began classes for preschool-aged handicapped children. Bobby was accepted in this program and attended a full day of school activities that emphasized language and cognitive development. The school district attempted to provide ongoing therapy services, but, due to the isolated location of the county, consistent services were not always available. During this school year, both boys received orthopedic evaluations, and several surgical procedures were recommended for Bobby's heel cords and muscles around the hips and upper legs. These operations were performed over the next 2 years. Special shoes, bracing following surgery, and continued therapy procedures implemented by Bobby's mother enabled him to be fully ambulatory with use of two canes by the age of 5. Bobby's mother then began to question why her son could not be educated in a regular school with non-handicapped children. The school district responded by providing partial mainstreaming in a regular kindergarten in combination with continued special education programming. Next year, at the age of 6, Bobby will attend a regular first-grade class in the school in his home district. Some modifications will be necessary (such as lifting him into the school bus), and Bobby needs to acquire more competence on stairs. But all in all, this little boy, under the loving and attentive care of his family, has grown up to be a normal child who walks with canes.

The prognosis for Ronny remains excellent. However, his more severe motor limitations and movement problems have prevented him from walking. Additional difficulties with arm and finger movement have made skills such as using a pencil difficult to manage. The twins' mother feels that Ronny is both challenged and frustrated by Bobby's motor competence. Furthermore, the surgical procedures which assisted Bobby are not likely to help Ronny to the same extent because of the postural tone deviations in the head, trunk, and arms. His mother continues to provide daily exercise and therapy activities with the hope that, in the future, Ronny's postural tone and movement patterns will improve enough for him to walk with assistive devices. Until then, the parents are considering the purchase of an electric wheelchair so that Ronny can keep up with his brother.

The progress of Ronny and Bobby can be attributed largely to the teaching done by their family. The importance of the family in ensuring security, providing care, and fostering growth cannot be minimized—particularly when the child requires specialized parenting because of a handicapping condition. Specialists can help by providing therapy, education, and specialized medical/surgical procedures. But no number of specialists can replace good parenting of children with special needs.

# Case Study 2: Carlos

Carlos' family members arrive at school eager to share information on Carlos' new movements or actions. Change for him comes in little steps because 32-month-old Carlos has multiple handicaps that are very severe. He has limited vision and hearing and is unable to make voluntary or directed body movements because of his abnormal muscle tone. Carlos has stiffness in his arms and legs, and his muscle tone fluctuates from stiff to floppy in his head and trunk. (Diagnostically this is referred to as spastic quadriplegia—stiffness in all four limbs.) Carlos has also been diagnosed as microcephalic, which means that the head is abnormally small due to retardation in head and brain growth. Carlos' retarded growth and physical problems most likely resulted from a viral infection his mother contracted during her pregnancy.

Carlos' mother says that she felt so overwhelmed by Carlos' problems that she waited until he was 19 months old before she enrolled him in an early intervention program. She admits that she wishes she had been guided to find a program sooner, not only to facilitate Carlos' development but also to obtain the support that the program has provided her and her husband. Opportunities for talking with other parents, participating in parent support groups and workshops, and receiving instruction on teaching techniques are all offered to parents in Carlos' early intervention program.

Carlos' parents have learned to be patient about the rate of his development. Due to the severity of his handicaps, his progress is slow. During the year that Carlos has been "going to school," however, he has acquired new skills. Carlos is beginning to follow an object for a short distance with his eyes, bring his hands to midline position with assistance at the shoulders, and hold his head up in an erect position while held or seated supported. He is also beginning to smile when certain sounds are made, to vocalize, and to show a change in his behavior (such as an increase in his body activity) when favorite toys are presented to him.

Perhaps most important, Carlos' parents are now able to position and handle him in a more therapeutic and convenient manner. Special attention has been given to making feeding less difficult by introducing strategies such as jaw control techniques to decrease Carlos' excessive jaw and tongue thrust. These skills allow Carlos to adopt more normal movement patterns and also help Carlos' parents to work with him in a less stressful and time-consuming manner—an especially important consideration given the recent brith of Carlos' new baby brother.

Carlos' family, encouraged by his progress, is preparing for Carlos to "graduate" to a preschool program for severely handicapped youngsters that is located in a regular public school in their community.

# Case Study 3: Jamila

Jamila is almost 2 years old. She can sit independently, creep on all fours, and is pulling herself up to a standing position using furniture. While Jamila clearly has some motor delays, she is continuing to make progress in her motor development, even though the rate of development is slower than that of her peers.

Jamila was born 3 weeks early and weighed 5½ pounds. She was sent home on the third day of her life but returned to the hospital several days later because she was having difficulty sucking her bottle and getting formula into her stomach. Upon her return to the hospital, Jamila was placed in the neonatal intensive care unit (NICU) where feeding via a tube through her nose and into her stomach (gavage-feeding) was begun. At this time, it was noted by the medical staff that Jamila had extremely low muscle tone or hypotonia. A series of medical tests was performed, including a brain scan, or CAT scan. All tests were normal. Because of the extreme hypotonia, the physicians wanted to perform a muscle biopsy, which would have required that Jamila be placed under general anesthesia. Due to her very weak condition and feeding difficulties, her parents were reluctant to submit their tiny daughter to this procedure at this time.

Jamila came home from the hospital (for the second time) at 3 weeks of age. Her parents continued to gavage-feed her because she was still not strong enough to suck from a bottle. At 7 weeks of age, Jamila was evaluated by a physical therapist at a university-affiliated child development center. In addition to noting the extreme hypotonia, the physical therapist also suspected that Jamila might have a genetic syndrome because her facial appearance was slightly suggestive of other children with specific genetic syndromes. The developmental pediatrician was called in to evaluate Jamila and recommended to her parents a special chromosome analysis of Jamila's blood. The chromosome analysis would allow the medical staff to look at special banding patterns on each of the chromosomes. The results of this test would take 6 to 8 weeks.

In the meantime, Jamila was referred to a developmental therapy center at a children's hospital for weekly therapy sessions. The therapist worked directly with her and taught her parents to handle and position her optimally. The therapist also showed the parents techniques for trying to improve or build up Jamila's muscle tone and suggested different positions for working on her head control—which was very floppy, even for a young infant.

Jamila's chromosome analysis came back positive for a fairly uncommon genetic disorder that begins with profound congenital hypotonia (very low muscle tone at birth). In other words, the laboratory tests confirmed the diagnosis made clinically by the medical staff based on Jamila's facial appearance, hypotonia, and medical history. Jamila continues to receive developmental physical and occupational therapy twice weekly. She has recently started speech therapy as well because of delays in her language milestones. When she turns 2 years old in a few months, she will be enrolled in an early intervention program where she will continue to receive physical, occupational, and speech therapy.

In Jamila's case—when she was referred for evaluation as an infant with hypotonia and severe motor delay—a definite medical diagnosis was possible. But in less than half of the cases of children with developmental delay who come to hospitals or child developmental centers for evaluations, it is not possible to make a clear diagnosis. This is very frustrating to both parents and professionals. Nonetheless, regardless of whether a diagnosis can be made, it is important to refer such a child for early intervention services in the hope that early treatment will help to minimize the impact of those early delays.

# Case Study 4: Dan

Dan is one of the "star pupils" in an early intervention program. Twenty-six-month-old Dan has been in the program for a year. He was referred to the program because of hypertonicity (or stiffness in his arms and legs), limited vision, and general developmental delay. Dan has subsequently been diagnosed as having cerebral palsy, specifically spastic diplegia (stiffness in all four limbs, especially lower limbs) with additional problems of limited vision resulting from retrolental fibroplasia (RLF), a condition that sometimes occurs when babies are given a lot of oxygen shortly after birth.

Dan's difficulties stem from complications during his birth. He was born 2½ months prematurely at 26–28 weeks gestational age. This 2-pound, 5-ounce baby boy suffered respiratory distress syndrome (RDS), resulting in multiple chest tubes, seizures, feeding difficulties, and general inactivity. Dan had to be given oxygen for 2 months and was hospitalized for over 3 months, at a total expense of over $200,000.

Despite the tremendous complications surrounding his birth, Dan was a lucky little boy because he had good medical care and parents who were watchful and concerned about his development. At 1 year of age, because Dan was generally delayed in his development, Dan's parents and pediatrician began seeking an early intervention program. This decision was made because of the stiffness in Dan's legs, his visual problems, and the delays he showed in developmental skills, such as rolling over. For example, when placed on his stomach Dan held his head up and rolled over at 5–6 months, crawled at 10–12 months, and began pulling himself up to a standing position at 12 months. Smiling began at 5 months, and he started watching his mother and others at 12 months. These observations indicated that Dan's development was delayed in several areas.

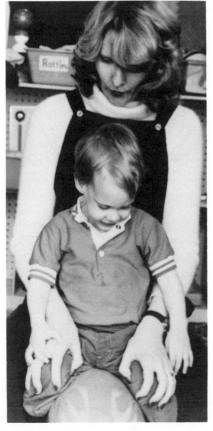

**Figure 3.2**

Dan's family interviewed the staff in several major intervention centers in the large city in which they live and selected a program with a transdisciplinary approach to training. Here therapists, teachers, and psychologists all work together with the parents in developing programs for each child. When Dan began the training program at 14 months, extensive interviews and home visits were scheduled with his family. During these discussions, the parents indicated that two of Dan's favorite activities were standing in his walker and jumping on their laps—both activities that in the judgment of the physical and occupational therapists were inadvertently reinforcing Dan's abnormal movement patterns. Already at 14 months, Dan had developed some "bad habits" in his motor movements that would have been easier to correct with therapy at an even earlier age. Dan's parents are excellent parents—very loving and attentive to their children. Nevertheless, they found it necessary to seek technical assistance for the special developmental needs of their child. Today they are working together with the teachers and therapists at the infant intervention program to facilitate Dan's development. Dan's intervention program focuses on working with parents to identify children's needs and to design training programs for the children that can be done at home during play and caregiving time.

After 12 months in the early education program, Dan has learned to assume a hands-and-knees position and creep to explore his environment, use trunk or body rotation to move in and out of this position, use trunk rotation to roll from his back to his stomach, and pull to a standing position from a half-kneeling position. He is also able to sit independently and rotate his body when in this position. Prior to intervention Dan was unable to turn or rotate his body, but this skill has improved, as have other body-righting and balance reactions.

In the areas of fine-motor and cognitive skills, Dan has begun manipulating objects (e.g., taking toys in and out of containers), understanding that objects are still present even when they are hidden, and imitating motor movements. He is also following objects visually with his eyes, imitating several words, and labeling and requesting actions and objects in the world around him. In feeding, Dan now assists in bringing a cup or spoon to his mouth and has begun finger-feeding; in dressing activities, he also is beginning to assist his parents and teachers. Dan can attend to activities for a longer period of time than when he began "school"—another major goal. He also shows more interest in the other children in the classroom and initiates interactions with them.

Dan's mother and grandmother participate in the classroom training program with Dan and attend a parent meeting every other week during his school time. The whole family is involved in home visits and in periodic parent workshops sponsored by the program. Dan's mother and father report that they have a better understanding of Dan's behavior and developmental problems as a result of program participation.

A more detailed description of Dan's educational program is provided in the following examples of program records. The first example (Figure 3.3) is Dan's Individualized Education Program (IEP). IEPs are written annually for each child at the beginning of the school year and are updated periodically throughout the year. Staff members and parents plan together and set annual goals and short-term objectives for the child's intervention program. These goals and objectives are listed on the IEP. All of these objectives were achieved by Dan during the past year in the early intervention program. Additionally, an example from the charts of Dan's progress as recorded by his parents is shown in Figure 3.4. These records give examples from one intervention program; other programs may use different formats and procedures.

# Individualized Education Program

1. **Name:** Dan                                    **Age:** 1 year, 3 months

2. **Health and Physical:**                          **Birthdate:** 5/22/83
   No specific precautions or medications
   Operation 9/23/84 to have both eye muscles loosened — sliding stitch
   Preterm — 26 weeks gestation
   Limited vision in left eye (no peripheral vision on left side), full vision in right eye
   Stiffness of hips and both legs
   Tone changes from floppy to stiff in trunk

3. **Mode of Communication:**
   Uses vocalization, fussing/crying, and nonverbal gestures to indicate likes and dislikes

4. **Behavioral Characteristics:**
   Very sociable and alert child. Explores physical environment.

5. **Effective Reinforcers:**
   Social reinforcement, toys, adult vocalizations

6. **Extent of Contact with Normal Peers**
   Swim program at Recreation Center, friends in the neighborhood
   Friends — normal peers at school program (3 days/week)

7. **Transportation:**
   Furnished by parents

8. **Additional Services:**

| Services | Initiation Date | Anticipated Date of Completion | Personnel |
|---|---|---|---|
| Special Education | 9/1 | 7/31 | Eve C. |
| Physical Therapy | 9/1 | 7/31 | Karin S. |
| Speech Therapy | 9/1 | 7/31 | Dr. Goldberg |
| Hearing Evaluation | 9/1 | 10/1 | Dr. Franklin |

Conference attended by:

_____          _____
Parent                                                            Teacher

_____          _____
Parent                                                            Therapist

_____          _____
Other                                                              Administrator

9. **Educational Assessment**

   **Gross Motor:**
   Dan pulls to a stand at furniture or on people, but he pulls up onto his toes with stiffening in both legs. He leads more easily with his left leg than his right leg. He cruises in both directions, but more frequently to his left. He has difficulty getting down from standing and generally falls. He assists with his arms and tummy in pull to sit. He sits steadily for 10 minutes. Often he will "W" sit, although this is being discouraged. He is beginning to assume hands-and-knees position.

   Dan is interested in physically exploring his environment and is an active child.

**Figure 3.3**

**Fine Motor:**

Dan's mouthing of toys is decreasing as he learns to explore new objects in different ways. His repertoire of object-manipulation skills includes batting, shaking or moving, banging (i.e., hitting the object on a surface). He also is beginning to push and/or pull a toy and visually examine a toy closely.

Dan displays an accurate reach-and-grasp pattern. He reaches for objects presented in different directions. When Dan has an object in each hand and is offered a third, he tends to drop one of the objects in order to obtain the new one. Dan is beginning to pick up objects using a raking motion. He empties objects from a container by tilting it but does not display total container rotation. He appears to enjoy this activity. He is also beginning to place a ring on a stacking pole.

**Cognitive:**

Dan is a very active and sociable child. He actively explores new objects and new environments. Dan has limited vision in his left eye and full vision in his right eye. His hearing appears intact. He attends well to people as well as to objects. The amount of time he attends to specific tasks is increasing. He has some difficulty tracking people moving around in his environment and would prefer to attend to objects or people that are near him.

Dan locates an object that is partially covered by a screen. He also pulls on a string to obtain an object on a horizontal surface.

In motor imitation, Dan imitates an action that is already in his repertoire. He is beginning to imitate actions that are unfamiliar to him (both actions involving objects and actions involving his body). Dan also demonstrates beginning anticipation of familiar routines.

**Pre-Academic:**

Dan does not point to preferred objects or people when asked to do so.

**Communication:**

Dan currently has limited expressive language at school, but makes more vocalizations at home, especially to familiar people. Now that he is mouthing objects less often, more vocalizations are expected. He has good auditory skills and differentiates Mom, Dad, and Gramma's voices from other people's voices in the room. He is using vowel and consonant sounds in his babbling and says some words in imitation.

**Self-Help/Social**

Dan finger-feeds (assists in spoon-feeding and cup-drinking). Foam inserts on either side of his hips and body are used to provide a narrower highchair.

He also appears to know the difference between being wet and dry.

Dan is a sociable child. He does not appear to fear strangers but demonstrates recognition of those familiar to him. He is an active and curious child, spending much time moving around in space and examining new objects. Dan shows as much curiosity in a familiar environment as in an unfamiliar environment.

Dan is showing more awareness of his peers in a large group setting and during a play situation. He is beginning to initiate interactions with them and will attempt to take away their toys.

Dan will fuss when tired or hungry. He expresses pleasure through smiling. He loves being rough-housed and tickled. He enjoys many kinds of toys, particularly the cloth ball, bells, and blocks.

# Gross Motor

| Goals | Objectives | Anticipated Date of Completion |
|---|---|---|
| 1. Dan will move on hands and knees up at least two stairs. | 1.1 Dan will move to a hands-and-knees position, support his weight in this position, and rock backward and forward for 1 minute on 80% of the trials for two of three consecutive days. | November |
| | 1.2 Dan will independently move forward for 2 feet in an alternating pattern on hands and knees (creeping—one hand and opposite knee forward, then other hand and opposite knee forward, and so on) on 80% of the trials for two of three consecutive days. | January |
| | 1.3 Dan will reach forward with one arm to obtain a toy placed 1 foot in front of him while supported on one hand and both knees on 80% of the trials for two of three consecutive days. | February |
| | 1.4 Dan will creep on hands and knees up two stairs on 80% of the trials for two of three consecutive days. | June |
| 2. Dan will roll independently. | 2.1 Dan will reach with hands and touch knees when lying on his back with feet in the air on 80% of the trials for two of three consecutive days. | December |
| | 2.2 Dan will roll continuously from side to side (turning first at the shoulders, then at the chest, then at the waist, then at the hips and legs) within 60 seconds when placed lying on the floor on 80% of the trials for two of three consecutive days. | March |
| 3. Dan will move into supported standing position from lying position. | 3.1 Dan will raise self from lying on back to sitting by rotating to the side, pushing up on straight arms, rotating the hips and upper legs, and straightening to a sitting position on 80% of the trials for two of three consecutive days. | December |
| | 3.2 Dan will raise self independently from lying on stomach to sitting by pushing onto straight arms, rotating the hips backward, and straightening to a sitting position on 80% of the trials for two of three consecutive days. | June |
| | 3.3 Dan will stand (support own body weight, feet flat on the floor) with minimum support, when held at the hands by parent for 1 minute on 80% of the trials for two of three consecutive days. | March |
| | 3.4 Dan will pull himself to standing by coming to kneeling, pulling to half-kneeling, then to a straight standing position using a furniture support for 80% of the trials for two of three consecutive days. | June |
| 4. Dan will move into and maintain correct sitting position. | 4.1 Dan will move from standing to half-kneeling, then to kneeling and into a sitting position on 80% of the trials for two of three consecutive days. | June |
| | 4.2 Dan will bring his hands and arms from sides to midline when prompted at the hips to assume a sitting position on 80% of the trials for two of three consecutive days. | June |
| | 4.3 Dan will move to a sitting position from a creeping position on hands and knees by rotating hips backward and down on 80% of the trials for two of three consecutive days. | June |
| | 4.4 Dan will maintain a good sitting posture (legs apart, turned slightly outward, and sitting flat on bottom) for 3 minutes while attending to a book on 80% of the trials for two of three consecutive days. | June |

# Communication

| Goals | Objectives | Anticipated Date of Completion |
|---|---|---|
| 1. Dan will turn toward a familiar voice and to an unfamiliar sound. | 1.1 Dan will make eye contact within a few seconds after parent says, "Look at me" on 80% of the occasions for two of three consecutive days. | October |
| | 1.2 Dan will turn his head to the side toward a sound within 10 seconds after the sound is presented on 80% of the trials for two of three consecutive days. | November |
| | 1.3 Dan will look toward the sound source and vocalize when his name is called on 50% of the occasions for two of three consecutive days. | December |
| 2. Dan will make sounds and gestures in response to changes in his environment. | 2.1 Dan will make at least five currently unknown sounds on two of three consecutive days. | December |
| | 2.2 Dan will laugh in response to various verbal or physical stimulation on 50% of the occasions for two of three consecutive days. | December |
| 3. Dan will vocalize and gesture to indicate his desires and needs. | 3.1 Dan will vocalize in response to the removal of a favorite toy on 50% of of the occasions for two of three consecutive days. | December |
| | 3.2 Dan will make five new sounds to request preferred objects and people on 50% of the occasions for two of three consecutive days. | March |
| | 3.3 Dan will combine three different pairs of gestures and vocalizations on 50% of the occasions for two of three consecutive days (e.g., says "uh" and lifts arms to be picked up). | March |
| | 3.4 Dan will say 10 words that are understandable to others (e.g., "water," "dog," "bye-bye") on two of three consecutive days. | June |
| 4. Dan will respond to verbal requests and suggestions. | 4.1 Dan will lift his arms in anticipation of being picked up on 50% of the occasions for two of three consecutive days. | November |
| | 4.2 Dan will momentarily stop what he is doing when commanded "no" on 80% of the occasions for two of three consecutive days. | November |
| | 4.3 Dan will use three gestures to respond to simple requests (e.g., shakes head to indicate "no") on 50% of the occasions for two of three consecutive days. | January |
| | 4.4 Dan will point to five objects or pictures as directed on 80% of the occasions for two of three consecutive days. | March |
| | 4.5 Dan will look toward family member when asked (e.g., "Where's Mom/Dad?") on 80% of the trials for two of three consecutive days. | March |
| | 4.6 Dan will follow five different one-component directions (e.g., "wave bye-bye," "put toys away," "dressing, arm up," "go get") on 80% of the occasions for two of three consecutive days. | June |
| | 4.7 Dan will point to himself immediately when asked on 80% of the occasions for two of three consecutive days. | |
| | 4.8 Dan will point to five different body parts on himself when asked on 80% of the occasions for two of three consecutive days. | June |

## Pre-Academic

| Goals | Objectives | Anticipated Date of Completion |
|---|---|---|
| 1. Dan will identify people and objects in his environment. | 1.1 Dan will point to family members and at least two other persons when asked on 80% of the occasions for two of three consecutive days. | December |
| | 1.2 Dan will point to an object placed within a group of objects within 30 seconds after he is asked on 80% of the occasions for two of three consecutive days. | March |
| | 1.3 Dan will differentially demonstrate the use of five different objects within 1 minute after he is asked (for example: "What do you do with a cup?") on 80% of the occasions for two of three consecutive days. | June |

## Fine Motor and Cognitive

| Goals | Objectives | Anticipated Date of Completion |
|---|---|---|
| 1. Dan will visually track objects. | 1.1 Dan will visually follow an object continuously from side to side on 80% of the trials for two of three consecutive days. | December |
| | 1.2 Dan will visually follow an object being moved in a circular motion on 80% of the trials for two of three consecutive days. | March |
| | 1.3 Dan will visually follow an object being moved vertically (up and down) on 80% of the trials for two of three consecutive days. | March |
| 2. Dan will reach and grasp objects presented at midline. | 2.1 Dan will look at a tiny object for 10 seconds when object is presented on 80% of the trials for two of three consecutive days. | December |
| | 2.2 Dan will grasp (nonreflexively) a small object when it is presented using his palm as well as his fingers on 80% of the trials for two of three consecutive days. | January |
| | 2.3 Dan will use a raking motion with his hand to bring a pellet-sized object to him on 80% of the trials for two of three consecutive days. | February |
| | 2.4 Dan will reach and grasp an object presented in midline at arm's length (elbow extended) on 80% of the trials for two of three consecutive days. | March |
| | 2.5 Dan will reach and grasp an object by reaching across midline on 80% of the trials for two of three consecutive days. | April |
| | 2.6 Dan will grasp a tiny object using thumb, index, and middle fingers on 80% of the trials for two of three consecutive days. | May |
| | 2.7 Dan will grasp a tiny object using a pincer grasp (thumb and index finger) on 80% of the trials for two of three consecutive days. | June |
| 3. Dan will explore toys and objects by moving them in and out of containers and grasping and releasing them voluntarily. | 3.1 Dan will hold a small object in each hand for 5–10 seconds when objects are placed in his hands on 80% of the trials for two of three consecutive days. | January |
| | 3.2 Dan will grasp and manipulate a small toy using rotary wrist movements on 80% of the trials for two of three consecutive days. | February |

| Goals | Objectives | Anticipated Date of Completion |
|---|---|---|
| | 3.3 Dan will bang/hit together two objects held in hands on 80% of the trials for two of three consecutive days. | March |
| | 3.4 Dan will extend his wrist during play with objects 50% of the time he is playing with objects for two of three consecutive days. | March |
| | 3.5 Dan will let go of object from his grasp voluntarily on 100% of the trials for two of three consecutive days. | April |
| | 3.6 Dan will use his index finger to poke at objects or holes in a board on 80% of the trials for two of three consecutive days. | April |
| | 3.7 Dan will remove a peg from a pegboard within 30 seconds after they are presented on 80% of the trials for two of three consecutive days. | June |
| | 3.8 Dan will remove three small toys or objects from a medium-sized container within 60 seconds after they are presented on 80% of the trials for two of three consecutive days. | June |
| | 3.9 Dan will place three small toys in a medium-sized toy container within 60 seconds after they are presented on 80% of the trials for two of three consecutive days. | June |
| | 3.10 Dan will push a ball or toy truck across a flat surface within 30 seconds after the toy is presented on 80% of the trials for two of three consecutive days. | June |
| | 3.11 Dan will stack two rings on a peg within 60 seconds after they are presented on 80% of the trials for two of three consecutive days. | June |
| | 3.12 Dan will put a tiny object into a very small container within 30 seconds after it is presented on 80% of the trials for two of three consecutive days. | June |
| | 3.13 Dan will place circle, square, and triangle shapes into a formboard within 30 seconds after each is presented separately on 80% of the trials for two of three consecutive days. | June |

## Self-Help

| Goals | Objectives | Anticipated Date of Completion |
|---|---|---|
| 1. Dan will drink from a cup and use a spoon. | 1.1 Dan will lick food off upper lip independently on at least 80% of the occasions for two of three consecutive days. | October |
| | 1.2 Dan will hold a small cup with one hand and drink from it with little spillage on 80% of the occasions for two of three consecutive days. | January. |
| | 1.3 Dan will use a napkin to wipe his mouth after drooling or eating on at least 50% of the occasions for two of three consecutive days. | January |
| | 1.4 Dan will engage in mouth-closing exercises when instructed (e.g., kissing, humming, verbal reminders) on 80% of the occasions for two of three consecutive days. | June |
| | 1.5 Dan will scoop food with spoon, bring food to mouth, and remove spoon with few spills on 80% of the occasions for two of three consecutive days. | June |

**Chart of Dan's Progress
Through a Training Program***

**GOAL:**

*Brings hands to midline when prompted (facilitated) to assume sitting position.*

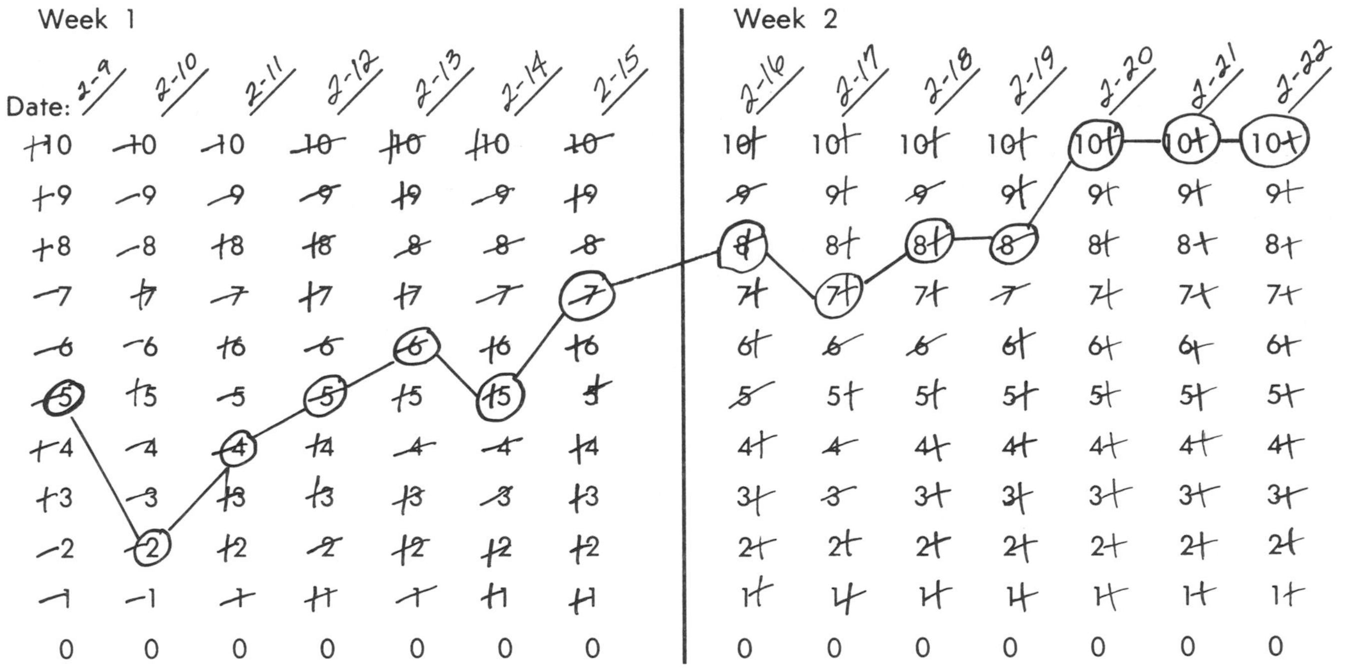

| | Week 1 | | | | | | | | Week 2 | | | | | |
|---|---|---|---|---|---|---|---|---|---|---|---|---|---|---|
| Date: | 2-9 | 2-10 | 2-11 | 2-12 | 2-13 | 2-14 | 2-15 | | 2-16 | 2-17 | 2-18 | 2-19 | 2-20 | 2-21 | 2-22 |

*The charting system is the same as that described in Chapter 6.

**Figure 3.4**

# CHAPTER 4

# Interacting and Teaching

**A**ll parents express concerns about the development of their young children. Are the children happy? Are they healthy? What will they be like when they grow up? Will they have a good job? Will other people like them? Most parents wonder at the same time what they can do to assist their children through the trials and joys of growing up. One of the first steps in this process of raising a child is establishing a relationship with the infant—getting to know the baby. Even in the first few hours of the baby's life a relationship between parent and child begins.

A number of researchers have shown that babies from birth are capable of perceiving and interacting with their environment, especially the people in it—their parents (Appleton, Clifton, & Goldberg, 1975; Stone, Smith, & Murphy, 1973; Sherrod, Vietze, & Friedman, 1978).

As most parents know, babies can signal their family members in many ways. One cry means "I'm hungry"; another cry means "I want my diapers changed." A look can bring a mom or dad across the room, and a baby's smile can begin a game. Researchers have studied these signaling systems and the way in which infants and their caregivers interact with one another (Bell, 1968; Lewis & Rosenblum, 1974).

Though parents and babies signal each other, at times each is confused about the behavior of the other. To reduce the baby's difficulties in understanding the parent, the parent must provide consistent loving care. The parent, on the other hand, can try to understand the baby by recognizing that babies, like adults, are different in terms of their temperament and behavior. Just as babies vary in size, skin color, and the amount of hair on their heads, they vary in behavior and temperament. Some are described as happy-go-lucky, others as fussy and moody. Even brothers and sisters may vary in this way. It is not uncommon to hear a parent remark: "My first baby was so easy to take care of—always happy and so able to entertain herself. But my second one, she's something else. She's into

**Figure 4.1**

everything all the time. She really keeps me on the go." It is certainly fascinating to observe how radically different even young babies can be. However, these differences and changes may also be perplexing to parents as they try to "read" their infant's emotional responses and mood changes, especially at the time when families are adapting to the addition of this new member.

This adaptation may be particularly stressful if complications occur during the baby's birth or if the baby is born with medical and/or developmental problems. Children born prematurely, for example, often sleep a great deal and show irritability and difficulties in feeding. Likewise, children for whom medical interventions are necessary, such as surgery, the delivery of medications, or the use of special apparatus (drainage or feeding tubes), may also be more drowsy, irritable, and/or subject to sleeping and feeding difficulties.

As children grow and develop over the first year of life, some of these early conditions may stabilize; others may not. As parents have the opportunity to observe their baby, they can become better at understanding their infant's needs and behavior. Infants also develop common ways to signal or communicate with their parents, like eye gazes and specific cries and sounds. Again, for those parents whose children have developmental problems, these signals may develop later than usual or may differ from the signals that most infants provide. For example, in extensive observations of blind babies, Selma Fraiberg and her colleagues found blind babies often showed delays in motor development, such as reaching for an object; delays in smiling; and fewer readable expressive facial signs when compared with sighted infants (Fraiberg et al., 1977). The parents of these infants were unable to understand their infants' requests and responses with the usual signals of smiling and eye contact. Instead, through observations of the children's habits, parents learned to read the infants' intentions and wants by watching their hand movements.

A dramatic example of a special communication system between a mother and an infant is the case of Julie and Sherry. Due to genetic errors during her development, Sherry was born with missing arms and feet, facial deformities that included the absence of a true oral cavity (mouth), and visual problems. She had to be fed through a tube in her stomach (a gastrostomy tube) and had few ways of signaling her mother. However, Sherry's mother Julie spent a lot of time caring for and observing her daughter. After several months Julie learned to read Sherry's requests and intentions, which were signalled through the body movements and sounds Sherry made. From these signals, Julie could identify when Sherry was hungry, when Sherry was fussy, and when Sherry wanted her diapers changed (regardless of whether the diapers were wet or dirty!). Though Sherry was limited in the ways she could signal her mother, she and her mother developed a complex communication system with each other. With time and patient observation parents and infants (even infants with severe medical and developmental disorders) can establish a relationship and actively get to know one another. Likewise, children can teach their parents, and parents can teach their children.

## Teaching Your Child

As Kirk walked past David's crib, David squealed and raised his arms. "Hey, do you want Daddy to pick you up?" Kirk smilingly asked his year-old son as he lifted him from the crib. Kirk was teaching David, and David was teaching his father. David "taught" his daddy because he used the "arms up" gesture each time he wanted to be picked up and held. That initiation, coupled with smiles and coos, is likely to train most fathers to respond! Likewise, weeks before, when caring for and playing with his son, Kirk would ask David if he wanted to be picked up, and then would smile and raise him up if the child made any gesture to signal "up." Gradually David learned to use this action to signal his request.

A similar teaching interaction took place between Beverly and her son, Rory. Rory also "told" his mother when he wanted up—but because of stiffness in his arms, Rory used finger movements and a "Hi, Mom, pick me up!" facial expression. Teaching babies to use gestures to communicate is a major developmental goal. Thus, important training was occurring during these early daily caregiving and play activities.

We teach people around us all the time. The purpose of this chapter is to introduce some general strategies and techniques to help you effectively interact with and teach your child. Many of the strategies may be methods you already use. When applied systematically and constantly, they will help you more effectively teach your child.

# General Teaching Strategies

Parents can best help their babies to learn if they use the following strategies:

**Be responsive to your baby and treat your baby as an active learning partner.** As was discussed earlier, even very young babies are able to give their parents signals, such as "I want to be picked up" and "I am hungry." Watch for your baby's signals and respond to them. Even a baby with significant motor problems will be able to signal you; it may just take some time for you to learn to read the signals.

For an infant one of the most powerful signals is the child's cry. Young babies use their cries and later their coos and eye contact to convey many different needs and wants. Respond to your baby's cries. At this early age don't worry about spoiling the child. With the older infant you will be able to tell when your child is "conning" you; it is at that point that you may wish to ignore the cries that are just manipulative.

**Teach your baby through social experiences.** Children learn best (like adults!) through highly motivating experiences. For babies, these experiences are social experiences. Try making the learning activities and motor exercises into positive social interactions and games whenever possible. Use your attention and smiles and hugs as a way of indicating to your child that you like what he is doing.

Young children learn most about the world through play—play with their parents and sisters and brothers and play with toys and other objects in their environment. Parents can assist this learning by being responsive to the child's social initiations. Some initiations like smiles, hugs, and touches are easy to read. Others may be subtle, such as the child's eye glance toward you. This glance may mean that the child is looking to you for praise or confirmation of what she has just done, or it may mean that the child is asking for more information through an eye glance. You must be alert to the child's means of engaging you so that you don't miss these valuable and enjoyable learning opportunities. These experiences are especially important for the child with physical disabilities. Motor problems may limit the child's ability to point or orient toward an activity; eye glances and smiles may be the child's major way of conveying information or questioning you!

Play also provides the child opportunities to learn new things, such as all about objects and their relationships to one another. For example, it is through exploring and playing with toys and objects that the child learns important concepts like big, small, round, under, over—concepts the child must master to be able to interact normally in our world. The more you allow your child to safely move around the environment and explore new items, the more likely the child is to learn new things!

**Take turns when you interact with your baby.**  We all learn by listening or watching and then by initiating or responding. This is true for young children as well. Give your child enough time to "process" the situation and then respond by moving or talking, before you assist the child. For example, if you put a toy in front of the baby, give the baby time to reach for it. If the baby is unsuccessful, put the toy closer, or move the toy to make it more interesting to the baby, or give the baby a small prompt or physical guide to reach the toy. These actions are all preferable to doing the activity for the child. Above all, wait for the baby to try the activity before you jump in to teach him! This *turn-taking* is especially important for speech and language activities. Conversation most definitely involves turn-taking, and young children learn this very quickly. When your baby coos, imitate her, then give her time to coo again. You may also try making a sound, then waiting and giving the baby time to look at you and maybe attempt a sound or a smile. Practice imitating the baby's sounds or actions and give the baby time to try to imitate your sounds and actions. Imitation activities will help you remember to take turns and will also help you develop a turn-taking rhythm with your baby. Take turns with your baby in playing, talking, and all activities.

**Be consistent with your baby.**  Babies are new to the world and need to learn about the environment. They learn best and learn to be secure if they have a consistent and predictable environment. They need to have one or several caregivers whom they know—not a different person every day! They need to have caregivers or parents who respond consistently. For example, if the baby gives a "hungry" cry, the baby needs to be fed—not yelled at, not ignored, or not ignored one time and fed another. Babies need to know that they can count on their caregivers to be there for comfort and basic needs. That goes for social needs, too. Babies need to know that a social smile or coo will result in a smile from Mom or Dad, not a yell sometimes, a smile another, or ignoring at yet another time.

To help promote consistent interactions in your life, insofar as possible, establish routines with your baby. Then your baby will come to expect feeding time, bath time, time to go to day care, time for Mom and Dad to return, shopping time, and bedtime. Other suggestions include making a special place or places for your baby's toys or treasures. These special places should always be safe, within reach of the child, and constructed such that the child can have access to the toys inside (e.g., not too deep). In this way your baby always knows where she can find special items. Finally, try to schedule play and interactions with your baby that are in tune with your baby's rhythms. Play and bounce when the baby is alert, not drowsy. Provide quiet time when the baby is grumpy and tired. Be aware of your baby's moods and try to adjust your interactions accordingly. Your baby will come to love you as a parent and as a safe and secure person to whom she can turn.

**Give your baby varied, everyday learning experiences.** Take your child on walks or outings to the supermarket or to a friend's house. Give the child many sensory experiences. (*Note:* Consult your physician and physical therapist about providing this type of stimulation if your child is very stiff or tactilely defensive.) Let the child feel soft things and rough things such as cotton or fur or coarse cloth. Place your child on different-textured materials, such as terry cloth or a fuzzy rug. Present the child with warm, cold, wet, and gooey substances (like lotions). Don't forget different smells and tastes. Let the child smell an onion or vanilla or an orange. Give the child a taste (just a drop) of grapefruit or something salty. Present the child with a wide variety of shapes and sounds. Furthermore, if your child has a weak side due to low muscle tone and doesn't move that arm often, place a mobile or toy so that the child must hit, touch, or pull it to make it wiggle. Notice that you are helping the child to move by not doing it for him. In general, give the child the opportunity to be in different locations and situations. Position him on stomach, side, and back and move the child around the crib. Also try moving the crib so that the child can see different things. Remember to feed and change the child from different directions. Spend time in conversations with your baby or playing with your baby. Talk to your child throughout the day and describe your activities. Perform these activities naturally as part of your general routine, but not as a constant bombardment upon a poor unsuspecting baby! Overstimulation can be as much of a problem as understimulation. If the baby's environment is constantly filled with noise, such as the blasting of stereo or television, or if the baby is constantly being engaged in activities, he may learn to "tune out." Watch for your baby's signals to know when he is ready and able to interact.

**Maintain a positive attitude about teaching your child.** Both authors have worked with children with very severe and multiple handicaps. However, neither of us has ever met a child who could not learn. Sometimes it can be very difficult and frustrating to work with a disabled child, especially if you are the parent and have responsibility for the child day in and day out. In addition to the rough times, though, there are minutes and days of pure joy! Moments when you watch your child reach for the first time, smile, look at you, play with a toy, greet you when you come home! All children can learn and do! Be confident that your child can learn many things and that you will be the most important teacher your child ever has!

The following sections will introduce you to teaching terms and techniques that you can use effectively to teach your baby new behavior. These techniques have been utilized in many different teaching programs and have been tested by both parents and teachers alike. Remember the six strategies you just learned when applying these techniques. Learning should always be fun and natural for both you and your child. Every day won't be easy, but the relationship you develop with your child will make every minute worth it!

# Teaching Terms

Now let's introduce a few key terms that will be used frequently in this book.

## Behavior or Response

A behavior or response is simply any action of a person. If you turn the light on in a dark room or make a loud sound, your child will probably behave or respond by moving. When your child cries and you go to the crib, you are responding to a change in your environment—the child's cries.

## Learning

Most actions, such as dressing, talking, and walking, are learned or acquired through practice and interaction in the world. Children with developmental delays learn, but do so at a slower rate or in a different way. Special strategies and techniques are often utilized to facilitate their learning. Many of these techniques will be described in this guide and can be used by you to teach your child new actions.

## Environment

The environment is simply your surroundings, the people and things around you. Our environment affects the way we behave. For example, if you hang a mobile or cradle gym 1 to 2 feet above your baby's crib, your baby may begin to look up at it, but it is unlikely that the baby will reach for it because the mobile is too high to touch. However, if the mobile is within the baby's reach, the baby will probably begin to swat at it to make it move.

## Objective or Goal

Before we teach something, we have to have a specific idea about what we want to teach. This idea is an objective or goal. For example, our objective might be to teach the child to follow an object with her eyes as the object is moved from side to side. Your objectives/goals for your child will change as the child gets older and gains new skills.

## Consequences

A consequence refers to anything that follows a response or behavior. For instance, your child might respond to a new toy by reaching out for it. You may praise the child for reaching and also squeak the toy. Praising and squeaking the toy are consequences of your child's response of reaching. The use of consequences is very important in teaching your child and influences the likelihood that your child will do the behavior again. Let's take the example once more and look at your behavior. If your child responds to your behavior of squeaking the toy by crying, you probably won't continue to squeak the toy. On the other hand, if she smiles and coos, you will most likely squeak the toy again.

### Prompt or Cue

A prompt or cue is any action or signal given to get the child to respond in a certain way. For example, the verbal prompt/cue "Hold still" may be used to signal your child during diapering. You may then use a physical prompt/cue to help your child pull to a sitting position after the diaper has been changed.

# Teaching Techniques

This section will present an overview of teaching techniques. Techniques are grouped into two categories: consequation and prompting or cueing. These techniques or methods are used for effectively teaching children.

### Consequation

Consequences (anything that follows a behavior) can either strengthen the behavior they follow (make a behavior more likely to occur) or weaken the behavior they follow (make a behavior less likely to occur).

**Consequences that strengthen the behavior they follow.** These consequences are called *reinforcers*. The use of reinforcement following a child's behavior is the most important strategy we will discuss. Most of the teaching programs presented in the second part of the book incorporate reinforcement as a major part of training because it is useful in building new behavior, such as sitting or playing pat-a-cake.

There are many types of reinforcers—different ones for different people. There are social reinforcers, such as praise ("Good girl," "I like that," "I love you," "Wow"). Physical contact can be reinforcing also (e.g., hugging, touching, patting, stroking). An expression—smiling, nodding, clapping—can be a reinforcer. Even just being near someone or watching someone can be socially reinforcing to them.

Other types of reinforcers are objects (tangible reinforcements). These include items such as food, money, toys, gifts. Doing a favorite activity, like helping Mommy or Daddy in the kitchen, could also be reinforcing to a child. With a young baby many of the reinforcers just named would not be appropriate because the baby has not had time to learn to be "social." However, babies seem to like faces or pictures of faces, bright and shiny objects, colorful items, objects with patterns (checks or plaids, circular patterns, and other prints), and a change of activity (sounds, ball rolling, mobile moving). A baby's bottle can be a reinforcer as can other foods or drinks when the baby is a little older. Family members certainly will become reinforcing to the baby with their smiles and praise.

When selecting effective reinforcers, try different things with the child to see what your child likes best, then follow the behavior you want to strengthen with that reinforcer. For example, let's pretend you are teaching your baby to raise her head up off the blanket when lying on her stomach. You could present a shiny toy for the child to see when the child lifts the head up. Try pairing your social reinforcers—praise, smiles, touches—with the tangible item such as the toy. In addition, change the reinforcers often so that the child does not become bored with them and so that they continue to be reinforcing. For example, don't always use the same squeaker toy; rather, use different toys at different times.

Now list three things that would reinforce you and three things that would reinforce your child.

|  | Parent |  | Child |
|---|---|---|---|
| 1. |  | 1. |  |
| 2. |  | 2. |  |
| 3. |  | 3. |  |

**Your answers might look something like this:**

| | Parent | | Child |
|---|---|---|---|
| 1. | New clothes (tangible reinforcer) | 1. | A shiny bell (tangible reinforcer) |
| 2. | A kiss (social and physical reinforcer) | 2. | A smile and praise from parent like "Good sitting" (social reinforcer) |
| 3. | Going to a movie or concert (activity reinforcer) or Baby says first word, "Mama" or "Dada" (social reinforcer) | 3. | A bite of a cookie or a sip of apple juice (tangible reinforcer) |

To be effective in strengthening or increasing a behavior, a reinforcer must be given immediately after the behavior occurs (but only when the behavior you want to strengthen occurs). For instance, reinforce your child the moment she sits up alone, not after she falls or lies down after sitting. Otherwise you could strengthen some other behavior, such as lying down. When you are first training a behavior, it is important that you reinforce the behavior every time that it occurs. Once the child does the new behavior most of the time, shift to reinforcing that behavior just occasionally. For example, reinforce the behavior after the second, third, or fourth time it occurs.

Reinforcement can also be used to "shape" a new behavior. By shaping we mean reinforcing approximations of the behavior, actions like the behavior being taught. For example, pretend you are trying to teach your child to say the word "ball" when she sees a toy ball. Present the ball and say "ball." You might reinforce the child at first for making any sound, later for saying "b," then for saying "ba," and, finally, when the child says "ball." The key is to gradually require more and more from the child until you have reached your teaching goal or objective. It would be unrealistic to require the child to begin by saying "ball" perfectly the first time so the behavior must be taught in small steps, a little at a time.

**Consequences that weaken the behavior they follow.** There are several ways to weaken a behavior. One way is simply to ignore it. If your child continually whines, ignore it. Look at or attend to the child only when she is not whining. At first, the behavior may increase while your child "tests" out the new situation. However, you'll be surprised at how quickly it decreases if you use this consequence every time whining occurs.

Another method is called *time-out*. This means removal from all reinforcement. Having the child sit in a corner with her back to everything can be a form of time-out. Typically time-out is used when problems such as tantrums occur. If your 3-year-old throws a fit, it might be effective to remove the child to a place where there are no toys, people, or fun activities. Then require the child to stay there until the crying or tantrum stops or for several minutes if the child is already quiet. Do this with as little fuss as possible. Merely say, "No, you can't climb on the bookshelf" and remove the child to the time-out space.

Consequences that weaken the behavior and are applied immediately following a behavior are called *punishers*. Hitting and scolding are punishers and are usually effective in weakening the behavior. However, there are many reasons not to use punishment. Punishment may teach children to escape or avoid the person punishing them. It also shows children how to be aggressive to other people. Why not use reinforcement instead to control your child's behavior? For example, try reinforcing behavior that is the opposite of the bad behavior before the bad behavior has a chance to occur. For instance, reinforce your child for scribbling in the coloring book. If she has an appropriate place to scribble, she won't be as likely to use the walls! Catch your child being good. Reinforce her for helping to pick up toys! In addition, if you want your child to stop throwing food, you could either punish the child when food is thrown or reinforce the child for eating nicely. "Throwing food" can't occur if the child is "eating nicely." Therefore, if your reinforcement is well chosen, your child will eat appropriately more often (behavior strengthened) and throw food less.

## Prompting or Cueing

Prompting or giving a cue to get the child to respond or behave in a certain way is the second major teaching technique. Prompts or cues can be *verbal* (e.g., "Laurene, come here," or "Brett, stand up") or *physical*, such as physically rolling the child over or touching the child's arm to assist in placing a ring on a peg. Many of the teaching programs presented in the second part of this book utilize both verbal and physical prompts. Some of these programs include forms of physical prompting called facilitation/inhibition techniques because the prompting is done to normalize tension in the muscles and to teach specific forms of reaching, looking, or talking. Typically the physical prompts are gradually removed until only a verbal prompt or cue is given. For instance, in teaching a child to pull from a kneeling to a standing position, a parent might begin by saying, "Stand, Cathie" (verbal cue). At the same time, the parent might apply pressure to help the child shift weight to one side and gently tug the child to a standing position (physical cue or prompt). Later the parent might give just the verbal cue and a slight tug to encourage the child to stand, and still later, only a verbal cue (physical prompt or cue removed). A child will not be able to respond to the verbal cue alone until she is old enough to understand language, However, by using the verbal cue with the physical cue a parent can help teach the child to understand verbal instructions.

Other things in our environment are also cues to behave in various ways. Paper and a pencil might be a cue to write or draw. A red light is a cue for us to stop our car when we are driving. Likewise, placing blocks in front of a child might become a cue to the child to stack the cubes once the child has learned how to do this. Ideally the child's actions will eventually come as responses to the entire environment so that verbal and physical teaching cues provided by other persons will not be necessary. For example, it is important that a child learns to walk whenever she wants, not only in response to the parent's verbal cue "Walk."

Here are some examples of the use of prompting or cueing in training programs:

**Example 1:** Teaching child to finger-feed herself.

Begin physically assisting your child by holding her hand (physical prompt or cue) in bringing the food to the mouth. Release child's hand just before the food reaches the mouth. Later release the child's hand 2 inches from the child's mouth, then later 4 inches from the mouth. Then try only a touch on the child's hand to get the child to pick up the food and bring it to the mouth independently. See how prompts/cues can be gradually removed in the course of a training program. Your child's progress will indicate to you how quickly this can be done. At the end of the program, just seeing the food should be a cue to the child to pick up the food (if the child is hungry).

Can you see that you are also "shaping" your child's eating behavior? The baby gets reinforcement, food, and your praise after lifting the food to the mouth. You have gradually required the child to make closer and closer approximations to your goal of finger-feeding. Therefore, you have combined both strategies—reinforcement and prompting. Typically these strategies will be combined in most of the training programs listed in this book.

**Example 2:** Teaching child to place a puzzle piece in proper spot.

You may begin by putting the puzzle piece almost in and directing the child to finish placing it by tapping it in the puzzle hole. The next step might be to place the piece next to the puzzle hole. Still later, you might hand the piece to the child in the correct position. Then, perhaps, you might place the piece in a random position on the table. After the child has mastered this task you may wish to introduce two puzzle pieces. The prompts/cues in this program are your verbal directions (e.g., "Put, Alan") and the physical placement of the puzzle piece. Again you have gradually removed the prompts/cues given your child in this training program.

**Example 3:** Teaching child to reach forward toward an object.

Begin by laying your child on her side or placing her in a sitting position using any equipment required to maintain normalized tone and normal body alignment. You may also wish to employ gentle shaking of the arm if tone is increased. Next prompt your child to reach forward by holding her at the shoulder and turning the arm out. Further prompting may be provided by holding the child's elbow with your other hand and slowly guiding the arm forward toward the object. Gradually remove the prompt at the elbow and at the shoulder as your child learns to reach with normalized tone and muscle coordination and control.

As your baby gets older and learns to imitate you, your behavior (e.g., clapping pat-a-cake) becomes a cue for the baby to respond by imitating—she, too, claps her hands. Imitation is a useful and quick way to teach new actions.

In this section, you have been introduced to two teaching techniques: using consequences (in particular, reinforcement) and using prompting or cueing to teach new behavior. Once a behavior is learned, you will want your child to do that behavior in different settings, with different people, and under many conditions. For instance, you will want your child to walk and talk at school, at the grocery store, and at Grandma's house, not just at your house. Therefore, give your child practice in different situations with different people assisting in teaching the child. As much as possible, arrange the environment to "cue" the child to do a particular behavior. Put the child's toys on top of things so that she must stand to reach them or ask for them. Don't teach the child to rely only on your cues or assistance—gradually remove it. Be creative!

# Problem Behavior

Although most of your teaching will be directed at teaching your baby new actions, there are occasional problems you may encounter even with the child under 2 years of age.

## Negative Behavior

Negative behavior includes such actions as kicking, throwing, and biting. Babies normally throw things for a period of time because they are learning that when they let go, something happens. The object crashes to the floor and usually makes a sound. However, if the child always throws food and other items, you might try the following procedures. Suppose your child is hungry and is given a dish of food and a spoon. The child dips the spoon in the food and throws it on the floor or spoons all the food onto the tray, not into the mouth. You might try saying "no" sternly and removing the food and ignoring the child for 20 or 30 seconds. In general, say "no" sharply, then remove the items. Ignore the child for a brief period of time, then begin again. Young children, of course, will be messy and will try out new behavior. If these actions start to happen all the time, or if your child's actions destroy things or hurt others, it might be necessary for you to use these strategies to weaken the behavior. However, don't forget to always reinforce your child for being nice to others and doing activities appropriately.

## Tantrums

It is unlikely that you will experience many full-fledged tantrums by your child when he is a young infant. However, if this becomes a problem later you might wish to use the time-out procedure discussed earlier. The books listed in Appendix 3 as references for managing child behavior will provide a more extensive discussion of this procedure to guide you in its use.

## Helplessness

Just as you can teach your child to talk and to feed herself, you also can teach her to be helpless and "retarded." You can do this by constantly waiting on the child and never demanding anything from the child. You can train your baby to be a tyrant over your whole family, to cry and whine helplessly until aid is given. If you don't want this behavior, teach your child many new skills so that she can actively explore the environment and interact with that environment relatively independently of you. Encourage actions your child makes, such as crawling into the kitchen, saying "Hi," even getting into your cupboards! Treat your child as normally as possible.

# Summary

Treat your child as you would treat any child. Although your child has some special problems and you will have to work harder than usual to teach your child, he needs the same treatment that anyone does—love, care, and quality learning experiences. Give your child time and opportunity to do things on his own. Attend to the initiations the child makes to you and to others. Finally, respond when the child coos, reaches, crawls, walks. Remember, as parents you are the most important people to your child and what you do *does* make a difference. The ideas and programs suggested in this book will not require you to change your lifestyle or work habits. They are merely guidelines to use in the course of your daily living to help your child's development.

# CHAPTER 5

# Breaking Behavior into Small Steps

**I**t is recommended that you read this chapter through several times and try to answer the questions in it before actually beginning to use the teaching programs in this manual. Then use the chapter as a reference when you need to adapt the teaching programs for your child. This chapter is technical, so do not worry if you have difficulty understanding it at first.

The chapter will introduce you to a procedure for teaching your child new activities. For example, when your child is a young baby, you may want to teach rolling over, head control, and reaching for a toy. Eventually, you will build on these beginning behaviors to help your baby learn more complex things such as sitting, crawling, standing, and walking. In addition to these physical behaviors, your baby may require teaching in other areas, such as communicating (speech) and identifying colors and shapes (concepts).

You are probably thinking: "Aren't all these things learned by children naturally as children grow up?" Well, yes and no. Children can and do learn as they grow up, through watching and listening to others, through experiencing and practicing behavior, and through gaining physical strength as they grow. However, some children require special teaching or therapy techniques to develop. These techniques can encourage children to learn more easily and at a younger age than would be expected without teaching.

You, as a parent, can teach your child a wide variety of behaviors by breaking each behavior into small, easily learned steps. This process of breaking a behavior into small steps is called *task analysis*. While this term sounds very technical and scientific, it is a fairly simple procedure. For

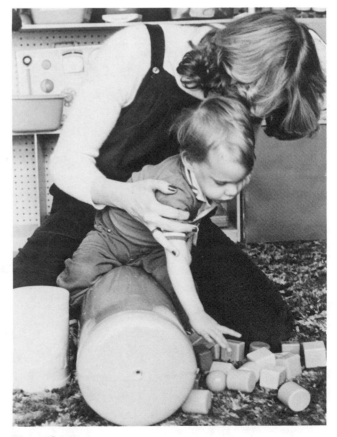

**Figure 5.1**

This chapter is adapted from N. M. Todd and M. J. Hanson, "Breaking Behavior into Small Steps," in Hanson, M. J. (1977) *Teaching Your Down's Syndrome Infant: A Guide for Parents.* Austin, TX: PRO-ED.

example, let's look at the steps that make up the task of washing your hands while standing at the sink.

1. Child turns on cold water.

2. Child turns on hot water so as to achieve warm water with which to wash hot hands.

3. Child removes soap from the soap dish.

4. Child holds soap between hands and places both hands and soap beneath the running water.

5. Child rubs both hands with soap.

6. Child places soap either back in soap dish or on side of sink.

7. Child rubs both hands together working up lather with soap.

8. Child rinses hands under water.

9. Child shuts off hot water.

10. Child shuts off cold water. (Adapted from Baldwin, Fredericks, & Brodsky, 1973)

See how a very simple behavior can be broken down into many steps? Washing hands is not usually considered to be complex, yet it has been broken down into 10 steps that can be broken into even smaller steps.

Now let's talk about how you can learn to break a behavior into its many parts. To help you understand task analysis, the process is separated into four basic actions:

1. Decide which behavior you want to teach and which cues and consequences you will use to teach the behavior.

2. Break the behavior into the necessary steps needed and order these steps.

3. Decide how well the child must do the behavior you are teaching.

4. See what your child can already do and then decide where in the sequence of steps you should begin teaching.

The remainder of this chapter will show you how to do these things, one at a time. Examples will be given so that you can practice each action.

# Action 1: Decide Which Behavior You Want to Teach

Before you can teach your child, you must *decide exactly what behavior you want to teach*. For example: "Jennifer will lift her head."

Next, *describe the behavior* in such a way that another person could sit down, watch the child, and tell you whether or not she was performing the behavior. This is called observing (watching) for the skill. For example:

**Precise Description:** "Jennifer will move her head up so that her chin is parallel to the floor."

**Child's Position:** "On her stomach over a wedge."

Thus, the beginning would be Jennifer moving her head off the floor. The ending would be her head up with chin parallel to the floor.

Behavior that has a definite beginning and ending can be counted (measured) to determine how often the child does the behavior. Responses such as pointing, naming, picking up, and matching are all observable and measurable. However, enjoying, appreciating, and understanding are not observable and measurable—they do not have a definite beginning and a definite ending.

Once you have described the behavior you want to teach, *decide upon a cue/prompt to tell your child when you want her to do the behavior*. This cue will tell the child that *now* is when you want her to do the behavior. It is important that you use the same cue each time you want the behavior done as you are teaching it.

Your cue can be a verbal cue (e.g., "Head up, Maria"), a physical cue (e.g., pushing up under her chin to begin her head movement while saying, "Head up, Maria"), or showing the child an object or toy and shaking it above her head (object cue). It is always important to combine the verbal cue with the physical or object cue. Later when your child learns to understand words you can use only the verbal cue. Here is an example:

**Behavior:** "Jennifer will lift her head."

**Precise Description:** "Jennifer will move her head up with chin parallel to the floor."

**Child's Position:** "On her stomach over a wedge."

**What Cues/Prompts?** Shake favorite toy (that makes noise) above eye level. Say "Head up."

After you have described the behavior and decided upon the cue or prompt that you will use to teach your child, you can then decide what *consequences you will provide when your child performs the required behavior*. In Chapter 4, you practiced identifying things that are reinforcing for your child. This list probably includes toys, foods, particular people, and certain activities and events. Now is the time when you will use one of these "known" reinforcers after your child's successful performance. If your child has many preferences, the most effective consequences are those that directly relate to the behavior you want to teach. For instance, food reinforcers fit well with teaching your child to eat, and favorite toys are most appropriate in grasping or looking activities or even when teaching your child to crawl or walk.

In reviewing Action 1, you have been introduced to the following procedures: describing a behavior, deciding on cues to tell the child when to do the behavior, and providing consequences for performance. Now you can practice using this approach by doing the following example. You can compare your answer with the answer included after the example. This is only *one* answer— it is okay if you come close to this example, although your steps and wording might differ somewhat.

## Example

### Behavior: CHILD REACHES FOR AN OBJECT

A. Decide which behavior you want to teach. (Write your complete description here.)

B. Decide on the cue/prompt you will use to tell your child when to do the behavior.

C. Decide on the consequences to the behavior.

## Answer

### Behavior: CHILD REACHES FOR AN OBJECT

A. Decide which behavior you want to teach.

   *Lamont will reach for a noise-making object placed 2 inches from his right or left hand.*

   Child's position: *Sitting in his adaptive corner chair with the tray attached.*

B. Decide on the cue you will use to tell your child when to do the behavior.

   *Give an object cue by shaking the object in front of the child for a few seconds while saying, "Reach, Lamont." Use physical prompt at shoulder to facilitate movement if Lamont does not initiate.*

C. Decide on the consequences to the behavior.

   *Lamont can play with the object for a few seconds.*

# Action 2: Break the Behavior into the Necessary Steps and Order These Steps

After you have decided on the behavior you want to teach your child, you will need to *determine all the small steps* that make up the behavior. You may want to look again at all of the small steps outlined earlier for the skill of washing hands. The emphasis here is on looking at the many actions we as adults consider to be simple, but which are actually very complex combinations of many smaller steps. While actions such as pouring milk and buttering bread may seem to be simple for us, to a child they are as complex as the number of steps into which we can divide those actions. Thus, when we teach a child to eat his cereal, or walk across the room, or drink from a glass, it has been found that it is best to break that action into small parts and teach each of the parts separately. For example, here is the skill of buttering a piece of bread broken into smaller steps.

1. Assuming you are right-handed, place your fingers around the knife with your forefinger extended on top of the knife.

2. Lift the knife from the counter and move it in the direction of the butter dish.

3. Assuming you have a one-quarter pound block of butter, place the blade of the knife approximately one-quarter of an inch from the square edge of the block, resting on top of the block of butter.

4. Press down with the forefinger, causing the knife to cut through the block of butter.

5. Move the knife slightly to the left, lifting the cut part of butter on the knife blade.

6. Balance the pat of butter on the knife blade; move the knife to the piece of bread.

7. Pick the piece of bread up with your left hand, letting it rest in the palm of your hand, being steadied by your fingers.

8. Place the pat of butter on the right edge of the bread.

9. Move the knife to the left, pressing the butter onto the bread.

10. Return the knife to the far edge of the bread, adjacent to the position in Step 8.

11. Repeat Steps 9 and 10 as many times as necessary until the bread is covered with butter.

12. Replace the bread on the board.

13. Move knife to butter plate.

14. Place knife on butter plate. (Baldwin, Fredericks, & Brodsky, 1973; pp. 14–19)

Buttering a piece of bread is just one example of how a very simple behavior can be broken into many small steps.

*Order the smaller steps in the sequence necessary to do the behavior.* Once you have broken the behavior into its smaller steps, it is important to sequence the steps in the order in which they occur logically when you do the behavior. The simplest way to determine this sequence is to perform the task yourself and write down each small step as you go along. Then to check yourself, you can perform each step as you read through your sequence. If the task is completed when you come to the end of your sequence, you have all the necessary steps—in the correct order. As you can see from the bread-buttering example, steps were listed in the order in which they occur as that task is naturally done.

Now it is your turn. To give you more practice, an example is given. An answer follows the example. Again, this is only one answer—your steps and wording might differ somewhat.

## Example

### Behavior: CHILD VISUALLY FOLLOWS A MOVING OBJECT

A. Decide which behavior you want to teach. (Write your complete description here.)

B. Decide on the cue you will use to tell your child when to do the behavior.

C. Decide on the consequences to the behavior.

D. Break the behavior into small steps and order the steps.

## Answer

### Behavior: CHILD VISUALLY FOLLOWS A MOVING OBJECT

A. Decide which behavior you want to teach.

*Child will look at and visually follow an object moved from side to side when in backlying position with head support.*

B. Decide on the cue you will use to tell your child when to do the behavior.

*Say, "Look, Steven," while presenting a favorite object directly in front of him.*

C. Decide on the consequences to the behavior.

*Activate the toy when Steven looks and follows to the side.*

D. Break the behavior into small steps and order the steps.

1. *Child looks at object for a few seconds.*

2. *Child looks at object and visually follows it from directly in front of face to 2 inches to one side (alternating sides each time done).*

3. *Child looks at object and visually follows it from directly in front of face to as far to the side as child can comfortably turn head. (Can do this going both directions.)*

4. *Child looks at object and visually follows it from one side completely over to the other side.*

# Action 3: Decide How Well the Child Must Do the Behavior You Are Teaching

After you have described the behavior and decided which cue to use, then broken the behavior into small steps and ordered these steps, you must decide how well the child must master this skill. In other words, you must decide when the child should do the behavior, how long and/or how far, and how many times.

First, this requires that you *decide how long (number of seconds) you will wait (following your cue) for the child to do the behavior*. This decision is based on your own judgment. For example:

**Behavior:** Kim will move her head up so that her chin is parallel to the floor.

**Child's Position:** On her stomach over a wedge.

**Cues/Prompts:** Shake toy (that makes noise) above eye level. Say, "Head up."

**Consequences:** Kim can play with toy for a few seconds.

**Within what time period?** 30 seconds after toy is presented.

Next, in order to decide whether she has done the task, you should *decide the distance she must go to do the behavior* and *the length of time she must do it*. For example:

**Precise Description:** Kim will move her head up so that her chin is parallel to the floor and maintain this position for 5 seconds.

Finally, *decide how often the child must do the behavior correctly* before you move on to a new teaching step. Often children are required to do the task on 8 out of 10 trials (or 80%) before moving to a new step. However, this decision is based purely on your own judgment.

Let's take the example of "CHILD VISUALLY FOLLOWS A MOVING OBJECT" again and add practice on Action 3.

---

## Example

### Behavior: CHILD VISUALLY FOLLOWS A MOVING OBJECT

A. Decide which behavior you want to teach.

*Child will look at and visually follow an object moved from side to side when in backlying position with head support.*

B. Decide on the cue you will use to tell your child when to do the behavior.

*Say, "Look, Steven," while presenting a favorite object directly in front of him.*

C. Decide on the consequences to the behavior.

*Activate the toy when Steven looks and follows to the side.*

D. Break the behavior into small steps and order the steps.

1. *Child looks at object for a few seconds.*

2. *Child looks at object and visually follows it from directly in front of face to 2 inches to one side (alternating sides each time done).*

3. *Child looks at object and visually follows it from directly in front of face to as far to the side as child can comfortably turn head. (Can do this going both directions.)*

4. *Child looks at object and visually follows it from one side completely over to the other side.*

E. Decide how well the child must do the behavior.
   1. The number of seconds you will wait following the cue.

   2. The number of seconds or distance required for the child to perform the behavior. (This will change for each teaching step.)

   3. The number of times the child should correctly perform the behavior.

## Answer

### Behavior: CHILD VISUALLY FOLLOWS A MOVING OBJECT

A. Decide which behavior you want to teach.

*Child will look at and visually follow an object moved from side to side when in backlying position with head support.*

B. Decide on the cue you will use to tell your child when to do the behavior.

*Say, "Look, Steven," while presenting a favorite object directly in front of him.*

C. Decide on the consequences to the behavior.

*Activate the toy when Steven looks and follows to the side.*

D. Break the behavior into small steps and order the steps.

1. *Child looks at object for a few seconds.*

2. *Child looks at object and visually follows it from directly in front of face to 2 inches to one side (alternating sides each time done).*

3. *Child looks at object and visually follows it from directly in front of face to as far to the side as child can comfortably turn head.*

4. *Child looks at object and visually follows it from one side completely over to the other side.*

E. Decide how well the child must do the behavior.

1. The number of seconds you will wait following the cue.

*The child will look at the object within 30 seconds after the object and verbal cues are given.*

2. The number of seconds or distance required for the child to perform the behavior. (This will change for each teaching step.)

*The child will look at the object and follow the object visually as it is moved 2 inches to the side.*

3. The number of times the child should correctly perform the behavior.

*The child will perform correctly on 8 out of 10 times. When the child does this 8 out of 10 times for 3 days in a row, he can go on to the next step.*

Need more practice? Try another example.

## Example

**Behavior: CHILD ROLLS FROM BACK TO STOMACH**

A. Decide which behavior you want to teach. (Write your complete description here.)

B. Decide on the cue you will use to tell your child when to do the behavior.

C. Decide on the consequences to the behavior.

D. Break the behavior into small steps and order the steps.

E. Decide how well the child must do the behavior.

    1. The number of seconds you will wait following the cue.

    2. The number of seconds or distance required for the child to perform the behavior. (This will change for each teaching step.)

    3. The number of times the child should correctly perform the behavior.

## Answer

### Behavior: CHILD ROLLS FROM BACK TO STOMACH

A.  Decide which behavior you want to teach.

*Child will roll continuously from back to stomach without assistance.*

B.  Decide on the cue you will use to tell your child when to do the behavior.

*Say, "Roll over, Jerome," while physically assisting child. Favorite toys are lying out of reach in direction child will roll to encourage rolling.*

C.  Decide on the consequences to behavior:

*Play with toy obtained through mobility of rolling.*

D.  Break the behavior into small steps and order the steps.

1.  *When the child is lying on his back, physically bring his arm across his chest and by bending child at knee gently roll the child all the way over from back to stomach.*

2.  *Child is physically rolled three quarters of the way over; rolls the last one quarter of the roll on his own.*

3.  *Child is physically rolled one half of the way over; rolls the last one half of the roll on his own.*

4.  *Child is physically rolled one quarter of the way over; rolls the last three quarters of the roll on his own.*

5.  *Child rolls on his own from back to stomach with only a slight physical cue to begin the roll.*

6.  *Child rolls on his own from back to stomach.*

*Note:* The verbal cue "Roll over, Jerome" is used during each step.

E.  Decide how well the child must do the behavior.

1.  The number of seconds you will wait following the cue.

*Child will roll within 30 seconds of cue.*

2.  The number of seconds or distance required for the child to perform the behavior. (This will change for each teaching step.)

*Child will roll one half the distance of the roll (as illustrated in step 3 above).*

3.  The number of times the child should correctly perform the behavior.

*Child will perform correctly on 8 out of 10 times. When the child does this 8 out of 10 times for 3 days in a row, he can go on to the next step.*

## Action 4: See What Your Child Can Already Do and Then Decide Where You Should Begin Teaching

Although you may have outlined 15 small steps in your skill sequence, your child may already be able to do the first 7 steps. Therefore, it is important that you observe the child performing or attempting to do the behavior before you begin teaching it.

To do this, simply position the child in such a way that he would be likely to perform the behavior if he knew how. Put your sequence of steps close by and place a check by any of the steps he is able to do. Generally it is a good idea to set up this situation a few times a day for 2 or 3 days so you can get an accurate idea of his behavior. With this information you can decide exactly where in the sequence of steps you should begin teaching.

Now, using your "CHILD VISUALLY FOLLOWS A MOVING OBJECT" example, show where in the sequence of steps you would begin teaching if, for instance, your child could already visually follow an object moved from in front of face over 2 inches to the side. The answer follows.

### Answer

**Behavior: CHILD VISUALLY FOLLOWS A MOVING OBJECT**

A.  Decide which behavior you want to teach.

*Child will look at and visually follow an object moved from side to side when in backlying position with head support.*

B.  Decide on the cue you will use to tell your child when to do the behavior.

*Say, "Look, Steven," while presenting a favorite object directly in front of him.*

C.  Decide on the consequences to the behavior.

*Activate toy when Steven looks and follows to the side.*

D.  Break the behavior into small steps and order the steps.

1.  *Child looks at object for a few seconds.*

2.  *Child looks at object and visually follows it from directly in front of face to 2 inches to one side (alternating sides each time done).*

★ ★ ★ ★ ★ **Start Teaching Here** ★ ★ ★ ★ ★

3.  *Child looks at object and visually follows it from directly in front of face to as far to the side as child can comfortably turn head. (Can do this going both directions).*

4.  *Child looks at object and visually follows it from one side completely over to the other side.*

E. Decide how well the child must do the behavior.

  1. The number of seconds you will wait following the cue.

     *The child will look at the object within 30 seconds after the object and verbal cue are given.*

  2. The number of seconds or distance required for the child to perform the behavior. (This will change for each teaching step.)

     *The child will look at the object and follow the object visually as it is moved 2 inches.*

  3. The number of times the child should correctly perform the behavior.

     *Child will perform correctly 8 out of 10 times. When the child does this 8 out of 10 times for 3 days in a row, he can go on to the next step.*

---

You have been introduced to the following guides or actions for task analyzing and teaching a behavior:

1. **Deciding which behavior you want to teach and which cues and consequences to use.**

2. **Breaking the behavior into steps and ordering those steps.**

3. **Deciding how well the child must do the behavior.**

4. **Seeing what your child can already do and then deciding where in the sequence of steps to begin teaching.**

As you become familiar with teaching programs in this book, you will realize that we used these same actions in writing our programs. However, every child is different. Therefore, we cannot possibly make every program suited to just your child. For this reason, it may be necessary for you to change the programs we have listed and break them into smaller steps. For instance, as in the "CHILD VISUALLY FOLLOWS A MOVING OBJECT" example, it might be necessary to begin by having the child follow the object just 1 inch or even ½ inch rather than the 2 inches recommended. Go ahead and change the programs to fit your child's needs.

Use this chapter as a reference or guide while you are teaching. Refer to it whenever you find that you must change a program or come up with a new one.

# CHAPTER 6

# Observing and Recording the Child's Progress

In the previous chapters you were introduced to some basic strategies and techniques for teaching children. You also learned how to break a behavior into small steps (task analysis) in order to teach it. The major focus of this chapter is on observing your child's development in specific areas and recording this progress in a systematic way. These strategies will assist you in utilizing the teaching activities presented in Part II. You may find it useful to reread Chapters 4 and 5 before working through this chapter.

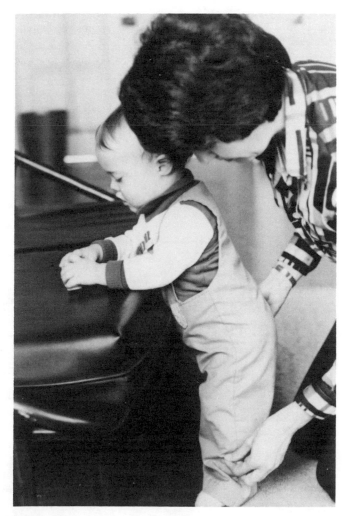

**Figure 6.1**

# Identifying Your Child's Needs

To identify your child's needs and decide which activities (presented in Part II) will benefit your child most, try the following four-step process: *planning, assessing, observing, deciding.*

**Planning** involves gathering the materials you need to do the activity and determining suggested positions or directions for the child. Once you have developed these preliminary plans you are ready to assess your child informally.

**Assessing** means that you introduce your child to the activity by placing the child in the appropriate position and showing the child the materials or giving the child the cues that are needed.

**Observing** is a very important skill to cultivate. When you are observing, watch to see how your child responds to the assessing/teaching situation. Does the child perform the behavior? Is the child able to do the task with a little assistance from you? How quickly or slowly does the child respond? Does the child enjoy the activity? Does the child maintain the appropriate position while doing the activity? These are all questions you must answer while observing so that you can move to the final step of deciding.

**Deciding** what to teach and how to teach is a difficult task. Use the programs suggested in the second part of this manual and also consult your child's physical or occupational therapist and/or teacher for assistance. After deciding on the appropriate program and then beginning your teaching, you may realize after a few days or a week that your child is not learning the task and that another procedure might work better. If so, repeat the four-step process and design a new program. Not all activities work for all children, and it is impossible to make the right teaching choice every time. That is why your observations of different situations over a long period of time are so important. Trust your observations and work with professionals who know your child so that you can design and update your teaching methods on a continuous basis.

For reference purposes, developmental milestone charts are presented in Appendix 1. These charts show skills typically accomplished by children from birth to 2 years of age. Some children with motor delays will grow and develop according to these developmental milestones and sequences and others will do so differently. However, these charts can provide a useful reference or guide for you in planning teaching activities.

# Recording Your Child's Progress

There are many reasons why it is important to gather information or collect data on a child's progress in a training program. First of all, since we want the child to progress as rapidly as possible, it is easy to think, "Oh, yes, my child is doing fine." However, it is important to be very objective and continue to teach a behavior until the child is able to perform it independently in different situations. Otherwise, we may omit teaching that is necessary for the child's best development. Second, collecting information helps us make decisions about our teaching. If we see from the data that a particular teaching program is not positively changing the child's behavior, then we can change the teaching procedure right then without frustrating the child and wasting more time. Third, a system for data collection allows parents to be active participants in their child's development and to convey information on the child's progress to other professionals. How many times has your doctor or a teacher or therapist asked about an aspect of your child's development? Now you can answer with specific information: "Julie walks 5 steps by herself"; "Max says 10 words so

TARGET SKILL:

Week 1                                                    Week 2

Date: /  /  /  /  /  /  /  |  /  /  /  /  /  /  /

| 10 | 10 | 10 | 10 | 10 | 10 | 10 | 10 | 10 | 10 | 10 | 10 | 10 | 10 |
|----|----|----|----|----|----|----|----|----|----|----|----|----|----|
| 9 | 9 | 9 | 9 | 9 | 9 | 9 | 9 | 9 | 9 | 9 | 9 | 9 | 9 |
| 8 | 8 | 8 | 8 | 8 | 8 | 8 | 8 | 8 | 8 | 8 | 8 | 8 | 8 |
| 7 | 7 | 7 | 7 | 7 | 7 | 7 | 7 | 7 | 7 | 7 | 7 | 7 | 7 |
| 6 | 6 | 6 | 6 | 6 | 6 | 6 | 6 | 6 | 6 | 6 | 6 | 6 | 6 |
| 5 | 5 | 5 | 5 | 5 | 5 | 5 | 5 | 5 | 5 | 5 | 5 | 5 | 5 |
| 4 | 4 | 4 | 4 | 4 | 4 | 4 | 4 | 4 | 4 | 4 | 4 | 4 | 4 |
| 3 | 3 | 3 | 3 | 3 | 3 | 3 | 3 | 3 | 3 | 3 | 3 | 3 | 3 |
| 2 | 2 | 2 | 2 | 2 | 2 | 2 | 2 | 2 | 2 | 2 | 2 | 2 | 2 |
| 1 | 1 | 1 | 1 | 1 | 1 | 1 | 1 | 1 | 1 | 1 | 1 | 1 | 1 |
| 0 | 0 | 0 | 0 | 0 | 0 | 0 | 0 | 0 | 0 | 0 | 0 | 0 | 0 |

Week 3                                                    Week 4

Date: /  /  /  /  /  /  /  |  /  /  /  /  /  /  /

| 10 | 10 | 10 | 10 | 10 | 10 | 10 | 10 | 10 | 10 | 10 | 10 | 10 | 10 |
|----|----|----|----|----|----|----|----|----|----|----|----|----|----|
| 9 | 9 | 9 | 9 | 9 | 9 | 9 | 9 | 9 | 9 | 9 | 9 | 9 | 9 |
| 8 | 8 | 8 | 8 | 8 | 8 | 8 | 8 | 8 | 8 | 8 | 8 | 8 | 8 |
| 7 | 7 | 7 | 7 | 7 | 7 | 7 | 7 | 7 | 7 | 7 | 7 | 7 | 7 |
| 6 | 6 | 6 | 6 | 6 | 6 | 6 | 6 | 6 | 6 | 6 | 6 | 6 | 6 |
| 5 | 5 | 5 | 5 | 5 | 5 | 5 | 5 | 5 | 5 | 5 | 5 | 5 | 5 |
| 4 | 4 | 4 | 4 | 4 | 4 | 4 | 4 | 4 | 4 | 4 | 4 | 4 | 4 |
| 3 | 3 | 3 | 3 | 3 | 3 | 3 | 3 | 3 | 3 | 3 | 3 | 3 | 3 |
| 2 | 2 | 2 | 2 | 2 | 2 | 2 | 2 | 2 | 2 | 2 | 2 | 2 | 2 |
| 1 | 1 | 1 | 1 | 1 | 1 | 1 | 1 | 1 | 1 | 1 | 1 | 1 | 1 |
| 0 | 0 | 0 | 0 | 0 | 0 | 0 | 0 | 0 | 0 | 0 | 0 | 0 | 0 |

NOTES:

From Hanson, M. J. (1977). *Teaching your Down's syndrome infant.* Austin, TX: PRO-ED.

**Figure 6.2.** Recording Sheet.

clearly that others can understand him." By recording your child's progress you can better evaluate your own progress in teaching your child and also evaluate the suggestions of others assisting you.

A data collection and recording system found to be useful and simple to read will be explained in this chapter. A sample recording sheet is included for reference (see Figure 6.2). This system is a modification of a recording system devised by Saunders and Koplik (1975) and used in the Down Syndrome Infant Parent Program (Hanson, 1977). Each recording sheet is divided into four boxes, each box representing 1 week of information. Each column in the box represents a particular day of the week, so there are seven columns per box. Thus, each sheet allows you to record data daily on one program for 4 weeks. Make copies of the recording sheet for use in working with your child at home.

Here's how easy it is to record your observations. Refer to Figure 6.3. Let's suppose that you are working on a reaching program and that the teaching step is: Child will reach 1 inch to touch object within 20 seconds after given the cue "Reach, Susan." Therefore, write "Reaching" by TARGET SKILL and record the date (e.g., "5–1" or "May 1") at the top of the first column. On the first trial (see "1" at the bottom of the column), the child succeeds and reaches the object placed 1 inch away within that time. Therefore, you record a plus sign ("+") because she made the correct response by reaching 1 inch. On the second trial, she also makes the correct response, so you score another "+" next to the number 2. However, on the third trial, she does not reach or else she looks away. Therefore, you score a minus sign ("−") beside the number 3, and so on. At the end of the day, if you have done 10 trials, you merely count the number of plus signs and circle that number. On the example below, there were 6 plus signs recorded, so the number 6 was circled.

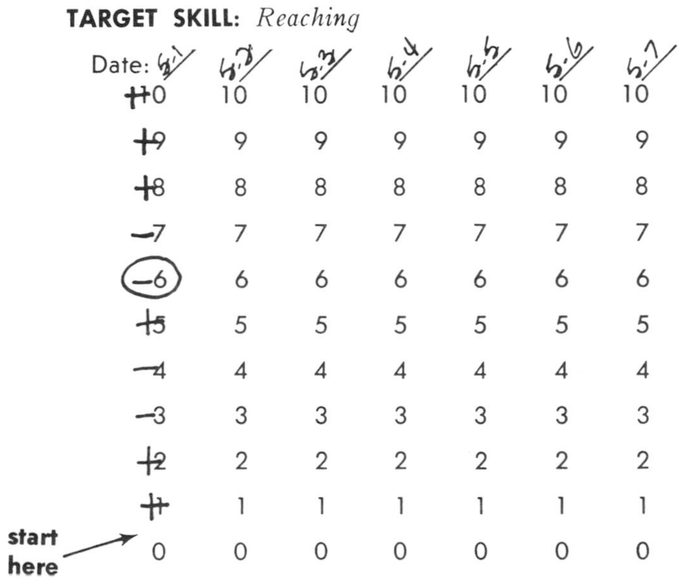

**TARGET SKILL:** *Reaching*

Figure 6.3

You are actually figuring out the percentage of correct responses for that day—which is usually found by dividing the number of correct responses (6) by the total number of trials (10). In this case, you just add a zero to the number you have circled (if you have done 10 trials) and that figure gives you the percentage. On each following day you record your observations in the same way, counting the number of plus signs per day and circling that number (see Figure 6.4). Connect the circles across days and you have a graph of your child's progress. If the graphed line is going up, you can see that your child is making progress; if not, it is time to change the procedures you're using.

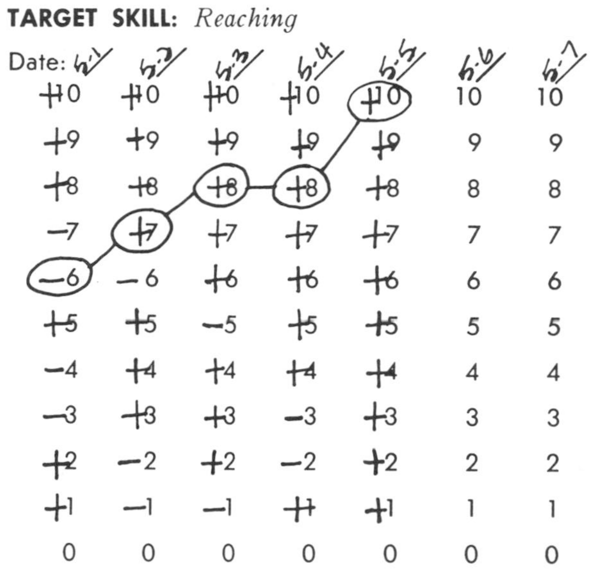

**TARGET SKILL:** *Reaching*

Date: 6/1  6/2  6/3  6/4  6/5  6/6  6/7

| ⊞0 | ⊞0 | ⊞0 | ⊞0 | (⊞0) | 10 | 10 |
| +9 | +9 | +9 | +9 | +9 | 9 | 9 |
| +8 | +8 | (+8) | (+8) | +8 | 8 | 8 |
| −7 | (+7) | +7 | +7 | +7 | 7 | 7 |
| (−6) | −6 | +6 | +6 | +6 | 6 | 6 |
| +5 | +5 | −5 | +5 | +5 | 5 | 5 |
| −4 | +4 | +4 | +4 | +4 | 4 | 4 |
| −3 | +3 | +3 | −3 | +3 | 3 | 3 |
| +2 | −2 | +2 | −2 | +2 | 2 | 2 |
| +1 | −1 | −1 | ++ | +1 | 1 | 1 |
| 0 | 0 | 0 | 0 | 0 | 0 | 0 |

**Figure 6.4**

Before you begin using this system, you will need to determine what your child already can and cannot do so that you can decide where to begin in the teaching program. You can determine this by doing *probes*. This is also called *collecting baseline data*. By this we mean that you observe the child without providing any teaching in the form of cues/prompts or reinforcement (see Figure 6.5). For example, place a favorite toy 1 inch from the child's hand and wiggle it so she can see it. On the first trial, let's suppose your child does not reach it, so you record a minus sign at the bottom of the first column. The child does touch the rattle on the second probe trial, so she gets a plus sign. But she is unable to touch the rattle on the remaining three trials, so three minus signs are recorded. From Figure 6.5 you can see that on four out of five probes your child does not perform the target behavior. Therefore, this seems to be a logical teaching step on which to begin. Suppose the child had received four or five plus signs; then it would have been necessary to move to the next teaching step, which might have been "reaches 2 inches." In general, if the child performs the specific behavior four or five times, move to the next step and probe that step. This method allows you to move quickly through the steps without wasting time on a skill the child has already mastered. In addition, we have set an arbitrary criterion or guideline for moving up through the steps of a program. Move to the next teaching step when the child makes the correct response on a step on 8 out of 10 (80) or more of the trials per day for 3 days.

**TARGET SKILL:** *Reaching*

Date: / / / / / / /

| 10 | 10 | 10 | 10 | 10 | 10 | 10 |
|----|----|----|----|----|----|----|
| 9 | 9 | 9 | 9 | 9 | 9 | 9 |
| 8 | 8 | 8 | 8 | 8 | 8 | 8 |
| 7 | 7 | 7 | 7 | 7 | 7 | 7 |
| 6 | 6 | 6 | 6 | 6 | 6 | 6 |
| 5 | 5 | 5 | 5 | 5 | 5 | 5 |
| 4 | 4 | 4 | 4 | 4 | 4 | 4 |
| 3 | 3 | 3 | 3 | 3 | 3 | 3 |
| 2 | 2 | 2 | 2 | 2 | 2 | 2 |
| 1 | 1 | 1 | 1 | 1 | 1 | 1 |
| 0 | 0 | 0 | 0 | 0 | 0 | 0 |

+
=  } Baseline   Reaching one inch
=

**Figure 6.5**

Now take a little break, then work through the following example. It's really very simple once you practice!

Using Figure 6.6 for practice, let's pretend that your child is 10 months old and that you have read through the teaching programs in the chapter on motor activities. Now you are ready to begin teaching. You observe your baby and determine that he needs to work on sitting with minimal support (Objective 4.1 in the gross motor section). Through observing you determine that your child has mastered the prerequisite skill of maintaining head up in a supported sitting position. You have also determined that your child can be positioned facing you, supported by your hands under his arms. Additionally, from your observations and probes you know that he is able to hold his head up in this activity for 2 seconds. Therefore, you start on training step 2—"child sits with head up and minimal support for 5 seconds." You decide to do 10 teaching trials throughout the day on step 2. On the 1st and 2nd trials the baby responds correctly, and you mark "+"; on the 3rd through 6th trials, he gets "−"; on the 7th trial, a "+"; on the 8th trial, a "−"; and on the 9th and 10th trials, a "+." After recording this information you circle the number 5 on the graph because your baby got 5 correct responses (5 plus marks) that day. Let's suppose you collect the following information for the remaining days. The second day, the baby makes 6 correct responses; the third day, 8 correct; the fourth day, 9 correct; and the fifth day, 8 correct. Connect the circles by a line to

**TARGET SKILL:** *Rolls, Back to Stomach*

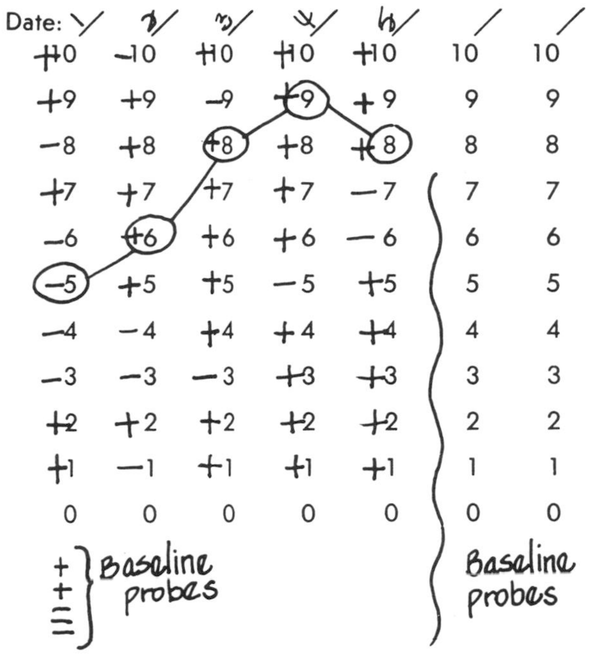

Date:

|  |  |  |  |  |  |  |
|---|---|---|---|---|---|---|
| +10 | -10 | +10 | +10 | +10 | 10 | 10 |
| +9 | +9 | -9 | +9 | +9 | 9 | 9 |
| -8 | +8 | +8 | +8 | +8 | 8 | 8 |
| +7 | +7 | +7 | +7 | -7 | 7 | 7 |
| -6 | +6 | +6 | +6 | -6 | 6 | 6 |
| -5 | +5 | +5 | -5 | +5 | 5 | 5 |
| -4 | -4 | +4 | +4 | +4 | 4 | 4 |
| -3 | -3 | -3 | +3 | +3 | 3 | 3 |
| +2 | +2 | +2 | +2 | +2 | 2 | 2 |
| +1 | -1 | +1 | +1 | +1 | 1 | 1 |
| 0 | 0 | 0 | 0 | 0 | 0 | 0 |

+ + = } Baseline probes

Baseline probes

**Figure 6.6**

form a graph of the baby's progress (see Figure 6.6). You can see that the baby has achieved a score of 8 out of 10 (or 80%) for 3 days in a row. Now it's time to move to the next teaching step, step 3. Draw a colored mark or squiggly line between steps on the graph so that you can see when you move to the next step. You now have a graph of your child's progress through the steps of the teaching program. Isn't it nice to see the line move up? Your baby is learning to sit with minimal support—step by step!

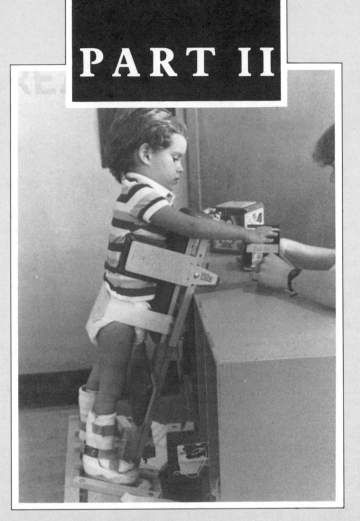

# PART II

# Teaching & Therapy Activities

This part of the book will show you how to facilitate your child's learning and movement by teaching the child new behaviors. This teaching approach centers around helping children to explore their environment motorically and to gain independence so that they can actively interact with the world around them.

These teaching and therapy activities are divided into three types: preparatory activities; motor activities; and social, cognitive, and communication activities. Chapter 7 discusses preparation for motor activities. These activities include different techniques for normalizing muscle tone as well as specific strategies for positioning and handling your child. Adaptive equipment and mobility devices are also discussed. Chapter 8 contains specific teaching programs for facilitating gross motor, fine motor, and oral-motor activities. These programs are functional in nature and developmentally sequenced. Chapter 9 describes activities you can use to teach your child social, cognitive, and communication skills, which typically require special attention when a child experiences motor delays.

## The Importance of Movement

Children under the age of 2 years interact with people and objects largely through the use of motor movements. Even the simple social expression of smiling requires coordination of the facial muscles. Young children typically cannot explain what they want, ask questions about what is going on around them, or even express their feelings without depending on motor coordination. For children to be able to talk, well-coordinated motor movements are necessary. These movements center on the muscles of the facial area and on coordination between breathing and movement of these muscles. A simple one-word statement like "Milk" can tell parents that more milk is desired, just as "No!" can indicate that the child does not want to do something. Before the child is able to talk, these same desires are expressed through use of the total body musculature. Placing the hands over the mouth can indicate "No more milk," and pointing to the glass (instead of saying "Milk") tells parents that the child is still thirsty. Even gross movements, such as climbing down out of the highchair, are used to indicate that the child does not want to sit any longer. For young children, movement is a crucial part of social and communicative expression.

Young children not only express themselves through motor coordination, but also gather information about objects and people through movement. The infant who is not yet able to roll over or crawl is dependent on adults to provide toys and other interesting activities that can be visually explored, moved by the arms or legs, or manipulated by the hands. Later, movement enables the child to initiate exploration rather than to be fully dependent on parents for information. Looking, sucking, listening, and holding are also simple ways in which young infants gain input. Parents also know that the young infant will not be restricted to

these simple ways and totally dependent on their parents for interesting objects and activities for very long! Increasing competence in arm and hand movements allows the child to begin to combine ways of gathering information. For example, the child may happen to move his arm when holding a noise-making object and begin to combine holding with arm movement (or shaking). Here the child combines movements to perform more complex skills as a means of activating the environment. Movement is thus important to the young child for social interactions, for communication, and as a means of learning through exploring the environment.

As noted in Chapter 4, the child with motor problems may have difficulties actively interacting with others and exploring his world in the way that other children do. The child with motor delay who is unable to create changes in his environment may remain dependent on adults. This dependence may further isolate the child and may limit his learning possibilities, resulting in a passive dependency cycle. Under these circumstances, a person can come to feel helpless in his world. This idea of "learned helplessness" has been studied by researchers (Seligman, 1975). The problem of helplessness may be worsened if the child has additional problems such as visual or hearing impairments. Visual information, for example, appears to be important in helping the young child coordinate his movements and learn purposeful behavior. Blind infants, in fact, are often delayed in acquiring many motor milestones such as reaching (Adelson & Fraiberg, 1974). Thus children with motor delay (particularly those with multiple problems that include sensory

impairment) may be particularly at risk for developing feelings of helplessness and for withdrawal from active involvement with the world around them. The teaching programs provided in the following chapters are designed to prevent overdependency and helplessness by teaching the child to interact with and modify his environment through motor actions.

# Developmental and Functional Approaches to Intervention

Whereas a nonhandicapped child is usually able to walk alone without support somewhere between the ages of 9 and 17 months (average age = 12 months), the child with a motor handicap may not develop this skill until much later. Children with Down syndrome may not walk alone until 20 to 30 months of age. A 12-month-old child with severe cerebral palsy may only be able to lift his head for a few seconds when placed on his tummy; he may never be able to walk alone without support.

Physical and occupational therapists who work with young children with motor handicaps usually follow a developmental approach to treatment or intervention. Rather than concentrating on the child's chronological age, they focus instead on the child's developmental age. For example, if a therapist is working with a 2-year-old girl who can roll from back to stomach (2- to 6-month milestone) and support herself on her arms when on her stomach (1- to 5-month milestone) but does not yet sit or crawl, it would *not* be developmentally appropriate to try to work on independent standing. Activities more appropriate to the developmental sequence for this child might include supported sitting and assuming a creeping position.

While it is helpful to use developmental milestones (see Appendix 1) as guidelines, parents and teachers should be aware that the sequence of motor development is not "lock-step" in every child. For example, some children may learn to walk without ever having crept on hands and knees. It is *not* necessary to go back to this earlier milestone and teach it if the child is walking independently and efficiently. Furthermore, it is helpful for parents and teachers to realize that children with *severe* motor handicaps may never learn to sit, stand, or walk independently. In such cases, it is still important to work toward developmentally appropriate activities. However, these activities should be supplemented with specific types of adaptive equipment that can help to compensate for the motor handicap. If the child has too inadequate control of the trunk and legs to stand without support, he may benefit from a prone board or parapodium to enable him to stand. Children as young as 2 to 3 years of age, with myelomeningocele (spina bifida) or severe cerebral palsy, have learned to operate their own electric wheelchairs to provide themselves with an independent form of mobility (Butler, Okamoto, & McKay, 1983). These examples represent a *functional* approach to treatment while still focusing on activities which are developmentally appropriate.

When working with young children with motor handicaps, it is important to provide intervention strategies that are both *functional* and *developmentally appropriate*. As you select the most beneficial strategies in this book to use with *your* child, you will want to determine whether they are both appropriate to your child's *developmental* level (not too difficult) and *functional* for your child. Functional movements will enable your child to grow up to become as independent and self-sufficient as possible. This type of movement is the most complex and highly organized. We use *functional* movement to move from one location to another, to manipulate objects with our hands, to take care of ourselves, and to communicate with other people. You may have to help your child learn to use movement *functionally* in all of these areas or in only some of these areas depending on how much difficulty your child has with movement. Some children with difficulties in moving their legs may only need assistance in learning how to walk. Other children may need help in additional areas, such as moving around their environment, exploring objects, self-care, and communication.

Furthermore, every child with movement problems may not learn to perform skills in exactly the same way as children without motor problems. For example, many children without movement problems achieve independent toilet habits with a minimum of instruction from their parents. However, the 5-year-old child with severe movement difficulties will require specific help in order to achieve similar independence. Some children with motor problems may never be able to walk to the bathroom and then get on and off the toilet by themselves. However, many children will be able to wheel a chair to the bathroom and use a sliding transfer board to get on and off the toilet by themselves. The teaching programs in this book will provide suggestions for teaching your child independence with movements as normal as possible. Where normal movement is not possible, guidelines are offered for using assistive devices and other means of achieving independence.

# Intervention Goals

The suggestions and activities presented in this book are based on several important intervention goals. These goals are:

1. To help the child to move as normally as possible.

2. To teach the child to use movement to initiate interactions with and to control aspects of her environment.

3. To provide opportunities that allow the child to grow and gain independence.

These goals emphasize teaching movement competence through structured experiences. Children acquire new skills not by just growing older but from experimenting with the many aspects of their environment. For instance, the young infant does not learn to balance better in sitting because he is older but because he has learned to experiment with the effects of gravity in sitting and to control his body posture in relation to gravitational effects. Therefore, the training and environmental adaptations that parents, therapists, and teachers provide young children are crucial for preventing delays in acquiring normal milestone skills and for assisting children to become competent and independent.

# Materials Needed

You will need very few materials for training that you don't already have around the house. Pots and pans, measuring cups and spoons, plastic containers (like cottage cheese containers), spoons, jar lids and rings, cereal, finger foods, pillows, towels, beads, corks, spools, little blocks or cubes, rattles, small balls, and boxes with and without lids all come in handy for these programs. You may need to purchase or make only a few items: simple toys that can be easily manipulated; books; musical toys and instruments; simple switches for operating toys and other devices; pillows, bolsters, and other moveable equipment; and perhaps some specialized equipment depending on the movement problems your child may have. Specific teaching materials needed are listed at the beginning of each program. Read through them now and ask friends, neighbors, and relatives to save items for you. Additional items you might find useful are a stopwatch or a watch with a second hand, a kitchen timer, and a notebook and pen. Here are some guidelines for other toy and equipment purchases:

1. Look for toys that have cause-and-effect components: for example, moving a screen reveals a picture, moving dials produces a sound, pushing a button makes a jack-in-the-box pop out. The result of the child's action (e.g., a sound or picture) should last only a few seconds so that the child must do the action again to produce an outcome or effect. It is important that the outcome produced is directly linked to the child's action.

2. Books should have simple, realistic (photograph-like), and colorful pictures so that you can use them in teaching. "Touch and feel" books are excellent for children.

3. Check all objects to be sure there are no detachable small parts that could be swallowed, no sharp edges, and no dangerous strings or cords. Purchase only items that are nonflammable and nontoxic. If you make the toys, use nontoxic, lead-free paint. Consult consumer publications and buying guides for guidelines to toy purchasing.

Vary the toys and materials you use as much as possible. If children have only one toy or play with the same toy over and over again, they will become bored with it. Also use just one or two toys or objects at a time. A whole crib full of toys may overload the child's senses.

# Consequences

Every motor action produces a consequence to that action. Twisting a knob on a music box results in a pleasurable sound; hitting a mobile results in movement of the objects on the mobile. Raising one's head produces a consequence of seeing something that could not be seen when the head is flat. Putting an arm out for support when sitting causes the body to stay upright instead of falling over!

Most of us prefer some consequences over others. For instance, we may prefer coffee rather than tea or a movie rather than a football game. Children are no different in this respect. Most prefer their parents over a stranger. Some young children laugh when being bounced or "rough-housed" while others cry. In Chapter 4 you learned that consequences are anything that follow a behavior (or response). You will recall that a consequence that is preferred by your child will *strengthen* the response that came before it; a consequence that is not preferred will *weaken* the response. Consequences are the most effective overall strategy you can use to teach your child movement skills.

Most young children relate to the objects and people in their environments through movement. A movement that produces an interesting or preferred consequence will be strengthened. Movements that result in no consequences, in nonpreferred consequences, or in punishing consequences will not be strengthened. Rather, the child may simply stop producing those movements. Consequences must be incorporated as a strategy in all of the movement activities that you will be teaching your child. Some movement patterns may be atypical, and these patterns can be weakened through providing nonpreferred consequences while *at the same time* providing highly preferred consequences for more normal ways of moving. By varying consequences, you can help your child to learn.

In Chapter 4, you practiced identifying some toys and activities that were preferred by your child.

You may have found that you were able to identify only a few toys, activities, foods, or people that might be reinforcing for your child. For instance, for some children who may have difficulty moving, finding toys with which the child can play may be a hard task. Or if your child has problems with seeing or hearing, activities that may be reinforcing for many children may not be interesting to your child. With careful observation of your child, however, in time you will be able to determine the toys, activities, and other situations that your child prefers.

Learning to perform new movements is very hard work for many children with motor delay. Therefore, you will want to structure your teaching so that your child will work to achieve consequences that are preferred. None of us would work hard to obtain nothing or to produce a result of no interest to us. The activities here will help you to structure your teaching so that your child receives big rewards for working very hard.

You may also have to learn to change your own behavior a little bit in order to provide consequences when teaching your child. If, for instance, your child gets ice cream for dessert every night for dinner, your child will learn that he can have ice cream without doing anything special. Ice cream will not be a treat. If, however, you teach the movements required for self-feeding with ice cream on the spoon, your child will probably work hard to learn to move the spoon to his mouth.

Using preferred activities, foods, or other materials to teach your child can be hard work for you if your child has difficulties with movement, with seeing or hearing, or in all three areas. But persistence in identifying reinforcing consequences and in providing those preferred consequences for specific movement responses will help your child learn more skills. Then *your* effort will be reinforced as your child learns to smile, to play, to feed himself, and to do other things that he might not have learned without your help.

# Meeting Your Child's Unique Needs

Remember that the teaching activities in the following chapters cannot cover everything for every child. All children with movement difficulties are different. Just knowing that your child has a condition such as cerebral palsy, for example, does not define the movement difficulty specifically enough to determine the methods and techniques that should be used to teach your child. You will have to select teaching programs that are appropriate in terms of your child's individual developmental needs and functional needs. You need only teach your child skills in those areas where problems exist; you do not need to do every program suggested here. Furthermore, you should feel free to change the activities as necessary to allow for individual differences.

You will also want to coordinate your teaching activities with others who may be involved in providing education or therapy. Your child's physical, occupational, or speech/language therapist and teacher can help you use this guide more effectively and can demonstrate activities described under each of the teaching program areas. These teaching programs are *not* intended to take the place of regularly scheduled physical therapy (PT) or occupational therapy (OT). Rather, it is suggested that you work closely with your PT or OT to decide which activities are most appropriate for your child. Together you can develop an ongoing program that will provide maximum benefit in minimizing the effects of your child's motor handicap.

Work with your child during your everyday routines. Space these teaching sessions throughout the day and perform them only when your child is ready to learn. From time to time, your child's illnesses may also slow the progress. Wait until the child is alert and healthy to begin teaching again. In addition, try to minimize distractions as much as possible during this teaching. It is also best to integrate your teaching into your daily schedule. For example, work on a program to teach the child to rise to a sitting position after a diaper change. Each teaching session takes only a few seconds! The amount of time it takes you to teach each day will vary depending upon the programs you select and on the habits of you and your child. The programs and activities in this book are to be used as a basic guideline for your teaching. Change them as necessary for your child's needs and according to your lifestyle.

# CHAPTER 7

# Preparation for Motor Activities

The strategies you will use to teach your child will vary in relation to the types of motor difficulties that your child experiences. For example, the child with high muscle tone requires an approach different from one suited to the child with low muscle tone. This chapter discusses different types of muscle tone problems and suggests ways of normalizing muscle tone to make movement easier for your child. Also included here is a discussion of positioning and handling techniques as well as specific adaptive devices and equipment for the child with motor impairments. Read this chapter carefully before beginning any of the teaching activities presented later. Seek professional guidance for more information about the techniques and aids described in this chapter.

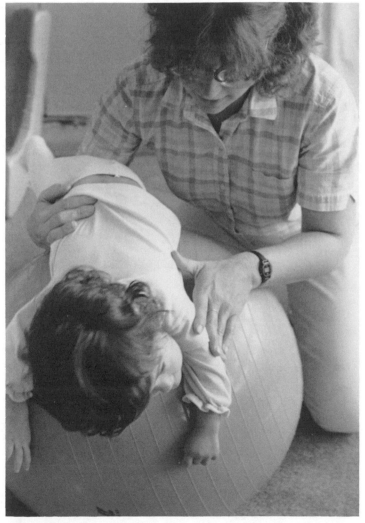

Figure 7.1

# Types of Muscle Tone Problems

Children with motor handicaps frequently have abnormal muscle tone, which may limit their ability to achieve developmental motor milestones. Muscle tone refers to the resistance of a body part to passive movement and is thought of as muscle tension. If you were to passively flex (bend) and extend (straighten) the arm of a child with normal muscle tone, there would be a slight resistance to your movement, but you would be able to completely flex and extend the arm. The ability to move the body against the force of gravity is referred to as postural tone. There are three basic types of abnormal muscle tone that may affect a child with a motor handicap: high tone or hypertonia, low tone or hypotonia, and fluctuating tone (fluctuates from low to high or high to low).

## Hypertonia

The child with hypertonia has too much muscle tone. Another name for hypertonia is spasticity. Many children with cerebral palsy have the spastic type of cerebral palsy. In children with hypertonia, the affected body parts are stiff and have limited ability to move. The muscles will feel hard and rock-like in the affected parts. If you try to passively move the affected arm, leg, or trunk, you will encounter resistance to your passive movement. In children with spastic hemiplegia, one side of the body is affected. In spastic diplegia, the legs are primarily affected, but the trunk and arms may also be involved. In children with spastic quadriplegia, all four extremities (arms and legs) and the trunk will be involved.

Children with hypertonia usually have limited movement (range of motion) in the affected body parts. Most of the motion occurs in the middle ranges of movement, such as partial bending (flexion) and straightening (extension) of the elbow or knee but not full motion, as in complete flexion and extension. Because of the limited motion and the "tightness" of the muscles, children with hypertonia are at risk for contractures (permanent shortening of the muscle tendon), dislocations (as in the hip), and deformities (such as curvature of the spine).

Motor milestones are frequently delayed in children with hypertonia. These children have difficulty assuming and maintaining positions that go against the force of gravity (antigravity postures), such as sitting, creeping, and standing. Because of the increased muscle tone in the chests of children with generalized hypertonia, breathing may be difficult due to decreased movement of the ribs. If the facial and oral muscles are also involved, as is often the case in spastic quadriplegia, articulation (the ability to speak clearly and distinctly) is also difficult.

## Hypotonia

The child with hypotonia or low muscle tone may be described as "floppy," like a rag doll. The infant with hypotonia has great difficulty assuming and maintaining positions against the force of gravity (antigravity postures). These infants lie flat against the surface on which they are placed and have difficulty lifting their heads, arms, and legs against gravity. Motor milestones such as sitting, creeping, and walking are usually delayed because of the generalized low muscle tone. Types of handicapping conditions usually characterized by hypotonia include Down syndrome, Prader-Willi syndrome, and the ataxic type of cerebral palsy. Children with the mixed type of cerebral palsy may have hypertonia in the limbs and hypotonia in the trunk muscles.

Children with hypotonia usually have very lax ligaments (ligaments help form the joints by connecting bone to bone), which results in excessive movement at the joints, referred to by laypersons as being "double-jointed." Because of the lax ligaments, these children may be at risk for dislocation of some joints, such as in the hip, jaw, and neck. When pressure is placed on the muscle belly of children with hypotonia, such as the biceps or calf muscle, the muscle feels soft and doughy.

Because of the low muscle tone in the chest and face muscles as well, breathing tends to be shallow, and these children have difficulty sustaining sounds when attempting to cry, babble, or talk. The low tone in the jaw and tongue muscles results in the jaw hanging open and the tongue hanging out because of the effect of gravity pulling the jaw and tongue down.

### Fluctuating Tone

Some children show variations in tone, ranging from hypotonia to hypertonia or vice versa. Tone may change in different body parts depending upon the child's position (e.g., back-lying vs. side-lying) or the activity in which she is involved. The most common type of motor handicap in which fluctuating muscle tone occurs is athetoid cerebral palsy. The child with athetoid cerebral palsy has wide-ranging, somewhat uncontrolled movements of the arms, legs, and face. Her tone will vary depending upon the position of her body or the difficulty of the task that she is trying to complete. These children, like children with hypotonia, may also appear to be "double-jointed" and are at risk for joint dislocations and subluxations (partial dislocations).

# Normalizing Muscle Tone

Before you can begin to teach developmental motor skills to your child, it is important to normalize the tone. Normal muscle tone serves as a background for acquiring normal movement patterns. Muscle tone will vary depending upon the activities in which your child is engaged. The ability of the muscles to work together to maintain antigravity postures, such as sitting and standing, is called postural tone. You will need to facilitate normal postural tone in your child before beginning to teach specific motor skills.

Before attempting activities to normalize tone, consult with your PT or OT about the type of tone differences, if any, that your child displays. Have the therapist describe the type of tone (hypertonia, hypotonia, or fluctuating tone) as well as variations in tone that occur when your child is placed in different positions. Listed below are some general activities for normalizing tone that you can try with your therapist's supervision. Note that in all activities you will be handling the child at either the head, shoulders, trunk, or hips. These are known as the **key points of control** (Bobath & Bobath, 1972) and are the best body parts to use in handling and positioning your child.

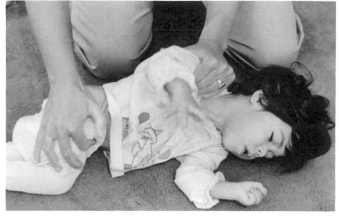

**Figure 7.2**

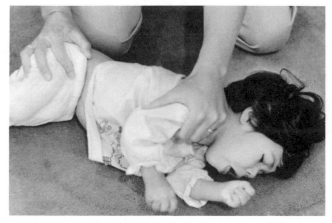

**Figure 7.3**

## Preparatory Activities for the Child with Hypertonia

The child with hypertonia or spasticity has muscle tone that is too high. To normalize the child's tone, you will want to reduce or relax the high tone. Listed below are three relaxation activities for reducing tone in the hypertonic child.

**Relaxation over the therapy ball.**  Place the child in prone position (on her tummy) over a large therapy ball or bolster. You will be behind the child either in standing or kneel-standing position. Support the child at her upper thighs (near hips). Rotate the thighs so the hips are separated (abducted) and the feet are pointed outward (external rotation at hips). Gently roll the child forward and backward while maintaining your control at the child's hips. You should feel the spastic tone relax throughout the trunk and hips as you gently roll the child (see Figure 7.1).

**Relaxation in side-lying.**  Place the child in side-lying position on a mat or padded floor. Kneel facing the child in front of her. Place one of your hands over the child's shoulder and one over her hip. Rotate the shoulder forward as you rotate the hip backward, thus passively rotating the child's trunk. Reverse and pull backward on the shoulder as you push forward on the hip. Repeat several times until you feel the tone relax or loosen up (see Figures 7.2 and 7.3).

**Relaxation in supine.**  Place the child in supine or back-lying position with a pillow under her upper head to extend or lengthen the back of the neck. Roll the child into a flexed position at the lower back, hips, and knees by supporting her on your knees as you are kneeling at her bottom. By flexing the child's entire body in this way, you can relax the muscle tone. Then you can work on rotation of the lower trunk by rotating her hips and knees from side to side (see Figure 7.4)

In reducing hypertonia, it is also important to minimize all extraneous stimuli in the child's environment—there should be no loud noises, bright lights, or quickly moving visual stimuli. The overall aim is to relax the child through a soothing, calm environment.

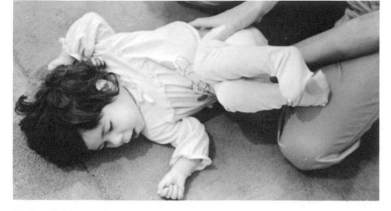

Figure 7.4

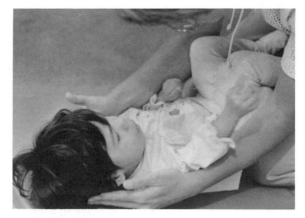

Figure 7.5

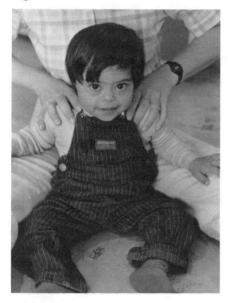

Figure 7.6

In general, it is wise to move slowly with the child with hypertonia. Quick or sudden movements will tend to increase tone even more. Work slowly and rhythmically and you will soon be able to feel the tone "give" as the child begins to relax. Use a calm, soothing voice when talking to your child and encourage him to make his muscles feel "soft" and relaxed.

## Preparatory Activities for the Child with Hypotonia

The child with hypotonia is floppy and has little stability for movement. To normalize the tone of a child with hypotonia, you will need to do preparatory activities aimed at increasing or building up muscle tone. Listed below are three activities for increasing muscle tone.

**Joint Compression.**  For the young infant or child with severe delays who does not yet sit independently, place the child in supine (on her back) on a firm surface with her legs flexed (bent up toward her trunk). Align the child's head in midline with her trunk. Place your knees against the child's buttocks and press down through the head and through the spine, applying counter-pressure at the infant's buttocks with your knees. Use firm pressure downward so that you are pushing the vertebrae (bones in the spine) together. This technique is called joint compression or joint approximation and is designed to increase the ability to contract the muscles on both sides of the neck and trunk (co-contraction) in order to maintain an upright position against the force of gravity (see Figure 7.5).

Joint compression can also be applied downward through the shoulders and into the buttocks (see Figure 7.6). For the older infant who can sit independently, joint compression may be applied in supine or sitting by applying pressure downward through the spine. Either continuous pressure (compression) can be applied or quick, short compressions can be repeated. *CAUTION:* For infants and young children with Down syndrome, do *not* apply joint compression through the head and neck unless the child has had an X-ray of the cervical spine (neck) to rule out instability of the first and second vertebrae (atlanto-axial instability).

**Bouncing.**   Bouncing your child firmly on a ball or on your knees will help to increase muscle tone in the trunk. Support the child at lower trunk or mid-trunk and bounce her on a firm surface. This is a fun game for most babies, and they will often coo or squeal in delight.

**Resisting movement.**   Resistance to movement helps to increase muscle tone as well as muscle strength. If your child has begun to move—either crawling on the belly, creeping on hands and knees, or walking—you can play a game with her by pushing gently against her as she tries to move forward. Don't do it so hard as to frustrate her, but make it into a playful activity.

For the infant who is able to walk with support or independently, have him push a child-sized cart full of 5 to 10 pounds of weighted objects. Pushing a load is one way of providing resistance to movement and should help to build up tone as well as strength (see Figure 7.7).

For the child with low tone or hypotonia, use activities that are brisk and stimulating. Frolic play or roughhousing is usually appropriate with the hypotonic child since it tends to increase tone. For the same reason, these activities are *not* appropriate for the child with hypertonia.

## Preparatory Activities for the Child with Fluctuating Tone

Activities for the child with fluctuating muscle tone will vary depending upon the type of tone he is showing at the time you are working with him. If he is showing low tone at a particular time or in a particular position, then you will want to engage in activities to increase tone using the preparatory activities described above for the child with hypotonia. If he is showing higher than normal tone, then you will want to work on the preparatory activities described for the child with hypertonia.

Only a few preparatory activities have been listed for each type of tone. Your PT or OT will be able to show you others as well. Remember to try these preparation activities *only* after you have consulted with your child's PT or OT to make sure that they are truly appropriate for your child.

# Positioning and Handling Your Child

While it is usually important to encourage movement as much as possible in the child with a motor handicap, there are also times when the child will need to remain in a static position. For very young infants or older youngsters with severe motor handicaps, the role of proper positioning is an extremely important addition to active teaching (Finnie, 1975). Improper positioning and handling may maximize the muscle tone differences that your child may already have. Appropriate handling and positioning, on the other hand, will provide an important carry-over of the goals you are seeking in carrying out the teaching programs described in the next chapters. Once again, your PT or OT will be the most important person to aid you in identifying appropriate positioning strategies for your child. For further suggestions on handling and positioning, refer to the book by Nancie Finnie entitled *Handling the Young Cerebral Palsied Child at Home* (see Appendix 2). This is an excellent reference for parents and

Figure 7.7

Figure 7.8

therapists of young children with *all* types of motor handicaps, including cerebral palsy.

## General Guidelines for Positioning and Handling

In addition to specific activities for positioning and handling your child, there are four general guidelines to keep in mind.

Use *key points of control* when handling or positioning your child. The key points of control are the more proximal parts of the body or those nearest the center of the body. These include the *head and neck*, the *shoulder girdle*, and the *hips*. You should begin to concentrate on using these key points whenever you move, carry, or position your child. This will help to normalize your child's muscle tone as well.

Work toward *symmetry* in handling or positioning your child. Symmetry means that both sides of the body are positioned similarly so that one side looks like a mirror image of the other. For example, if you were to position your child in prone (on her tummy), you would want her arms to be forward in the same position and her legs to be extended similarly to one another (see Figure 7.8). Her head should be in the middle or midline of the body.

Positioning the child symmetrically will help to normalize muscle tone and will also help to inhibit primitive patterns of movement that may be interfering with her ability to acquire normal movement. Primitive patterns of movement are those patterns normally seen in very young infants, such as the early baby reflexes, which should begin to disappear as the infant reaches 4 to 6 months of age.

Work toward *midline* positioning. Many young children with motor handicaps are unable to get their hands together in the midline of the body. Midline activities with the hands are important for developing fine motor and self-help skills. One position that helps to facilitate midline activities of the hands is

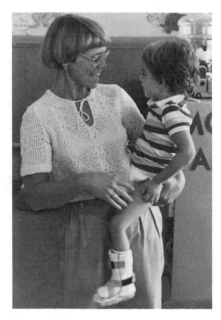

**Figure 7.9**

**Figure 7.10**

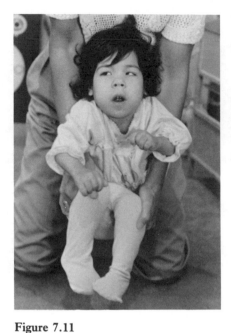

**Figure 7.11**

side-lying. The child may be positioned in side-lying with the use of pillows or placed in a commercially made or homemade side-lying positioner.

Use only the *minimal support* needed when handling or positioning your child. While it is important to provide adequate support when handling or positioning your child, providing more support than is needed will not allow the child to use the muscle control he has developed thus far. For example, if your child has developed adequate control of trunk muscles to be able to sit independently on the floor, you should allow him the opportunity to use those muscles whenever possible. When carrying the child, support should be given at the hips or lower trunk so that he will be actively using his upper trunk muscles to hold himself erect (see Figure 7.9). If you always place the child in a highchair or other chair with a back support to lean against, he will not be required to actively use his trunk muscles. By setting the child on a stool or bolster chair, he will be given the opportunity to use his trunk muscles for upright stability (see Figure 7.10).

In Figure 7.11 all four of the general guidelines listed above are being followed. Support is given at the hips (a key point of control), the child is carried in a symmetrical position, hands are forward toward the midline, and minimal support is being given to allow the child to actively use the trunk muscles.

## Specific Activities for Positioning

For the young child with a severe motor handicap who is unable to move actively on his own, proper positioning is an extremely important addition to his therapy program and his home management program. Likewise, very young infants will not display much active change of position and thus should be positioned properly by their parents.

There are four basic positions that are generally appropriate for the child with a motor handicap: *prone-lying*, *side-lying*, *suppported sitting*, and *supported standing*. For the child who is able to move little, if any, on his own, changing his position at least once every 30 to 45 minutes is extremely important. Such position changes will minimize the risks of developing redness or pressure sores over bony prominences (such as the elbow or ankle) and will give the child an opportunity to view his environment from different vantage points.

Once again, positioning activities should be developmentally appropriate (based on the child's developmental age) just as the teaching exercises should be geared toward the child's developmental level of functioning rather than his chronological age. If your baby is 4 months of age or younger, you will probably concentrate on prone-lying and side-lying positioning strategies. By 6 or 7 months of age, you will want to add supported sitting activities, providing your child has achieved adequate head control. By 12 or 13 months of age, it would be appropriate to add supported standing positions, providing your child has developed adequate head and trunk control.

**Prone-lying positions.**  In the normally developing newborn, head control in prone is one of the first motor activities to develop. During the first 1 or 2 months, the baby will be able to lift and turn her head while lying on her tummy. By 3 or 4 months, she will be able to support her weight on her elbows and hold her head up at a 45–90° angle and in the midline.

For the child with a motor handicap, these activities may be very difficult. Nonetheless, working to gain head control in prone is very important. To assist your child in accomplishing these early activities, proper positioning in prone is an important adjunct to the teaching programs described in this book.

There are two basic types of adaptive devices which are appropriate for facilitating prone positioning. One is a bolster and the other is a wedge (see Figure 7.12). Both the bolster and wedge are made commercially or can also be fabricated at home (see Appendix 2). Some authors have recommended that a hard, firm wedge be used for children with hypotonia and a softer, foam rubber wedge for children with hypertonia (Campbell, Green, & Carlson, 1977).

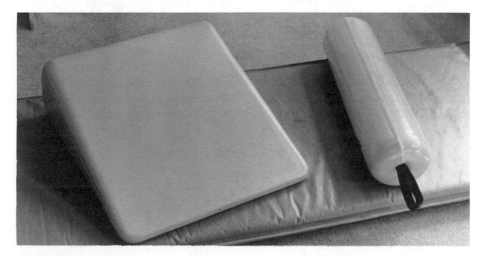

**Figure 7.12**

For the very young infant with a motor handicap, a rolled-up towel or flannel baby blanket may function as a "bolster" to be placed under the baby's arms. Sometimes this provides just the elevation needed to encourage the baby to lift her head, as was our experience with a 2-month-old infant with Down syndrome who was unable to lift her head when flat on the floor in prone but did so immediately with the aid of a rolled-up blanket.

**Side-lying positions.** Side-lying is an excellent position for facilitating midline activities with the hands. Many infants and young children with motor handicaps are unable to bring their hands together in the midline when lying on their backs or in a sitting position. By placing the child in the side-lying position, the arms are brought forward and gravity assists in bringing the hands together.

The normally developing infant does a lot of hand-to-hand and hand-to-mouth exploration. He will transfer objects from hand to hand and bring objects to his mouth to explore their taste, shape, and feel. It is important that young children with motor handicaps also have an opportunity to manipulate objects with their hands and mouth. By placing the child in a side-lying position, you can frequently facilitate these fine motor activities.

To place the infant or very young child in side-lying, you can use pillows, towels, or sandbags to help her maintain the position. Her head and trunk should be slightly flexed with one or both hips flexed as well; this is especially important for a child with a lot of extensor hypertonia. The child in Figure 7.13 is positioned in side-lying.

Homemade or commercially made sidelyers may also be used and may be necessary for children with more severe motor handicaps. Appendix 2 lists several commercial equipment companies that manufacture sidelyers.

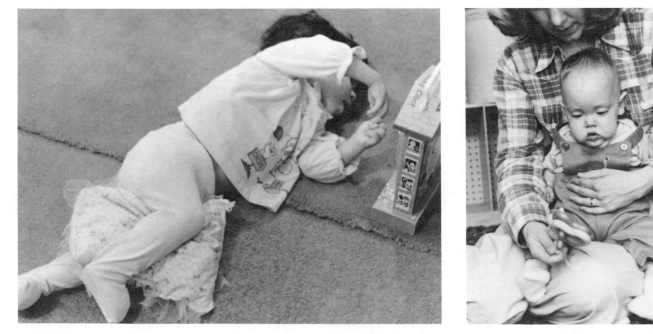

Figure 7.13                                                                                          Figure 7.14

**Supported sitting.** The normally developing infant will be able to sit with slight support by the age of 3 to 6 months and can sit independently by 5 to 9 months. The child with a motor handicap may achieve independent sitting at a much later age or may never be able to sit independently without some external support. For the young child who is delayed in achieving independent sitting or who does not have enough control of the trunk muscles to sit independently, some type of adaptive positioning or equipment may be needed. Adaptive seating is particularly important in providing the child the support needed in the trunk to free up the hands for functional activities, such as self-feeding or fine motor activities, and for play activities. There are a number of commercially made adaptive devices (see Appendix 2) as well as homemade versions. The four general guidelines should be remembered when making or buying an adaptive seating device for your child: (1) provide support at key points of control, (2) position the child symmetrically, (3) use only minimal support necessary, and (4) encourage midline activities.

In Figures 7.14 and 7.15, the baby's mother is providing optimal supported sitting positions with her own body. In Figure 7.16, the baby is seated in a special adaptive seating device. Both forms of adaptive positioning are appropriate when working with young children.

**Supported standing.** The infant with normal motor development will begin to pull up to stand at furniture between 6 and 12 months. Independent standing is achieved by 9 to 16 months. The infant with a motor handicap may learn to stand at a much later age or may never have adequate head and trunk control to stand without outside support.

The principles of symmetry, midline positioning, and minimal support at key points of control are also important when providing the infant with the

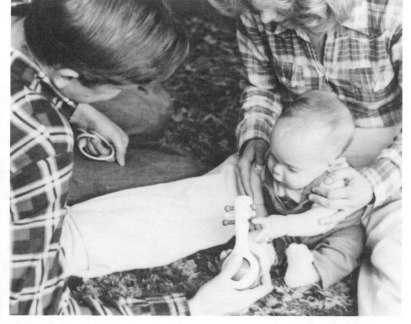

**Figure 7.15**

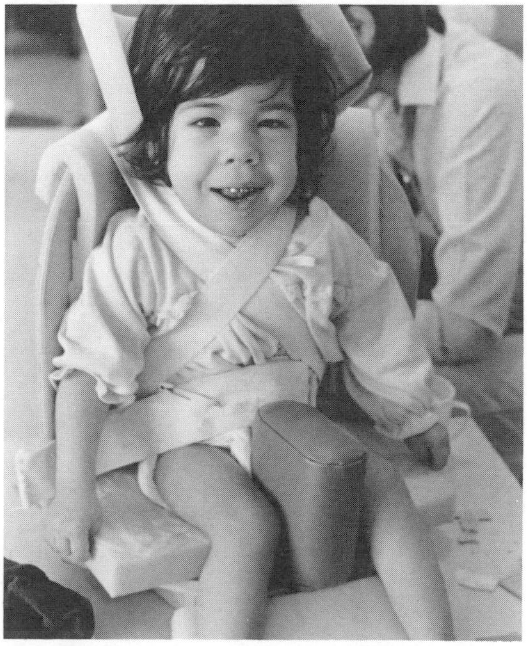

**Figure 7.16**

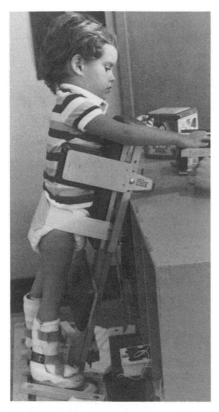

**Figure 7.17**

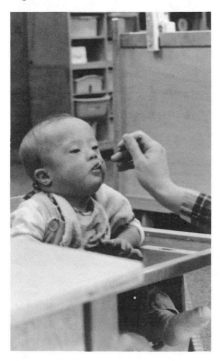

**Figure 7.18**

means to maintain supported standing. The most common piece of adaptive equipment used to provide supported standing for the child with a severe motor handicap is the prone board (see Figure 7.17). Instructions for making a prone board can be found in Finnie's book, *Handling the Young Cerebral Palsied Child at Home*. A number of commercially produced prone boards are also available (see Appendix 2).

The prone board enables the child to look at his environment from an upright posture. It also helps him to maintain his head up against gravity and to position his arms forward and in the midline. Functional fine motor activities may be engaged in by the child while he is positioned in the prone board.

## Positioning for Feeding

Proper positioning is a key element in feeding the child with a motor handicap. Prior to positioning and feeding, the child's muscle tone should be normalized, as much as possible, by carrying out some of the preparatory activities described earlier.

There are a number of different ways to position your child for feeding, depending upon his age and the severity of his motor handicap. Once again, much of the information included here is derived from Finnie's book, *Handling the Young Cerebral Palsied Child at Home*. Two of the general guidelines for positioning are important to remember in positioning your child for feeding: symmetry and midline positioning.

To facilitate symmetry and midline positioning in the very young infant or the child with a severe motor handicap, Finnie recommends that the parent sit in front of a table with feet resting on a stool. The child is positioned facing the parent, on her lap, with the child's head and back semireclined against a large pillow propped against the table. The parent can then present the food from the midline while keeping the child in a symmetrical position with hips and knees flexed (bent). By propping a child in a supportive chair and sitting facing the child, the same positioning goals may be accomplished (see Figure 7.18).

For the older infant or child with less severe impairments who has some sitting balance, placement in a highchair or specially adapted chair is preferable. For the child with hypertonia, a special abduction piece may be placed in the front of the chair seat to keep the hips separated (abducted). Care should be taken to have the child's feet firmly resting on the footrest or floor so that the hips and knees are at a 90° angle.

The child's arms should be brought forward by assisting her at the shoulders. The head should always be in midline with relation to the trunk. The adult should be seated directly in front of the child to encourage midline positioning (Mueller, 1972; Mueller, 1975). The children shown in Figures 7.18 and 7.19 are in appropriate positions for feeding.

Helen Mueller, a Swiss speech therapist, has developed specific handling techniques for feeding the child with a severe motor handicap (Mueller, 1972; Mueller, 1975). For the child who does not have enough head control to maintain the head in an upright or midline position, Mueller recommends jaw control as an adjunct to proper positioning. Jaw control can be provided from

**Figure 7.19**

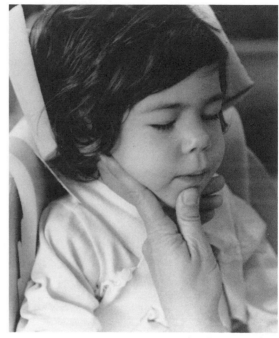

**Figure 7.20**

behind the child or from the front (Figure 7.20). If you are behind the child, place the index finger of your nondominant hand under the child's lower lip and your middle finger under the chin. Hold the head in midline and with slight flexion (lower the chin toward the neck). If you are in front of the child, place the thumb of your nondominant hand vertically in the middle of the chin below the lower lip; your index finger rests along the jaw and your middle finger rests firmly under the chin. Once again, the head is positioned in midline with slight flexion.

Have your PT or OT help you devise the most appropriate position for feeding your child at home. Remember, *your* comfort is important, too—so find a position that is optimal for both you and your child.

# Adaptive Equipment and Mobility Devices

In addition to proper positioning and handling techniques, adaptive positioning devices may enable your child to carry out important functional activities. Through the use of adaptive seating and feeding devices, it may be possible for a child with a severe motor handicap to eat independently. Furthermore, specially adapted communication devices, such as communication boards or head sticks, may enhance the child's ability to communicate with those around him. For the child with a severe motor handicap who cannot move around independently in his environment, special mobility devices such as the powered wheelchair may provide an important adjunct to therapy services. As you become more knowledgeable in the whys and hows of adaptive equipment, you will be able to work with your therapist in selecting and devising appropriate devices to meet your child's special needs. This equipment can give your child greater independence to explore and interact with his environment, thus providing a key to enhanced learning opportunities.

A great deal of adaptive equipment can either be made at home or purchased commercially (see Appendix 2). This equipment is designed to help children with motor handicaps to maintain correct positioning, acquire mobility skills, or perform various motor-related skills such as eating, dressing, toileting, communicating, or playing. Many therapists and teachers have creative ideas for equipment designed to help your child perform various activities. In addition, many new products are commercially marketed each year, so if you don't find the exact piece of equipment you need for your child in a current catalogue, keep checking with the distributor or with representatives of local health or medical supply companies. Appendix 2 lists commercial sources of adaptive equipment along with the types of equipment available through each company. Resources useful in designing and making your own equipment are also listed.

## Guidelines for selecting equipment

Many professionals are available to help you select and acquire the appropriate positioning and instructional equipment for your child. Physical and occupational therapists are the most likely to be familiar with your child's needs as well as the variety of local and national sources for specialized equipment. Local medical supply companies can also be helpful with equipment. However, these companies may only have access to certain equipment manufacturers and may not be able to acquaint you with all the types of available devices. Here are some guidelines to keep in mind when you consider purchasing specific devices.

**Quality of manufacture.** Some equipment is fabricated to withstand use indoors and out, use for daily transportation (such as between home and school), and use by a variety of people. In addition, some pieces of equipment have been designed to be used with a number of different children and include a number of highly adjustable features—which increases versatility of the equipment but also its cost. If your child is young and growing, a piece of equipment may be used for a short time only, and durability and high quality may not be needed. For many young children, homemade or makeshift equipment works quite well for the short period of time that the child may be using it. However, if your child is likely to be using a piece of adjustable equipment for a number of years (e.g., a transporter chair or wheelchair), durability and high quality may be essential.

**Durability.** Durability is related to the length of time the piece of equipment will be used as well as the overall usage that the equipment will tolerate. For instance, many nice chairs that can be used well at home or in a classroom are not durable enough to be moved from location to location or for use outside. Similarly, some mobility aids such as scooters, crawlers, and walkers are only durable enough for inside use. Decide how your child will use the equipment and which piece of equipment will best fit these usage needs. Durability and cost are also related. It is silly to spend a great deal of money for durability if your child will use equipment only in one location or if your child will need the equipment for only a year or so.

**Appropriateness.** Equipment must be selected on the basis of expected functional use. You must know what you expect the piece of equipment to do for your child and how long it must last in order to make an appropriate selection. For instance, if your child is learning how to control the muscles in his trunk but is frequently placed in equipment that provides trunk support through side supports, vests, or harnesses, the child will not have the opportunity to use the muscles in his trunk. This type of situation is frequently labeled "over-equipped." However, if your child has very poor trunk control that could lead to spinal deformities and the equipment does not provide trunk support, your child would be seen as "under-equipped." Most young children are continually acquiring movement abilities. Therefore, equipment will have to be frequently adjusted in order to be fully appropriate at any given time. Furthermore, most young children are growing, so equipment will need to be adjusted for appropriate fit as the child grows. A therapist can be of help to you in deciding what types of equipment are most appropriate for your child's movement abilities as well as to assist you with selecting the right-sized equipment. However, constant monitoring of equipment is required in order to ensure continuing appropriateness.

**Home construction vs. purchase.** Most adaptive equipment for home or school use can be easily made by an individual with some carpentry skills. Many therapists and agencies serving individuals with motor impairments have plans for building such equipment. Some agencies can even suggest resources such as retired individuals, vocational education classes, Bell Telephone Pioneers, and sheltered workshops which will build equipment for individual children. The disadvantages of home construction often include reduced durability, time required for someone to make the equipment, and less attractive appearance. However, lower cost is often a significant advantage. Home-constructed equipment can be fully appropriate for many young children.

**Cost.** The cost of adaptive equipment can be very high—particularly if your child will need adaptive equipment for a variety of functions like positioning, mobility, and communication or if equipment will be required throughout your child's lifetime. Therefore, cost-effectiveness of the equipment is an important factor to consider when selecting equipment.

Equipment that is very attractive, durable, well-built, and expensive is not cost-effective if your child will only use the equipment for a year or if a less expensive piece of equipment will provide the same function. For instance, transporter chairs, which fit over the seat of a car, position a child with a motor handicap safely for riding in a car or bus. However, chairs of this type are often not functional for other situations (in the classroom or at home) and may cost over $1,000. A car seat will cost significantly less but still position the child safely while being transported during the younger years. If your child will require positioning for safety in a car when he is 8 or 9 years old, the transporter chair would be a good cost-effective investment. However, if your child may sit independently enough to ride in a car with a harness and seat belt when he is 8 or 9 years old, a car seat may be a wiser choice.

**Figure 7.21**

## Community Resources for Adaptive Equipment

Many agencies maintain equipment-borrowing services and allow families to borrow (or rent) equipment for the time period required by the child. Local chapters of parent groups also often lend equipment among families in order to reduce the costs of equipment purchase. Check with your local agencies that serve children with motor handicaps (like Easter Seal, Muscular Dystrophy Association, United Cerebral Palsy) and with local parent groups to find out if equipment borrowing is possible in your local area.

Also check with your physician or social worker about programs that are available to financially assist families in purchasing equipment for their children. Many state Bureau of Crippled Children's Services provide funding for specialized equipment, and some agencies offer special financial assistance to families. If you or your child qualify for Social Security or Medicaid/Aid to Dependent Children, these programs sometimes pay full or partial equipment costs. Private insurance for medical and other health care (such as Blue Cross/ Blue Shield) often pay equipment costs in special instances or pay partial costs under major medical coverage. However, find out about funding resources *before* you begin purchasing any type of equipment because many of these resources may have special requirements to qualify for funding. For instance, most programs require physician prescription for equipment prior to determining coverage. Others may require prior approval for purchase and will not reimburse for already purchased equipment. Still others may have contractual relationships with only certain companies and will not cover equipment costs if not purchased from approved companies.

## Mobility devices

While positioning strategies and adaptive equipment help to provide stable postures for your child so that he can engage in fine motor, self-help, or play activities, providing mobility for your child is also very important. Some young children with severe motor handicaps are unable to move around freely in their environment. Finnie (1975) has recommended mobility aids such as scooter boards, tricycles, and adjustable walkers. She has provided instructions for making some of these aids as well. Once again, you should consult with your child's therapist for help in deciding which mobility aid would be most appropriate for your child.

Recently, powered wheelchairs have been recommended for very young children with severe motor handicaps (Butler, Okamoto, & McKay, 1983). Children as young as 2 to 2½ years old have been taught to propel their own electric wheelchairs and have thus been able to independently explore their environment. Powered wheelchairs are not appropriate for *all* children with severe motor handicaps, but they have provided a tremendous source of independence for some young children with cerebral palsy, meningomyelocele, and spinal muscular atrophy.

Developmental therapists and pediatricians frequently discourage the use of jumping chairs, swings, and walkers for infants and young children with motor handicaps (Holm, Harthun-Smith, & Tada, 1983). One of the reasons is that walking and jumping in such devices may increase muscle tone in the legs of the child who already has too much muscle tone (hypertonia). A second reason is that placing your child in one or more of these pieces of equipment for several hours a day may decrease the opportunities for her to move about on her own by crawling or creeping.

For these reasons, jumping chairs, swings, and walkers should be used only under the guidance of your child's therapist. There are some children with motor handicaps (especially some children with hypotonia) for whom these types of equipment may be very appropriate for strengthening the leg muscles, provided they also have plenty of opportunity to explore on their own while moving about on their tummies.

# A Typical Day with Your Child

You may now be wondering how to implement all these guidelines and activities into the daily care of your child, so let's describe a typical day. When your child wakes up in the morning, one of the first things you will do is change her diapers and get her dressed. If your child has hypertonia, you can use this time to build in some relaxation activities. Diaper-changing is a wonderful time to work on relaxation in supine combined with rotation of the lower trunk while you are fastening each side of the diaper. You can then roll the child over to side-lying while putting the rest of her clothes on. If your child has hypotonia, you can work on resisting movements during dressing in an effort to increase tone. You might also do some bouncing and tapping activities once the child is dressed.

When feeding your child breakfast, you will want to use one of the special positions for feeding that will encourage symmetrical and midline activities. After breakfast you may want to put your child in a static position, such as side-lying to play with a toy or prone-lying over a wedge, or you might want to encourage the child in mobility activities, either on the floor or with a specialized mobility device. During the morning nap, position the child in side-lying or on her tummy if possible. For the child with a motor handicap so severe that she cannot move about independently, remember to change her position every 30 to 45 minutes throughout the day during the time when she is awake.

Lunchtime provides a good opportunity to work on functional fine motor activities, such as self-feeding a cracker or cookie or working on independence in eating with a spoon. With a younger infant, you might want to work toward bringing the arms forward at midline to try to hold the bottle. The afternoon nap provides an opportunity to place the child in still another different position. When moving or carrying your child from place to place, remember to use only the minimal support necessary and to provide that support at key points of control, like the hips, shoulders, and trunk.

Following the afternoon nap, you might want to work on some of the specific teaching activities outlined in the following chapters. Dinnertime is a nice social time when most of the family is together—a good opportunity to work on your child's communication skills with others. After dinner, other members of the family may want to work on specific teaching activities with the child or just provide appropriate play and more social interaction.

Bathtime provides another opportunity to build in relaxation activities for the child with hypertonia. The warmth of the bath water can help to decrease muscle tone. Special seats that fit into the tub can help position your child symmetrically with hands in the midline during bathing. For the child with hypotonia, splashing and kicking in the water are actually resistive activities that should help to improve both muscle tone and muscle strength. Since these activities may have the opposite effect of relaxation, you may want to bathe the child with hypotonia in the morning rather than getting him excitedly kicking and splashing before bedtime! Reading your child a story before bed allows you a chance to position him in your lap—again using the general guidelines of symmetry and midline positioning. Encouraging him to look at the pictures, point, and babble are all important activities for facilitating learning in the young child.

Bedtime positioning is also important. For the child who has little active movement, side-lying is probably the most ideal position. You may want to reposition him to side-lying on the opposite side before you go to bed yourself.

The strategies you use throughout the day will vary depending on your child's needs and your family's lifestyle. However, preparatory exercises and positioning and handling techniques previously described will assist you in carrying out daily activities with your child in a more convenient and beneficial manner.

# CHAPTER 8

# Motor Activities

This chapter contains some specific motor activities that you can teach to your child. There are three types of motor activities included here: gross motor, fine motor, and oral-motor. Gross motor activities are those that involve large muscle movements such as sitting, crawling, and walking. Fine motor activities are those that require small muscle movement, such as the use of hands and fingers and eyes. Oral-motor activities involve interaction of the muscles of the neck, lip, tongue, cheeks, and jaw to produce the smooth movement needed to eat and to make sounds.

The motor activities listed in this chapter are both developmentally sequenced and functionally oriented. There are a number of general goals listed in each area with specific objectives or teaching activities listed under each goal. For example, the first goal under "Gross Motor Activities" is head control. There are 11 objectives or specific teaching activities listed under the goal of head control. These objectives are developmentally sequenced. In other words, it is expected that most children will learn to accomplish Objective 1.8 before they can accomplish Objective 1.11. However, it is important to remember that developmental sequences do not always occur in "lock-step" fashion, so it may be possible for your child to learn a higher-level motor activities *before* she has accomplished an earlier skill.

In addition to being developmentally sequenced, each of the motor activities listed is directed at functional movement. Even as simple an activity as lifting the head to a 45° angle while lying on the stomach (Objective 1.4) has functional significance for the child. First of all, this activity allows your baby to look around at her environment and, secondly, it gives her the opportunity to strengthen the muscles in the back of her neck to prepare her for the head control needed later on in sitting.

While it is important to remember that motor development is not always "lock-step," certain objectives or activities specifically list *prerequisite* programs. In these activities, it is wise to make sure that your child can accomplish the prerequisite objective before you begin the new activity. Once again, be sure to consult your physical or occupational therapist to decide which activities are the most

Figure 8.1

developmentally and functionally appropriate for your child.

At the end of each teaching activity are suggested consequences. A plus sign (+) indicates that the child has performed the activity correctly and should be rewarded or reinforced as described. A minus sign (−) indicates that the child was unable to perform the activity and suggests some alternate strategies for enabling the child to achieve success.

Before you actually begin the teaching programs, practice a few of them on your spouse or on other children. It will give you experience in reading the programs, following the directions, and in using the recording system.

# Gross Motor Activities

Gross motor activities are those involving the use of the large muscles in the body. Activities such as head control, sitting, crawling, creeping, and walking are all considered gross motor activities. Gross motor skills occur in a developmental sequence, proceeding in a cephalo-caudal direction (head-to-tail or head-to-toe). This means that the baby first develops control of the head, then of the upper trunk and arms, and finally of the legs. The following activities are designed to help you help your child progress in the gross motor area of development. In accomplishing these activities, you will enable your child to progress both functionally *and* developmentally.

## Goal 1: Head Control

### Objective 1.1: Child Lifts Head to Clear Chin

**Position:** Lying on stomach (prone)
**Materials Needed:** Favorite toy or object
**Teaching Activities:**
1. Place child on his stomach on a blanket or a wedge.
2. Present a sound stimulus, such as a bell or rattle, or a visual stimulus, such as a brightly colored toy, to encourage the child to lift his head. Say "Head up."
3. Practice this activity to both sides so that the child can lift his head and turn to either side.

**Consequences:**
(+) 1. Praise the child and stroke his back if he successfully lifts his head to clear his chin.
(−) 2. If the child does not lift his head, present the sound or visual stimulus again and physically lift the child's head to look at the object. Praise him for the assisted head-lifting.

### Objective 1.2: Child Turns Head from Side to Midline

**Position:** Lying on back (supine)
**Materials Needed:** Favorite toy or object, wedge

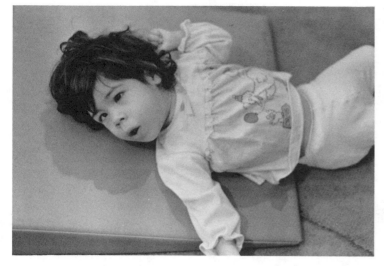

Figure 8.2

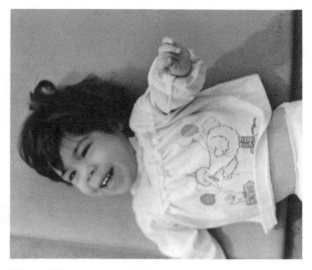

Figure 8.3

**Teaching Activities:**

1. Place child on her back on a blanket or a wedge. *Note:* If the child tends to "push back" with her head while lying flat on her back, you may want to position her in back-lying on a wedge to help to prevent this (see Figure 8.2).

2. Present a visual stimulus, such as a brightly colored toy, in the child's line of vision. (For children with visual impairment, you may use a sound stimulus, such as a bell or rattle.)

3. Hold the stimulus about 12 inches from the child's eyes and move it toward the midline. Say, "Watch the toy."

4. It is important to encourage the child to bring the head into midline because this position will help to decrease the influence of abnormal primitive reflexes that may serve to prevent normal movement.

**Consequences:**

(+) 1. Praise the child if she turns her head to follow the visual stimulus from one side toward the midline.

(−) 2. If the child does not turn her head, gently turn it for her with your fingertips on her chin. Praise her as you assist her through the motion.

### Objective 1.3: Child Maintains Head in Midline, Lying on Back

**Position:** Lying on back (supine)
**Materials Needed:** Blanket or wedge, favorite toy or object
**Teaching Activities:**

1. Place child on his back on a blanket or wedge (see note in Objective 1.2, Teaching Activity 1).

2. Encourage child to bring head to midline, as in Objective 1.2.

3. Maintain the visual or sound stimulus in the midline 12 inches above the child's eyes.

4. Steps:

(1) Child maintains head in midline for 2 seconds.

**Figure 8.4**

(2) Child maintains head in midline for 5 seconds.
(3) Child maintains head in midline for 10 seconds.
(4) Child maintains head in midline for 15 seconds.

**Consequences:**

(+) 1. Praise the child for maintaining his head in midline.
(−) 2. If the child moves head out of midline, remove the toy and turn away from him for 5 seconds, then go on to the next trial.

**Objective 1.4: Child Lifts Head 45°, Lying on Stomach**

**Position:** Lying on stomach (prone)
**Materials Needed:** Blanket, wedge, and favorite toy or object
**Prerequisite:** "Child Lifts Head to Clear Chin" (Objective 1.1)
**Teaching Activities:**

1. Place child on her stomach on a blanket or wedge.
2. Present a sound stimulus, such as a bell or a rattle, or a visual stimulus, such as a brightly colored toy, to encourage the child to lift her head. Say "Head up." Gradually raise the toy higher until head is at a 45° angle in relation to the floor.
3. Maintain the stimulus, in the midline, for as long as the child holds her head up at 45°.
4. Steps:
    (1) Child will raise head to 45° for 2 seconds.
    (2) Child will raise head to 45° for 5 seconds.
    (3) Child will raise head to 45° for 10 seconds.
    (4) Child will raise head to 45° for 15 seconds.
    (5) Child will raise head to 45° for 20 seconds.

**Consequences:**

(+) 1. Praise the child and stroke the back of her neck (from head downward toward shoulders) while head is up.
(−) 2. If child does not lift head to 45°, demonstrate by gently lifting her chin with your fingers until her head is at 45°. Praise the child for the assisted head-lifting.

**Figure 8.5**

**Objective 1.5: Child Maintains Head up in Supported Sitting**

**Position:** Supported sitting
**Materials Needed:** None
**Teaching Activities:**
1. Place child in sitting position, giving hand support at hips and lower trunk. You should be facing the child.
2. Talk to the child and encourage him to look at you. Say, "Head up" and keep your face at his face level. (Do *not* encourage the child to look *up* at you but rather to look straight ahead.)
3. Keep talking to the child for as long as he maintains his face up looking at you straight ahead.
4. Blowing gently on the child's forehead may encourage him to keep his head up.
5. Steps:
   (1) Child will raise head with eyes straight ahead for 2 seconds.
   (2) Child will raise head with eyes straight ahead for 5 seconds.
   (3) Child will raise head with eyes straight ahead for 10 seconds.
   (4) Child will raise head with eyes straight ahead for 15 seconds.
   (5) Child will raise head with eyes straight ahead for 20 seconds.

**Consequences:**
(+) 1. Praise the child and continue talking to him while his eyes are straight ahead.
(−) 2. If child does not lift head so eyes are straight ahead, gently lift up chin until face is vertical. Praise the child for the assisted head-lifting.

**Objective 1.6: Child Lifts Head 90°, Lying on Stomach**

**Position:** Lying on stomach (prone)
**Materials Needed:** Bell, rattle, brightly colored toy
**Prerequisite:** "Child Lifts Head 45°, Lying on Stomach" (Objective 1.4)
**Teaching Activities:**
1. Place child on her stomach on a blanket or wedge.
2. Present a sound stimulus, such as a brightly colored toy, to encourage the child to lift her head. Say, "Head up!" Gradually raise the toy higher until head is at 90° angle in relation to the floor.
3. Maintain the stimulus, in the midline, for as long as the child holds her head up at 90°.
4. Steps:
   (1) Child will raise head to 90° for 5 seconds.
   (2) Child will raise head to 90° for 10 seconds.
   (3) Child will raise head to 90° for 15 seconds.
   (4) Child will raise head to 90° for 20 seconds.

**Consequences:**
(+) 1. Praise the child and stroke the back of her neck (from head downward toward shoulders) while head is up.
(−) 2. If the child does not lift head to 90°, demonstrate by gently lifting her chin with your fingers until head is at 90°. Praise the child during the assisted head-lifting.

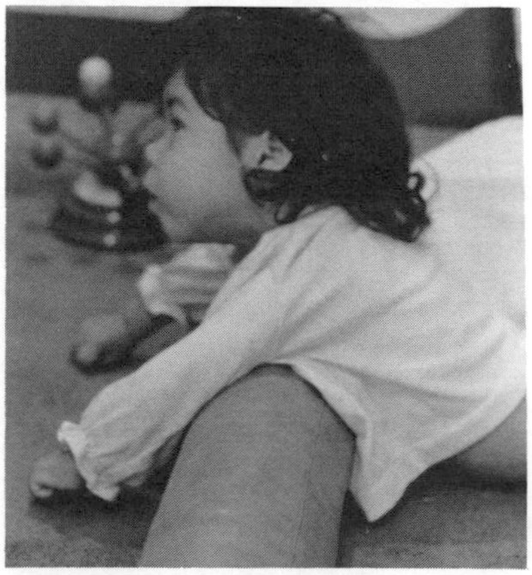

**Figure 8.6**

### Objective 1.7: Child Maintains Head in Line with Body, Tipping from Side to Side

**Position:** Supported sitting
**Materials Needed:** None
**Prerequisite:** "Child Maintains Head up in Supported Sitting" (Objective 1.5)
**Teaching Activities:**
1. Facing the child, place the child in sitting with support at hips and lower trunk.
2. Gently and slowly tip the child toward the right and observe the ability to keep the head in a line with the body.
3. Bring the child back to an upright sitting position, then slowly and gently tip toward the left.

**Consequences:**
(+) 1. Praise the child and smile when he maintains head in line with body.
(−) 2. If the child is unable to maintain head in line with body during tipping, continue to carry out this activity but tip the child very slightly and very slowly to each side to give the child more time to respond.

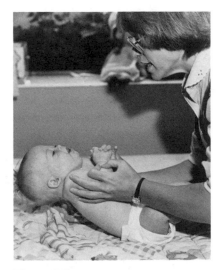

**Figure 8.7**

### Objective 1.8: Child Maintains Head in Line with Body During Pull-to-Sit

**Position:** Lying on back (supine)
**Materials Needed:** None
**Prerequisite Activities:**
1. If the child is unable to maintain head in line with body (shows a head lag), begin the activity with the child reclined at 45° rather than flat on her back. Sit on the floor with your feet on the floor and knees bent. Place the child on your thighs in supine facing you. Follow directions for Teaching Activities 2–4 (below) by positioning the child in this manner. This decreases the difficulty of maintaining the head in line with the body because the effects of gravity are reduced.
2. If the child is unable to flex her arms and assist in pulling up, place your hands around her shoulders and pull from the shoulders rather than the wrists.

**Teaching Activities:**
1. Lay child on her back facing you.
2. Give the child your thumbs to grasp and hold child at wrists.
3. Gently pull on the child's wrists while saying "Let's sit up."
4. Wait for the child to follow through by flexing her arms and assisting in pulling up.

**Consequences:**
(+) 1. Praise the child for pulling with her arms and maintaining head in line with body.
(−) 2. If the child is unable to perform this activity, do prerequisite activities instead.

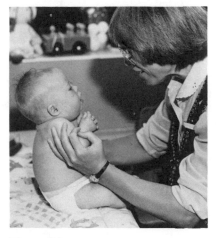

**Figure 8.8**

### Objective 1.9: Child Lifts and Maintains Head Up During Assisted Rolling

**Position:** Lying on back (supine)
**Materials Needed:** Favorite toy or object
**Prerequisite:** "Child Lifts Head to 45°, Lying on Stomach" (Objective 1.4)
**Teaching Activities:**
1. Place child in supine with head in midline.
2. Flex the child's left leg so the knee is up over the trunk.
3. Bring the left knee toward the child's right side (across his body) in an effort to help the child begin to roll over from back to stomach.
4. Bring the left knee all the way across the body and over to the floor on the right side.
5. Repeat all activities beginning with bending the right leg so that child can roll to opposite side as well.
6. Provide a toy and your attention to encourage the child to lift his head.

**Consequences:**
(+) 1. Praise the child for lifting and maintaining his head up while you are assisting in rolling him from back to stomach.
(−) 2. If the child is unable to lift his head during assisted rolling, provide a visual or auditory stimulus (e.g., bell, squeaker toy, yarn) to encourage head-lifting while rolling.

### Objective 1.10: Child Maintains Head Vertical, Tipping Side to Side

**Position:** Supported sitting
**Materials Needed:** Favorite toy or object
**Prerequisite:** "Child Maintains Head in Line with Body, Tipping Side to Side" (Objective 1.7)

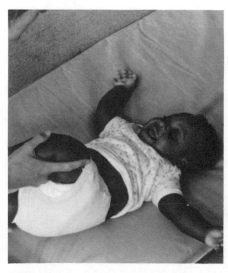

**Figure 8.9**

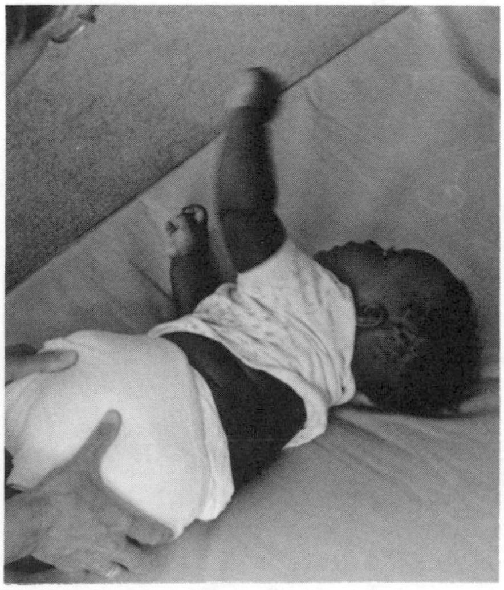

**Figure 8.10**

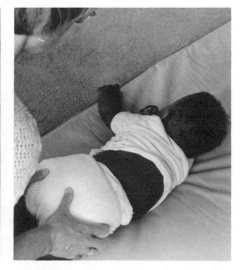

**Figure 8.11**

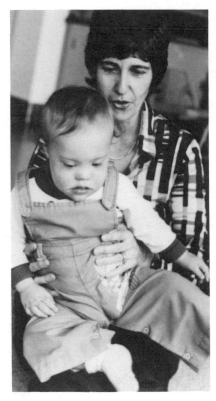

**Figure 8.12**

**Teaching Activities:**
1. Facing the child, place the child in sitting with support at hips and lower trunk.
2. Gently and slowly tip the child toward the right and observe the ability to keep the head in a vertical position with relation to the floor.
3. Bring the child back to an upright sitting position, then slowly and gently tip toward the left.

**Consequences:**
(+) 1. Praise the child and smile when she maintains head in a vertical position while being tipped to the side.
(−) 2. If the child is unable to maintain head vertical, continue to carry out this activity but tip the child more slowly to each side. Provide a visual or auditory stimulus to encourage bringing the head toward vertical.

**Objective 1.11: Child Maintains Chin Tuck During Pull-to-Sit**

**Position:** Lying on back (supine)
**Materials Needed:** Favorite toy or object
**Prerequisite:** "Child Maintains Head in Line with Body during Pull-to-Sit" (Objective 1.8)
**Teaching Activities:**
1. Lay child on his back facing you.
2. Give the child your thumbs to grasp and hold him at wrists.
3. Gently pull on the child's wrists while saying, "Let's sit up."
4. Wait for the child to tuck chin and flex arms to assist in pulling up.

**Consequences:**
(+) 1. Praise the child for tucking chin and pulling with his arms throughout the pull-to-sit.
(−) 2. If the child is unable to tuck the chin throughout the pull-to-sit, begin the activity with the child reclined at 45° rather than flat on his back. Sit on the floor with your feet on the floor and knees bent. Place the child in supine on your thighs and facing you. Repeat Teaching Activities 2-4 by positioning the child in this manner. This position will help to reduce the effects of gravity.

## Goal 2: Trunk Control

**Objective 2.1: Child Rolls from Stomach to Back (Prone to Supine)**

**Position:** Prone on extended arms
**Materials Needed:** Favorite toy or object
**Prerequisite:** "Child Lifts and Maintains Head Up During Assisted Rolling" (Objective 1.9)
**Teaching Activities:**
1. Place child in prone, allowing her to support herself on extended arms.

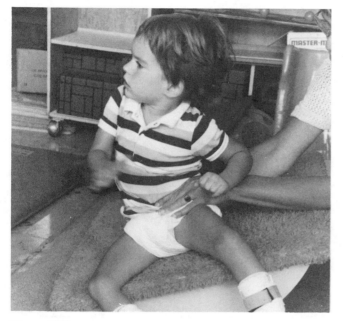

Figure 8.13

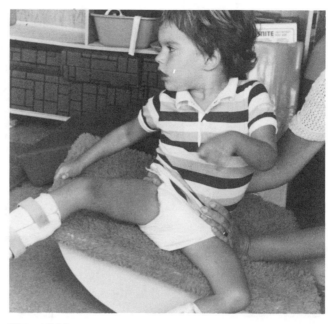

Figure 8.14

2. Present a visual stimulus (e.g., toy) in front of the child's eyes and say "Look at this."
3. Move the stimulus to the right and upward, bringing it around over the child's right shoulder. Say, "Roll over on your back."
4. Following each trial, reposition the child in prone and repeat the activity. Also repeat activity on the left side.

**Consequences:**

(+) 1. Praise the child and rub her tummy after she has successfully rolled from prone to supine.
(−) 2. Place your hand gently under the child's chin and rotate the head in the direction to which you want the child to roll. You can facilitate rolling over by using the head as a key point of control.

**Objective 2.2: Child Shows C-Curve in Trunk, Tipping from Side to Side**

**Position:** Supported sitting
**Materials Needed:** Beach ball
**Prerequisite:** "Child Maintains Head in Line with Body, Tipping Side to Side" (Objective 1.7)
**Teaching Activities:**

1. Place child (facing you) in supported sitting on a beach ball (with nonslip surface) or on your bent knees while you are sitting on the floor.
2. Support the child at the hips and slowly and gently tip him toward the right. Observe the ability to bring the head to vertical and curve the spine in a C-curve toward the left while tipping toward the right.
3. Bring the child back to an upright sitting position, then slowly and gently tip toward the left.

**Figure 8.15**

**Consequences:**

(+) 1. Praise the child and smile when he maintains head vertical and shows a C-curve in the trunk toward the opposite side to which he is being tipped.

(−) 2. If the child is unable to show a C-curve during tipping, continue to carry out this activity but tip the child very slightly and very slowly to each side.

### Objective 2.3: Child Flexes Trunk While Being Tipped Backward and Extends Trunk While Being Tipped Forward

**Position:** Supported sitting

**Materials Needed:** Beach ball

**Prerequisite:** ''Child Lifts Head 90°, Lying on Stomach'' (Objective 1.6) and ''Child Maintains Head in Line with Body during Pull-to-Sit'' (Objective 1.8)

**Teaching Activities:**

1. Place child in supported sitting on a beach ball or on your flexed knees while you are sitting on the floor.

2. Support the child at the hips; slowly and gently tip her backward. Observe the child's ability to bring the head forward and flex the trunk to compensate for being tipped backward.

3. Bring the child back to an upright sitting position, then slowly and gently tip her forward. Observe the child's ability to extend the trunk to compensate for being tipped forward.

**Consequences:**

(+) 1. Praise the child and smile when she flexes/extends head and trunk appropriately.

(−) 2. If the child is unable to flex or extend during tipping, continue to carry out this activity but move your hand support up to the lower trunk to make this activity easier.

**Objective 2.4: Child Rolls from Back to Side-lying**

**Position:** Lying on back (supine)
**Materials Needed:** Favorite toy or object
**Teaching Activities:**
1. Lay child on back and encourage him to track a favorite toy horizontally to the right.
2. Say, "Roll over this way."
3. Guide at key points (hip or shoulder) to encourage rolling.
4. Repeat toward the left.

**Consequences:**
(+) 1. Praise the child for rolling to correct side and give the child the toy he was tracking.
(−) 2. Say, "This is how we roll," and bend and bring the leg across the body in the direction toward which you want the child to roll. (See Objective 1.9: "Child Lifts and Maintains Head up during Assisted Rolling.")

**Objective 2.5: Child Rolls from Back to Stomach**

**Position:** Lying on back (supine)
**Materials Needed:** Favorite toy or object
**Suggested Preparatory Activity:** "Relaxation in Side-lying" (See "Preparatory Activities for the Child with Hypertonia" in Chapter 7
**Prerequisite:** "Child Rolls from Back to Side-lying" (Objective 2.4)
**Teaching Activities:**
1. Lay child on back and encourage her to track a favorite toy horizontally to the right.
2. Say, "Roll over this way onto your stomach."
3. Guide at key points (hip or shoulder) to encourage rolling.
4. Repeat toward the left.

**Consequences:**
(+) 1. Praise the child for rolling over and give her the toy to play with once she has rolled over completely.
(−) 2. If the child cannot roll over independently to her stomach, try preparatory activities first. Bend and bring the leg across the body in the direction toward which you want the child to roll.

## Goal 3:  Protective Extension Reactions

**Objective 3.1: Child Shows Forward Protective Extension**

**Position:** Prone over beach ball or bolster
**Materials Needed:** Beach ball or bolster, wall mirror (if possible)
**Teaching Activities:**
1. Place child in prone (stomach-lying) over a beach ball or bolster with

arms extended over his head. Hold the child at the hips, with hips abducted (separated) and feet turned out.
2. Roll the child quickly forward so that he will need to "catch" self on extended arms.
3. Use a wall mirror or standing mirror so you can observe the child's responses.

**Consequences:**
(+) 1. Praise the child for "catching" himself.
(−) 2. Move the child slowly through the movement and guide at shoulders to help him to put hands out.

**Objective 3.2: Child Shows Sideways Protective Extension on Forearm**

**Position:** Supported sitting
**Materials Needed:** None
**Teaching Activities:**
1. Place the child in sitting on firm surface with support at hips.
2. Tip child quickly to the right and observe whether she brings her arm out to the side and "catches" self on forearm.
3. Return child to upright sitting and repeat step 2 to the left side.

**Consequences:**
(+) 1. Praise the child and smile if she "catches" self on forearm or extended arm.
(−) 2. If the child does not show protective reactions automatically, tip her slowly to one side and abduct the arm by guiding at the shoulder. Place the child with weight bearing on the forearm and provide joint compression down through the shoulder.

**Objective 3.3: Child Shows Sideways Protective Extension on Extended Arm**

**Position:** Supported sitting
**Materials Needed:** None
**Teaching Activities:**
1. Place child in sitting on firm surface with support at hips.
2. Tip child quickly to the right and observe whether he brings his arm out to the side.
3. Return child to upright sitting and repeat step 2 to the left side.

**Consequences:**
(+) 1. Praise the child and smile if he "catches" self on extended arm.
(−) 2. If the child does not show protective reactions on extended arm, tip child slowly to one side and abduct the arm by guiding at the shoulder. Place the child with weight bearing on the extended arm and provide joint compression down through shoulder into the hand.

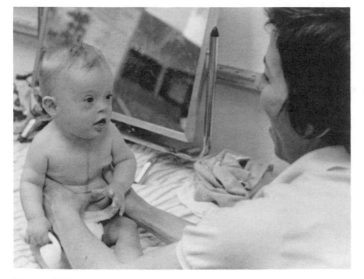

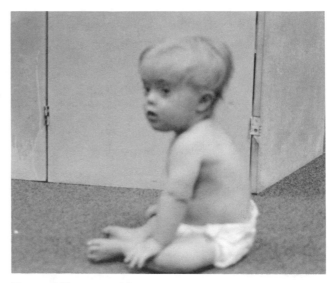

**Figure 8.16**                    **Figure 8.17**

**Objective 3.4: Child Shows Backward Protective Extension**

**Position:** Supported sitting
**Materials Needed:** None
**Prerequisite:** "Child Shows Forward and Sideways Protective Extension" (Objectives 3.1, 3.2, 3.3)
**Teaching Activities:**
1. Place child in supported sitting on firm surface with support at hips. Face the child while supporting at hips.
2. Rotate the child's trunk to the right and backward so that she will reach back with the right arm to "catch" self.
4. Return to upright sitting. Repeat step 3 to the left.

**Consequences:**
(+) 1. Praise the child for catching self when rotated backward to either side.
(−) 2. Rotate the child slowly backward toward right side. Place the extended right arm on the surface and provide joint compression through the shoulder and into the hand. Repeat to the left side.

## Goal 4: Sitting

### Objective 4.1: Child Sits with Minimal Support at Trunk

**Position:** Supported sitting
**Materials Needed:** Couch or easy chair or child-adapted seat, favorite toy or object
**Prerequisite:** "Child Maintains Head up in Supported Sitting" (Objective 1.5)
**Teaching Activities:**
1. Place child in supported sitting position, using the minimal support

needed. Supported sitting options include: (a) sitting supported by your hands while you are facing and talking to the child, (b) sitting propped in the corner of a couch or easy chair, (c) sitting in an adapted seat, such as a corner chair or adapted high chair (see Figure 8.16).

2. Praise the child while he maintains head up with support at the trunk. Provide a visual or auditory stimulus (e.g., toy) if needed.

3. Steps:
   (1) Child sits with head up and minimal support for 2 seconds.
   (2) Child sits with head up and minimal support for 5 seconds.
   (3) Child sits with head up and minimal support for 10 seconds.
   (4) Child sits with head up and minimal support for 15 seconds.
   (5) Child sits with head up and minimal support for 20 seconds.
   (6) Child sits with head up and minimal support for 30 seconds.

**Consequences:**
(+) 1. Praise the child for maintaining head up with minimal trunk support.
(−) 2. Provided the child has achieved Objective 1.5 ("Child Maintains Head up in Supported Sitting"), even the child with severe motor delay should be able to accomplish this objective with the correct adaptive seating. Failure to accomplish this objective suggests that the most appropriate adaptive seating device has not been located (see Appendix 2).

### Objective 4.2: Child Sits Supported on Arms

**Position:** Supported sitting
**Materials Needed:** Favorite toy or object
**Prerequisite:** "Child Sits with Minimal Support at Trunk" (Objective 4.1)
**Preparatory Activity:** Joint compression down through the shoulders while child is in sitting
**Teaching Activities:**
1. Place child in sitting on a firm surface with legs apart (see Figure 8.17).
2. Prop the child on extended arms with hands on knees or in front on floor. *Caution:* Prolonged propping (i.e., more than 30 seconds) is not to be encouraged because it does not allow for strengthening of trunk muscles.
3. Encourage the child to maintain this position by placing a favorite toy or other visual stimulus at eye level.
4. Steps:
   (1) Child will sit on propped arms for 2 seconds.
   (2) Child will sit on propped arms for 5 seconds.
   (3) Child will sit on propped arms for 10 seconds.
   (4) Child will sit on propped arms for 15 seconds.
   (5) Child will sit on propped arms for 20 seconds.
   (6) Child will sit on propped arms for 30 seconds.

**Consequences:**
(+) 1. Praise the child and present visual stimulus while she maintains sitting.
(−) 2. If child starts to slump down toward the floor, straighten up the back

and provide repeated joint compressions again for about 30 seconds; then begin a new trial.

**Objective 4.3: Child Sits Independently**

**Position:** Sitting
**Materials Needed:** Favorite toy or object
**Prerequisite:** "Child Sits Supported on Arms" (Objective 4.2)
**Preparatory Activity:** Joint compression downward from the shoulders to facilitate co-contraction of the trunk muscles for independent sitting (see "Preparatory Activities for the Child with Hypotonia" in Chapter 7)
**Teaching Activities:**
1. Place child in sitting on the floor or other firm surface.
2. Give the child a toy or favorite object to play with so he does not rely on arm support.
3. Steps:
    (1) Child will sit independently for 2 seconds.
    (2) Child will sit independently for 5 seconds.
    (3) Child will sit independently for 10 seconds.
    (4) Child will sit independently for 15 seconds.
    (5) Child will sit independently for 20 seconds.
    (6) Child will sit independently for 30 seconds.

**Consequences:**
(+) 1. Praise the child for maintaining sitting.
(−) 2. If child starts to lean forward to rely on arms for support, straighten up the back and provide joint compression again for about 30 seconds. *Note:* Some children sit easily when they are on the floor because of the wide base of support created by their legs. To increase the difficulty of independent sitting, have the child sit on a bench or on several telephone books or on a bolster. Children will often sit up straight if their base of support is decreased in this manner.

**Objective 4.4: Child Moves out of Sitting to Lying on Stomach**

**Position:** Independent sitting
**Materials Needed:** Favorite toy or object
**Prerequisite:** "Child Sits Independently" (Objective 4.3)
**Teaching Activities:**
1. Place child in sitting. Put a favorite toy off to the child's right side and encourage her to try to get it.
2. If the child does not rotate across, bringing both hands to the floor to try to go for the toy, encourage trunk rotation at the shoulders and place the child's hands to the right side. This should cause her to lean to the right and progress to lying on her stomach.
3. Repeat steps 2 and 3 to the left side.

**Consequences:**
(+) 1. Praise the child and allow her to play with the toy once it has been obtained.

(−) 2. Continue to facilitate trunk rotation and hand placement to the side. Gently lift up the child's hips to complete the move from sitting to lying on stomach.

### Objective 4.5: Child Rises from Lying on Stomach to Sitting

**Position:** Lying on stomach (prone)
**Materials Needed:** Favorite toy or object
**Prerequisite:** "Child Moves out of Sitting to Lying on Stomach" (Objective 4.4)
**Teaching Activities:**
1. Place child on stomach on the floor.
2. With a favorite toy, encourage child to push up on extended arms.
3. Continue to bring the toy around in front of the child's eyes and up to the right while facilitating trunk rotation at the right shoulder.
4. Allow the child time to help push up with his left arm.
5. Say, "Let's sit up" as you guide the action.
6. Repeat steps 2–6 to left side.
**Consequences:**
(+) 1. Praise the child and give him the toy once sitting is achieved. As the child gets better at doing this more independently, decrease your guidance at the shoulder.
(−) 2. Move the child through the entire transition from stomach-lying to sitting by guiding at shoulder and also providing counterrotation at hips on the same side.

## Goal 5: Mobility on Floor

### Objective 5.1: Child Will Maintain Weight on Extended Arms

**Position:** Prone (lying on stomach)
**Materials Needed:** Favorite toy or object, bolster or rolled towel or wedge
**Prerequisite:** "Child Lifts Head 90°, Lying on Stomach" (Objective 1.6)
**Teaching Activities:**
1. Place child in prone on a firm surface.
2. Encourage child to raise head to 90° and straighten arms by placing a favorite toy above eye level.
3. Steps:
   (1) Child maintains weight on extended arms for 2 seconds.
   (2) Child maintains weight on extended arms for 5 seconds.
   (3) Child maintains weight on extended arms for 10 seconds.
   (4) Child maintains weight on extended arms for 15 seconds.
   (5) Child maintains weight on extended arms for 20 seconds.
**Consequences:**
(+) 1. Praise the child for maintaining head up and arms extended. Dangle or shake the toy to maintain her attention.

**Figure 8.18**

(−) 2. If the child is unable to assume or maintain this position, try one or more of the following alternate strategies:
    (1) Place the child on a wedge that is the same height as the extended arms.
    (2) Place a small bolster or rolled-up towel under the child's arms.
    (3) Place the child in a prone-on-extended-arms position (over bolster, wedge, or across your legs) and provide joint compression down through the shoulders into the hands to give a feel for weight-bearing on extended arms.

### Objective 5.2: Child Will Reach from Position of Lying on Stomach

**Position:** Stomach-lying (prone)
**Materials Needed:** Favorite toy or object
**Prerequisite:** "Child Will Maintain Weight on Extended Arms" (Objective 5.1)
**Teaching Activities:**
1. Place child on his stomach on a firm surface.
2. Present a favorite toy at arm's length in front of the child's right hand.
3. Encourage the child to reach out for the toy with the right hand.
4. Repeat steps 2 and 3 on the left side.

**Consequences:**
(+) 1. Praise the child for reaching out and touching the toy.
(−) 2. If the child is unable to shift weight over to one side in order to reach out with the opposite hand, assist the child by facilitating weight-shifting at the hips. Gently rotate the right hip up off the floor to enable the child to lift and reach with the right hand. Repeat to the left side.

### Objective 5.3: Child Will Pivot on Stomach

**Position:** Stomach-lying (prone)
**Materials Needed:** Favorite toy or object
**Prerequisite:** "Child Will Reach from Stomach-lying Position" (Objective 5.2)
**Teaching Activities:**
1. Place child in prone on firm surface.
2. Present a favorite toy at the child's right side about 12″ away from the body.
3. Encourage the child by saying, "Get the toy." Shake or rattle the toy to make it more enticing.
4. Repeat to the left side.
5. Steps:
    (1) Child will pivot 45° to get the toy.
    (2) Child will pivot 90° to get the toy.
    (3) Child will pivot 180° to get the toy.

**Consequences:**

(+) 1. Praise the child and allow him to play with the toy.

(−) 2. If child is unable to shift weight from arm to arm and pivot toward the toy, facilitate weight-shifting by alternately lifting up either hip. If child is trying to move to the right, lift the right hip first to free the right arm to move, then lift the left hip so the left arm can be moved in the same direction.

**Objective 5.4: Child Crawls Forward (Stomach on Floor)**

**Position:** Stomach-lying (prone)
**Materials Needed:** Favorite toy or object
**Prerequisite:** "Child Will Pivot on Stomach" (Objective 5.3)
**Teaching Activities:**

1. Place child on stomach on floor.
2. Place a favorite toy or interesting object at varying distances on the floor in front of the child.
3. Provide upward pressure alternately on soles of the child's feet to encourage reciprocal crawling (alternating pattern). In other words, push on one foot, then the other.
4. Steps:
   (1) Child crawls 6″ with guidance at feet.
   (2) Child crawls 12″ with guidance at feet.
   (3) Child crawls 18″ with guidance at feet.
   (4) Child crawls 24″ with guidance at feet.

**Consequences:**

(+) 1. Praise the child and allow her to play with the toy once it is obtained.

(−) 2. If the child is unable to move forward, place her head down on a wedge or other incline so that gravity will assist the movement. Move each leg alternately through the entire crawling sequence.

**Figure 8.19**

**Objective 5.5: Child Rocks Back and Forth on Hands and Knees (Quadruped)**

**Position:** Quadruped (hands and knees)
**Materials Needed:** Favorite toy or object, scooter board (optional)
**Prerequisite:** "Child Crawls Forward (Stomach Down)" (Objective 5.4)
**Teaching Activities:**
1. Place child in quadruped (on hands and knees)
2. Place a favorite toy a few inches in front of the child and encourage him to try to get it.
3. Steps:
   (1) Child rocks in quadruped for 5 seconds.
   (2) Child rocks in quadruped for 10 seconds.
   (3) Child rocks in quadruped for 15 seconds.
   (4) Child rocks in quadruped for 20 seconds.

**Consequences:**
(+) 1. Praise the child for maintaining quadruped and rocking. Rub his back.
(−) 2. Place the child in quadruped and give joint compression down through the shoulders into the hands and down through the hips into the knees to give a feel for the quadruped position. After providing joint compression, gently rock the child back and forth.
(−) 3. For children who do not have adequate trunk control to assume quadruped, place them in prone on a scooter board to give them a feel for a position with the stomach up off the floor.

**Objective 5.6: Child Creeps (Stomach off Floor)**

**Position:** Quadruped (hands and knees)
**Materials Needed:** Favorite toy or object
**Prerequisite:** "Child Rocks Back and Forth on Hands and Knees" (Objective 5.5)
**Teaching Activities:**
1. Place child in quadruped (on hands and knees)
2. Place a favorite toy at varying distances in front of the child and encourage her to try to get it.
3. Steps:
   (1) Child creeps forward 6 inches.
   (2) Child creeps forward 12 inches.
   (3) Child creeps forward 18 inches.
   (4) Child creeps forward 24 inches.

**Consequences:**
(+) 1. Praise the child and allow her to play with the toy once it is obtained.
(−) 2. If the child is unable to move forward in quadruped, you can facilitate creeping by alternately lifting at the hips and bringing either knee forward.
(−) 3. If the child does not have adequate trunk control to assume quadruped and creep, place her in prone on a scooter board to encourage forward movement.

**Objective 5.7: Child Creeps Up Stairs**

**Position:** Quadruped (hands and knees)
**Materials Needed:** Safe stairway, favorite toy or object
**Prerequisite:** "Child Creeps (Stomach Up)" (Objective 5.6)
**Teaching Activities:**
1. Place child at bottom of stairs and put a favorite toy on the third step.
2. Encourage the child to pull up to knee-standing at the first step and continue on up.
3. Steps:
   (1) Child creeps up 1 step.
   (2) Child creeps up 2 steps.
   (3) Child creeps up 3 steps.
4. Guard the child carefully during this activity.

**Consequences:**
(+) 1. Praise the child and allow time to play with the toy once it is obtained.
(−) 2. If the child is unable to creep up stairs, facilitate this activity by lifting first one hand and then the other up on the first step. Then gently lift first one knee up to the first step and then the opposite hand up to the second step. Continue to facilitate climbing in this manner.

**Objective 5.8: Child Creeps Down Stairs**

**Position:** Quadruped (hands and knees)
**Materials Needed:** Safe stairway, favorite toy or object
**Prerequisite:** "Child Creeps Up Stairs" (Objective 5.7)
**Teaching Activities:**
1. Once the child is able to creep up one step, begin to work on creeping down backwards (head facing top of stairs).
2. Place the favorite toy on the floor and encourage the child to creep down to get it.
3. Steps:
   (1) Child creeps backwards down one step.
   (2) Child creeps backwards down two steps.
   (3) Child creeps backwards down three steps.
4. Guard the child carefully during this activity.

**Consequences:**
(+) 1. Praise the child and allow time to play with the toy once it is obtained.
(−) 2. If the child is unable to creep backwards down stairs, facilitate this activity by bringing one knee down first, followed by the opposite hand. Then repeat with alternate knee and alternate hand. Continue to facilitate creeping down the stairs in this manner.

## Goal 6:  Rising to Stand with Support

### Objective 6.1:  Child Rises to Kneel-Standing

**Position:**  Quadruped (hands and knees)
**Materials Needed:**  Stairway or low bench, favorite toy or object
**Prerequisite:**  "Child Rocks Back and Forth on Hands and Knees" (Objective 5.5)
**Teaching Activities:**
1.  Place child in quadruped at bottom of step or low bench. Place a toy on the step and encourage the child to pull up from quadruped into kneel-standing.
2.  Steps:
    (1) Child pulls up to kneel-standing at 6 inch height.
    (2) Child pulls up to kneel-standing at 10 inch height.
    (3) Child pulls up to kneel-standing at 12-14 inch height.
**Consequences:**
(+) 1.  Praise the child and allow him to play with the toy in kneel-standing.
(−) 2.  If the child does not reach up, push down and rotate left hip while facilitating lifting and reaching with right arm. Repeat on opposite side.

### Objective 6.2:  Child Shifts Weight from Side to Side in Kneel-Standing

**Position:**  Kneel-standing
**Materials Needed:**  Step or low bench
**Prerequisite:**  "Child Rises to Kneel-Standing" (Objective 6.1)
**Teaching Activities:**
1.  Place child in kneel-standing.
2.  Encourage her to lift each knee alternately to shift weight from side to side. You can make this into a game or "dance" to music.
**Consequences:**
(+) 1.  Praise the child if she is weight-shifting correctly and continue to make it a game.
(−) 2.  If the child is unable to weight-shift in kneel-standing, gently facilitate this activity by pulling sideways down on the left shoulder to encourage lifting of the right knee. Repeat to opposite side and continue to alternate.

### Objective 6.3:  Child Rises to Half-Kneeling

**Position:**  Kneel-standing
**Materials Needed:**  Step or low bench
**Prerequisite:**  "Child Shifts Weight Side to Side in Kneel-Standing" (Objective 6.2)
**Teaching Activities:**
1.  Place child in kneel-standing at step or bench.

2. Facilitate weight-shifting by pulling sideways up and down on left shoulder.
3. As child shifts weight over left knee, lift right leg and place foot flat on floor, then return to kneel-standing.
4. Repeat on opposite side.

**Consequences:**
(+) 1. Praise the child for getting into half-kneeling. Give him a toy to play with in this position.
(−) 2. If child is unable to assume this position, facilitate activity by repeating steps 2 and 3. Once the child is in half-kneeling position, provide joint compression down through the knee and into the foot on the leg that is up in half-kneeling. Repeat on opposite side.

### Objective 6.4: Child Rises to Standing through Half-Kneeling

**Position:** Half-kneeling
**Materials Needed:** Step or low bench, favorite toy or object
**Prerequisite:** "Child Rises to Half-Kneeling" (Objective 6.3)
**Teaching Activities:**
1. Child is in half-kneeling on right foot at step or low bench. Hold an object up above the child's eye level and encourage her to stand up to get it.
2. Repeat activity with child in half-kneeling on left foot.

**Consequences:**
(+) 1. Praise the child and give her the toy or object to play with.
(−) 2. If child is unable to rise to standing, give a physical prompt upward underneath the buttock of the weight-bearing leg. Provide joint compression down through the knee on the weight-bearing foot as the child stands up.

## Goal 7: Standing

### Objective 7.1: Child Stands Without Support

**Position:** Supported standing
**Materials Needed:** Favorite toy or object
**Prerequisite:** "Child Rises to Standing through Half-Kneeling" (Objective 6.4)
**Teaching Activities:**
1. Place child in standing in the middle of the floor.
2. Slowly release your support and say, "Stand all by yourself now!"
3. Stay close by to guard against falling.
4. Steps:
   (1) Child stands without support for 2 seconds.
   (2) Child stands without support for 5 seconds.
   (3) Child stands without support for 10 seconds.
   (4) Child stands without support for 15 seconds.
   (5) Child stands without support for 20 seconds.

**Consequences:**
(+) 1.  Praise the child and hold a favorite toy in his line of vision to encourage him to maintain standing.
(−) 2.  If the child falls forward and catches himself, pick him up and try again.

### Objective 7.2: Child Rises to Stand Without Support

**Position:** Sitting or quadruped (hands and knees) on floor
**Materials Needed:** Favorite toy or object
**Prerequisite:** "Child Stands Without Support" (Objective 7.1)
**Teaching Activities:**
1.  Place the child in sitting or quadruped (hands and knees) in the middle of the room.
2.  Hold a favorite toy or musical object up above the child's reach and say, "Get the toy."

**Consequences:**
(+) 1.  Allow the child to grab the toy and play with it in standing. Praise her by saying, "Nice standing-up!"
(−) 2.  If the child is unable to stand up by herself, give her your finger for support and provide as little assistance as possible. Repeat this activity several times, then move a few feet away and say, "Now *you* stand up all by yourself!"

### Objective 7.3: Child Squats and Resumes Standing

**Position:** Standing without support
**Materials Needed:** Favorite toy or object
**Teaching Activities:**
1.  Place the child in standing in the middle of the room (or encourage him to rise to stand without support as in Objective 7.2).
2.  Put a favorite toy or brightly colored ball on the floor next to the child's feet.
3.  Stand in front of the child and say, "Pick up the toy/ball and give it to me."

**Consequences:**
(+) 1.  Praise the child and say, "Thank you for giving me the toy/ball."
(−) 2.  If the child can squat to get the toy but cannot return to standing without support, give him your finger to help him to resume standing.

### Objective 7.4: Child Stands on One Foot with Support

**Position:** Standing at a small chair
**Materials Needed:** Chair or low table
**Teaching Activities:**
1.  While allowing your child to stand using one hand for support at a chair or low table, encourage her to lift the right foot several inches off the ground.

**Figure 8.20**

2. Demonstrate the activity by saying, "See how I hold up one foot?"
3. Repeat steps 1 and 2 but have child lift the left foot.
4. Steps:
    (1) Child lifts foot up momentarily.
    (2) Child holds foot up 1–2 seconds.
    (3) Child holds foot up 3–4 seconds.
5. Put different shapes, stickers, or colored tape on either shoe and say, "Show me the foot with the dog on it!"

**Consequences:**

(+) 1. Praise the child by saying, "Good, you're holding your foot up *just like Daddy/Mommy!*"
(−) 2. If the child does not voluntarily lift her foot, gently lift her foot up for her and tell her what you are doing.

**Objective 7.5: Child Stands on One Foot Independently**

**Position:** Standing without support
**Materials Needed:** None
**Prerequisite:** "Child Stands on One Foot with Support" (Objective 7.4)
**Teaching Activities:**
1. Have child stand in middle of the room.
2. Demonstrate holding up right foot, then repeat for left foot.
3. Use stickers or colored tape on tips of shoes as suggested in Objective 7.4.
4. Steps:
    (1) Child lifts foot up momentarily.
    (2) Child holds foot up 1–2 seconds.
    (3) Child holds foot up 3–4 seconds.

**Consequences:**

(+) 1. Praise the child by saying, "Good, you're holding your foot up *just like Daddy/Mommy!*"
(−) 2. If the child does not voluntarily lift his foot, say, "Show me the shoe with the clown on it."

# Goal 8: Walking

**Objective 8.1: Child Walks with Support**

**Position:** Supported standing
**Materials Needed:** Favorite toy or object
**Prerequisites:** Good trunk and hip control and ability to rise to stand with support (Goal 6)
**Teaching Activities:**
1. There are several different methods for helping the child walk with support:
    (1) For the child with cerebral palsy primarily in the legs (spastic diplegia), hold the arms outstretched at the shoulder and rotated so her thumbs are pointing up. This will facilitate abduction (separation) of the legs.

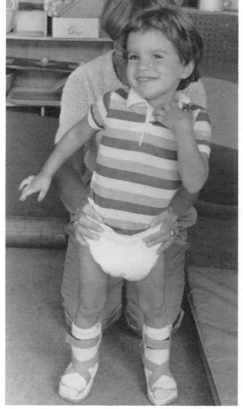

**Figure 8.21**

**Figure 8.22**

(2) For the child with cerebral palsy on one side of the body (spastic hemiplegia), hold the affected arm outstretched at the shoulder and rotated so the thumb is up.

(3) For some cases of hypotonia or fluctuating muscle tone, support the child at the hips and walk behind the child as she walks (see Figure 8.21).

(4) For the child with a very slight motor handicap, support at one hand may be all that is needed, or you may wish to give support at the shoulders while standing behind the child (see Figure 8.21).

2. Steps:

(1) Child moves 2 steps forward with support.

(2) Child moves 5 steps forward with support.

(3) Child moves 10 steps forward with support.

**Consequences:**

(+) 1. Praise the child and encourage her to walk toward a favorite toy (on a chair) or a favorite person.

(−) 2. For the child with a severe motor handicap who is unable to walk even with support, work on this objective using the child's preferred method of mobility (i.e., tricycle, scooter board, powered wheelchair). Rather than having the child move forward 2 steps, have her move forward 2 feet.

### Objective 8.2: Child Cruises Around Furniture

**Position:** Supported standing
**Materials Needed:** Low furniture, favorite toy or object
**Prerequisite:** "Child Rises to Standing through Half-Kneeling" (Objective 6.4). *Note:* Although it is possible to place a child in a standing position at furniture before he can rise to stand himself, it is wise to wait to work on cruising until he is pulling up to stand by himself.
**Teaching Activities:**
1. Place the child near low furniture so he can pull to stand.
2. Place a favorite toy or cracker about 12 inches to the right of the child and say, "Come and get the toy/cracker!" Repeat to the left side.
3. Steps:
   (1) Child cruises 1–2 steps to one side (right or left).
   (2) Child cruises 3–4 steps to one side (right or left).
   (3) Child cruises 5–6 steps to one side (right or left).

**Consequences:**
(+) 1. Allow the child to eat the cracker or play with the toy once he reaches it.
(−) 2. Facilitate side-stepping (abduction of the leg). To facilitate side-stepping to the right, put your hands over both of the child's hips and put slight pressure down on the left hip in order to free the right leg to abduct (see Figure 8.21).

### Objective 8.3: Child Walks Alone

**Position:** Supported or independent standing
**Materials Needed:** Chair or bench, favorite toy or object
**Prerequisites:** "Child Walks with Support" (Objective 8.1) and "Child Cruises Around Furniture" (Objective 8.2)
**Teaching Activities:**
1. Place a toy or cookie on a chair or bench just beyond the child's reach. Say, "Come and get the toy/cookie!" As the child becomes more skilled at walking alone, place the object farther away from her.
2. Steps:
   (1) Child takes 1–2 steps.
   (2) Child takes 3–4 steps.
   (3) Child takes 5–6 steps.
   (4) Child takes 7–8 steps.

**Consequences:**
(+) 1. Allow the child to play with the toy or eat the cookie.
(−) 2. If the child is reluctant to walk alone, give *very* slight support with your fingers at her shoulders and encourage her to walk on her own.

### Objective 8.4: Child Walks Sideways

**Position:** Standing without support
**Materials Needed:** Low chair, favorite toy or object

**Prerequisites:** "Child Cruises Around Furniture (Objective 8.2) and "Child Walks Alone" (Objective 8.3)

**Teaching Activities:**

1. Place a favorite toy or a low chair about 2 feet to the right of the child. Demonstrate taking steps sideways to reach the toy. Repeat to the left.
2. Steps:
    (1) Child walks 1 or 2 steps sideways.
    (2) Child walks 3 or 4 steps sideways.

**Consequences:**

(+) 1. Praise the child and allow him to play with the toy.
(−) 2. If the child does not walk sideways on his own, stand behind him and give a slight sideways prompt to the left shoulder to facilitate side-stepping to the right. Repeat to opposite side.

**Objective 8.5: Child Walks Backwards**

**Position:** Standing without support
**Materials Needed:** Pull toy
**Prerequisite:** "Child Walks Alone" (Objective 8.3)
**Teaching Activities:**

1. To encourage the child to walk backwards, demonstrate by pulling a pull-toy along the floor and walking backwards yourself.
2. Steps:
    (1) Child takes 1 or 2 steps backwards.
    (2) Child takes 3 or 4 steps backwards.
    (3) Child takes 5 or 6 steps backwards.

**Consequences:**

(+) 1. Praise the child for walking backwards and allow her to continue to play with the pull toy.
(−) 2. For the child who does not grasp the idea of walking backwards, stand behind her and guide her backward with light pressure at her shoulders while she pulls the pull toy.
(−) 3. For the child with a severe motor handicap who does not walk independently, encourage her to go backwards with her tricycle, scooter board, or powered wheelchair so she can learn the concept of "backwards."

## Goal 9: Running

**Objective 9.1: Child Runs with Support**

**Position:** Standing
**Materials Needed:** None
**Prerequisite:** "Child Walks Alone" (Objective 8.3)
**Teaching Activities:**

1. Hold the child's hand and run slowly with him down a hallway or

**Figure 8.23**                    **Figure 8.24**

across a room. Play games of running side by side or chasing one another.

2. *Caution:* For children with muscle tone that is higher than normal (hypertonia), running may increase their tone even further and should be discouraged. If running causes the child to stiffen his legs and stand on his tiptoes, it is probably not good to encourage it. Check with your PT or OT for further advice.

**Consequences:**

(+) 1. Praise the child and make running into a game. Run with him on different surfaces, like grass or sand, or run barefoot together.

(−) 2. If running is difficult for the child or if it causes an increase in muscle tone, use other forms of mobility to play games like tag. Use a scooter board or tricycle or play walking tag games.

**Objective 9.2: Child Runs Alone**

**Position:** Standing
**Materials Needed:** None
**Prerequisite:** "Child Runs with Support" (Objective 9.1)
**Teaching Activities:**

1. Start running, holding the child's hand until she begins to run also. Then let go and allow her to continue to run by herself.

2. See caution under Objective 9.1.

**Consequences:**

(+) 1. Praise the child and make games of running and stopping quickly, running in circles, turning corners, etc.

(−) 2. If the child cannot run independently, work on other mobility activities and games. Although running is *fun* and developmentally appropriate for the young child, it is not certainly a requirement for later, independent functional living!

## Goal 10: Jumping

### Objective 10.1: Child Jumps Down

**Position:** Standing on step or low bench
**Materials Needed:** Step or 2-inch thick board
**Teaching Activities:**
1. Start out with the child standing on a 2-inch step or board. Demonstrate jumping down with both feet together.
2. If the child is fearful, give him your hand or finger for support.

**Consequences:**
(+) 1. If the child jumps down, either with one foot leading (less mature response) or with both feet together (more mature response), praise him for jumping.
(−) 2. If the child has trouble grasping the concept of jumping down, stand in front of him, hold him under the arms, and "jump" him down off the step.

### Objective 10.2: Child Jumps in Place

**Position:** Standing on the floor
**Materials Needed:** None
**Prerequisite:** "Child Jumps Down" (Objective 10.1). *Note:* Developmentally, jumping down precedes jumping in place. However, some children are able to jump in place before they can jump down.
**Teaching Activities:**
1. Stand next to the child and demonstrate jumping in place.
2. Hold her hand and say, "Let's jump together." It may be helpful to put a line of masking tape on the floor and to try to encourage the child to jump *over* the tape (see Figure 8.24).

**Consequences:**
(+) 1. Praise the child for jumping in place, even if both feet are not together.
(−) 2. If the child is unable to jump in place, stand in front of her and lift her under the arms to help her "jump" in place.

## Goal 11: Stairs

### Objective 11.1: Child Walks up Stairs

**Position:** Standing at bottom of stairs

**Materials Needed:** Stairs with low railing (if possible)
**Teaching Activities:**
1. Either hold one of the child's hands or encourage him to hold onto a railing or wall.
2. Say, "Step up." Place a favorite toy at the top of the steps. The young child will step up and lead with one preferred foot for each step and then bring the second foot up behind him.
3. Steps:
   (1) Child walks up one step.
   (2) Child walks up two steps.
   (3) Child walks up three steps.

**Consequences:**
(+) 1. Praise the child for stepping up.
(−) 2. If the child does not step up on his own, gently lift his leg by tapping up from behind his knee. Help him to "lead" with his hand by reaching up on the railing before stepping up.

**Objective 11.2: Child Walks down Stairs**

**Position:** Standing at top of stairs (2–3 steps high)
**Materials Needed:** Stairs with low railing (if possible)
**Prerequisite:** "Child Walks up Stairs" (Objective 11.1)
**Teaching Activities:**
1. Either hold one of the child's hands or encourage her to hold onto a railing or wall.
2. Say, "Step down" and place a favorite toy at bottom of stairs. The young child will always step down first with one foot and then bring the other foot down to that step before going further.
3. Steps:
   (1) Child walks down one step.
   (2) Child walks down two steps.
   (3) Child walks down three steps.

**Consequences:**
(+) 1. Praise the child for stepping down and allow her to play with the toy.
(−) 2. If the child does not step down on her own, start by having her step down off a low bench (2–3 inches high) with one hand held.

# Fine Motor Activities

Fine motor activities involve the use of the smaller muscles of the body. Activities such as visual following and tracking as well as coordinated hand and arm activities—such as reaching, grasping, releasing, and manipulating objects—are all within the fine motor domain. Fine motor skills in the upper extremities occur in a proximal-to-distal sequence. This means that control of the shoulders and upper arms, which are *proximal* or closer to the trunk, develops before control of the fingers and hands, which are *distal* or farther away from the trunk.

When working on fine motor activities, be sure to try alternate positions besides supported sitting or lying on back or tummy. For the child with a

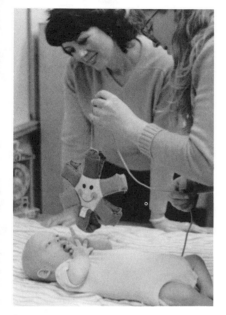

**Figure 8.25**

severe motor handicap, fine motor activities can be taught with the child lying on his tummy on a wedge or standing in a prone board or standing table.

The fine motor activities included here are just *examples* of activities that are both developmentally and functionally appropriate for your child. You may want to modify these or come up with other activities that can both provide fun and serve a specific goal you may have for your child. For example, young children love to poke their fingers into holes, bottle openings, and dials. They should have opportunities to play with objects of different textures—cornmeal, shaving cream, dried beans, corduroy, sandpaper, etc. "Busy boxes" offer lots of fine motor opportunities—patting, poking, turning, and spinning. The list is endless! Be creative—work with your child's teacher and therapist to "invent" new and exciting fine motor activities.

## Goal 1: Visual Following and Looking

### Objective 1.1: Child Follows Objects Short Distances

**Position:** Lying on back or supported sitting
**Materials Needed:** Brightly colored toy, black and white high-contrast picture, flashlight
**Teaching Activities:**
1. Place child on his back or in supported sitting position (or lying partly reclined in an infant seat).
2. Present a variety of visual stimuli, such as a bright red ball, simple pictures with sharp contrast, or a flashlight in a darkened room.
3. Begin with the child's head centered and place the object 8–12 inches from the child's face. Try to keep the chin slightly tucked so the child does not get too much extension of the neck.
4. Once the child has focused on the object, move it slowly from side to side a few inches in each direction.

**Consequences:**
(+) 1. Smile and praise the child ("Good looking!") when he looks at the object and follows it.
(−) 2. If the child does not look at the object, shake it gently in his field of vision. Try using an object that makes sound, such as a brightly colored rattle or jingle-bells, to get the child's attention initially. Make the sound, then stop to see whether the child follows the object visually.

### Objective 1.2: Child Follows Objects Horizontally

**Position:** Lying on back or in supported sitting
**Materials Needed:** Brightly colored toy, black and white high-contrast picture, flashlight
**Prerequisite:** "Child Follows Objects Short Distances" (Objective 1.1)
**Teaching Activities:**
1. Place the object 8–12 inches from the child's face with her head cen-

tered and chin slightly tucked.
2. Once the child has focused on the object, move it several inches to the right, then back to the center, then several inches to the left.
3. Steps:
    (1) Child follows object 2–3 inches to right and to left.
    (2) Child follows object 45° to right and 45° to left (head is rotated halfway to each side).
    (3) Child follows object 90° to right and 90° to left (head is rotated completely to each side).

**Consequences:**
(+) 1. Praise the child and smile, saying, "Good looking!"
(−) 2. Use an object that makes noise (a bright rattle or bell) and shake it several times while you move it back and forth across the child's field of vision horizontally. Also try to get the child to follow your face horizontally; some babies are much more interested in *people* than in objects! *Note:* If your child does *not* focus on your face or on a noise-making object, be sure to have her vision tested by an eye doctor (ophthalmologist). Some children with motor delays may also have visual impairments.

### Objective 1.3: Child Follows Objects Vertically

**Position:** Lying on back or in supported sitting
**Materials Needed:** Brightly colored toy, black and white high-contrast picture, flashlight
**Prerequisite:** "Child Follows Objects Short Distances" (Objective 1.1)
**Teaching Activities:**
1. Place the object 8–12 inches from the child's face with his head centered.
2. Once the child has focused on the object, move it slowly several inches upward, then back to eye level, then several inches downward.
3. Steps:
    (1) Child follows object 2–3 inches upward and 2–3 inches downward.
    (2) Child follows object through complete arc of motion upward and downward but loses sight of it once or twice.
    (3) Child follows object *continuously* through complete arc of motion upward and downward.

**Consequences:**
(+) 1. Praise the child and smile, saying, "Good looking!"
(−) 2. Use an object that makes noise and shake it gently several times as you move it upward and downward. Also try to get the child to follow your face upward and downward. *Note:* For *some* children with cerebral palsy, especially those with hypertonia, following objects in an upward direction may cause an increase in their muscle tone and may encourage them to "push back" with their heads. Check with your PT or OT to make sure this activity is appropriate for your child.

### Objective 1.4: Child Follows Objects in a Circular Motion

**Position:** Lying on back or in supported sitting
**Materials Needed:** Brightly colored toy, black and white high-contrast picture, flashlight
**Prerequisites:** "Child Follows Objects Short Distances, Horizontally, and Vertically" (Objectives 1.1, 1.2, and 1.3)
**Teaching Activities:**
1. Place child on her back or in supported sitting.
2. Place the object 8–12 inches from her face with her head centered (in the midline).
3. Slowly move the object around in a fairly large circle (10–12 inches). Move it to the right as well as around to the left.
4. Steps:
   (1) Child follows object part of the time through a circular motion.
   (2) Child follows object through a full circular motion losing sight of it 1–2 times.
   (3) Child follows object *continuously* through a circular motion without losing sight of it.

**Consequences:**
(+) 1. Praise the child for following the object.
(−) 2. If the child does not follow the object through the large circular motion, make a smaller circle (diameter of 5–6 inches) or use an object that makes noise.

### Objective 1.5: Child Looks at Object on Table or Tray

**Position:** Supported sitting
**Materials Needed:** Favorite large toy (5–6 inches in size), small cube or toy (1–2 inches), raisin or Cheerio
**Prerequisites:** "Child Follows Objects Short Distances, Horizontally, Vertically, and in a Circular Motion" (Objectives 1.1, 1.2, 1.3, and 1.4)
**Teaching Activities:**
1. Place the child in supported sitting in a highchair or specially adapted chair.
2. Place a favorite object on the tray or table directly in front of the child and point to it, wave it, or bang it gently.
3. Remove your hand from the child's view.
4. Steps:
   (1) Child looks at a fairly large (5–6 inches) toy for 3–5 seconds.
   (2) Child looks at a 1–2 inch object for 3–5 seconds.
   (3) Child looks at a small object (i.e., a raisin, a Cheerio) for 3–5 seconds.

**Consequences:**
(+) 1. Smile and praise the child for looking at the object. Give it to him to play with after he has successfully looked at it for 3–5 seconds.

**Figure 8.26**

(−) 2. If the child does not look at the object, gently move his head down so his eyes are directed at the table or tray. Then shake or bang the object while you are holding his head in a position to see it.

### Objective 1.6: Child Follows Moving Object Across Table or Tray

**Position:** Supported sitting
**Materials Needed:** Ball, toy car, or wind-up toy
**Prerequisite:** "Child Looks at Object on Table or Tray" (Objective 1.5)
**Teaching Activities:**
1. Place child in supported sitting in a highchair or specially adapted chair.
2. Place a ball, toy car, or wind-up toy on the tray or table directly in front of the child.
3. Slowly push the toy from the middle of the table to the right or left.
4. Steps:
   (1) Child follows moving object from middle of table to right side.
   (2) Child follows moving object from middle of table to left side.
   (3) Child follows moving object from left to right or vice versa.

**Consequences:**
(+) 1. Smile and praise the child for visually following the object. Allow the child to play with it after it has moved across the table or tray.
(−) 2. If the child does not continue to follow the object as it moves, gently prompt the child to direct his eyes to the object and wiggle or shake the object to make it more interesting to the child as it moves.

## Goal 2: Reaching and Hands-to-Midline

### Objective 2.1: Child Makes Random Pre-Reaching Motions

**Position:** Lying on back or in supported sitting
**Materials Needed:** Ring on a string, dangling rattle
**Teaching Activities:**
1. Place the child on her back, in an infant seat, or in a highchair or specially adapted chair.
2. Dangle a ring on a string or other favorite toy within easy reach (not more than a few inches) from the child's arms. Start with the object at midline and then move it slowly to the left and to the right.

**Consequences:**
(+) 1. Praise the child if she "swipes" at the object or reaches out in its general direction. Place the object in her hand after she has "swiped" at it several times and give her time to play with it.
(−) 2. If the child is unable to make pre-reaching motions while lying on her back, try this activity in sitting (where the force of gravity is reduced). Gently bring the child's shoulders forward with your hands so her arms will be brought forward to facilitate reaching.

**Objective 2.2: Child Brings Hands Together in Midline**

**Position:** Supported sitting or lying on back
**Materials Needed:** Soft, fuzzy toy
**Teaching Activities:**
1. Place the child in supported sitting or lying on his back. Since the effects of gravity are reduced in sitting, it will be easier for your child to bring his hands together in this position. However, you should work on this activity in both positions.
2. Start out by bringing the child's hands together by bringing the shoulders forward (a key point of control). Allow him to experience rubbing his hands together and fingering one with the other.
3. Remove your hands and allow the child to continue to play with his hands in midline.
4. Steps:
    (1) Child brings hands to midline in sitting following facilitation at shoulders.
    (2) Child brings hands to midline independently (without facilitation or assistance) in sitting.
    (3) Child brings hands to midline in back-lying following facilitation at shoulders.
    (4) Child brings hands to midline independently in back-lying.

**Consequences:**
(+) 1. Praise the child and allow him time to explore his own hands. Give him a soft, fuzzy object to hold and play with.
(−) 2. If your child is unable to bring hands together in midline independently, continue to provide facilitation by bringing the shoulders forward. An infant seat will help to position the shoulders forward to encourage this activity. If your child's hands are tightly fisted, as may happen in some children with hypertonia, hold the forearm (just below the elbow) and gently shake the hand up and down. This is a facilitation technique to help relax and open the hand so that he may explore his own fingers and hands in midline.

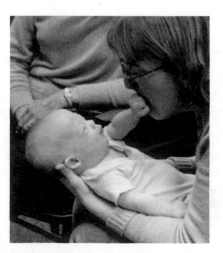

**Objective 2.3: Child Reaches Out and Touches Object**

**Position:** Supported sitting or lying on back
**Materials Needed:** Ring on a string, favorite toy
**Prerequisite:** "Child Makes Random Pre-Reaching Motions" (Objective 2.1)
**Teaching Activities:**
1. Place the child in supported sitting or in back-lying. Dangle a ring in front of or above the child (within arm's reach) or place a favorite object on the tray or table in front of the child.
2. Say, "Reach out and get the toy!"
3. Steps:
    (1) Child reaches out and touches object 1–2 inches from hand.
    (2) Child reaches out and touches object 3–4 inches from hand.
    (3) Child reaches out and touches object at arm's length.

**Figure 8.27**

(4) Child reaches out and touches object at arm's length in midline.

**Consequences:**

(+) 1. Praise the child for touching the object and then place it in her hand so she can play with it.

(−) 2. If the child is unable to reach out and touch the object, you can help her by facilitating at the shoulder. Bring the shoulder(s) forward, thereby guiding the hand(s) to touch the object. If the child's hand is fisted, gently "shake it out" first (see Objective 2.2).

### Objective 2.4: Child Reaches Out for Second Object

**Position:** Supported sitting or lying on back
**Materials Needed:** 1-inch cubes, small 1–2-inch toys, spoons.
**Prerequisite:** "Child Reaches Out and Touches Object" (Objective 2.3)
**Teaching Activities:**

1. Present one small object to the child and encourage him to reach for it and retain it.

2. While the child is still holding the first object in one hand, present a second object in the midline or near the other hand.

3. Steps:
   (1) Child reaches out for second object.
   (2) Child reaches out and touches second object.
   (3) Child reaches out and grasps second object while maintaining grasp on first object.
   (4) Child maintains grasp on both objects for 3–5 seconds.

**Figure 8.28**

**Figure 8.29**

**Consequences:**

(+) 1. Praise the child for reaching for the second object.

(−) 2. If the child does not reach for the second object, facilitate reaching by bringing the shoulder forward. If he is still unable to grasp it, place it in his hand so he can practice holding two objects at the same time.

## Goal 3: Grasping

### Objective 3.1: Child Grasps Rattle or Ring

**Position:** Lying on back or in supported sitting
**Materials Needed:** Rattle, brightly colored ring, or embroidery hoop
**Teaching Activities:**
1. Place the child in sitting or on her back.
2. Place a rattle, brightly colored ring, or embroidery hoop in the child's hand (see Figure 8.28).
3. If the child does not grasp the object automatically (the palmar grasp reflex), curl her fingers around the object to help her hold on.
4. Steps:
   (1) Child maintains grasp 1–2 seconds.
   (2) Child maintains grasp 3–4 seconds.
   (3) Child maintains grasp 5–6 seconds.
   (4) Child maintains grasp 10 seconds or longer.
5. Practice this activity with right and left hands.

**Consequences:**

(+) 1. Praise the child and keep talking and smiling while she maintains the grasp (see Figure 8.29).

(−) 2. If the child will not maintain her grasp, place your hand over hers and help her to hold on. Shake the rattle or wave the ring in front of her face as you help her maintain her grasp.

### Objective 3.2: Child Reaches Out and Grasps Dangling Object

**Position:** Supported sitting
**Materials Needed:** Ring on a string or embroidery hoop
**Prerequisite:** "Child Reaches Out and Touches Object" (Objective 2.3)
**Teaching Activities:**
1. Place the child in supported sitting and dangle a ring or embroidery hoop in front of the child within arm's reach.
2. Say, "Reach out and get the ring!"
3. Steps:
   (1) Child reaches out and grasps ring 1–2 inches from hand.
   (2) Child reaches out and grasps ring 3–4 inches from hand.
   (3) Child reaches out and grasps ring at arm's length.
   (4) Child reaches out and grasps ring at arm's length in midline.

**Consequences:**

(+) 1. Praise the child for grasping the ring and give him an opportunity to play with it.

(−) 2. If the child reaches out but is unable to grasp the ring because his hand remains fisted, gently shake the hand up and down by holding it at the forearm (see Objective 2.2).

**Objective 3.3: Child Grasps Cube Placed in Hand**

**Position:** Supported sitting
**Materials Needed:** Cubes (1 inch)
**Teaching Activities:**

1. Place child in supported sitting in a highchair or at a table.
2. Place cube on table or tray in front of child to give her the opportunity to reach for it.
3. If the child is unable to secure the cube, place it in her hand and allow her to grasp it.
4. Steps:
    (1) Child grasps cube momentarily.
    (2) Child grasps cube 1–2 seconds.
    (3) Child grasps cube 3–4 seconds.
    (4) Child grasps cube 5–6 seconds.
5. Alternate right and left hands.

**Consequences:**

(+) 1. Praise the child for as long as she maintains her grasp of the cube.

(−) 2. If the child is unable to maintain grasp, curl your hand over her hand and help her to hold on, praising her as you hold onto the cube together.

**Objective 3.4: Child Reaches Out and Grasps Cube**

**Position:** Supported sitting
**Materials Needed:** Cubes (1 inch)
**Prerequisites:** "Child Reaches Out and Touches Object" (Objective 2.3) and "Child Grasps Cube Placed in Hand" (Objective 3.3)
**Teaching Activities:**

1. Place child in supported sitting in a highchair or at a table.
2. Place a cube on table or tray in front of the child in the midline.
3. Steps:
    (1) Child reaches out and grasps cube with fingers and palm (palmar grasp).
    (2) Child reaches out and grasps cube with fingers and palm with thumb opposite fingers (radial-palmar grasp).
    (3) Child reaches out and grasps cube with fingertips and thumb opposed (radial-digital grasp).

**Consequences:**

(+) 1. Praise the child and give him ample time to bang the cube or wave it around.

(−) 2. If the child reaches out for the cube but does not succeed in grasping it, try using a tray with edges or build a barrier on the tray so that the child has a confined space in which to work in trying to secure the cube. Help him by guiding him at the shoulder. If his hand is fisted, "shake it out." (see Objective 2.2) *Note:* This is a developmental sequence that occurs over a 4-month period (between 5—9 months of age) in the nonhandicapped child. It may take weeks or even months to progress from step 1 to step 2 or from step 2 to step 3, so don't get discouraged.

### Objective 3.5: Child Grasps Small Object

**Position:** Supported sitting
**Materials Needed:** Cheerios, raisins, ½-inch cubes.
**Prerequisite:** "Child Reaches Out and Grasps Cube" (Objective 3.4)
**Teaching Activities:**
1. Place child in supported sitting in a highchair or at a table.
2. Place a small object (Cheerio, raisin, ½-inch cube) on the table in the child's midline.
3. Steps:
    (1) Child scoops or rakes the object into her palm using only her fingers.
    (2) Child picks up object using several fingers and thumb in opposition.
    (3) Child picks up object using thumb and index finger only.
**Consequences:**
(+) 1. Praise the child for grasping the object and allow her to eat it if it is food. (Be very cautious with nonedible small objects to make sure they do *not* go into the mouth!)
(−) 2. If the child is unable to grasp the object, use a tray with edges or build a barrier around the tray. Another strategy is to hold the object up in the air and have the child grasp it from your fingers. This is a good way to encourage more mature grasp patterns. *Note:* This is a developmental sequence that occurs over a 5-month period (7–12 months of age) in the nonhandicapped child. It may take months to progress from one step to the next, so be patient!

## Goal 4:  Releasing

### Objective 4.1: Child Exchanges Object Hand-to-Hand

**Position:** Lying on back or in supported sitting
**Materials Needed:** Ring, embroidery hoop, rattle
**Prerequisite:** "Child Grasps Rattle or Ring" (Objective 3.1)

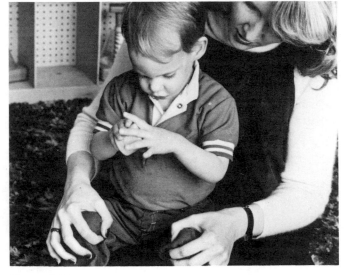

**Figure 8.30**

**Figure 8.31**

**Teaching Activities:**

1. Place the child on his back or in supported sitting and encourage him to grasp a ring or rattle (a ring is usually the easiest toy to transfer at first).

2. Allow the child ample time to play with the toy. Most early exchanges from hand to hand are accidental and occur as the child is playing with the toy in midline.

3. Steps:
   (1) Child exchanges object from one hand to the other *once* in 1 minute.
   (2) Child exchanges objects from one hand to the other *twice* in 1 minute.
   (3) Child exchanges object from one hand to the other three or four times in 1 minute.

**Consequences:**

(+) 1. Praise the child and allow him time to continue playing with the toy.

(−) 2. If the child does not exchange the toy hand-to-hand, this may be due to several different reasons. If the child is unable to bring hands together at midline, encourage this by bringing shoulders forward (work from behind the child). If the child still has a strong grasp reflex in the hands, it will be hard to exchange objects. Try using a large, soft object (stuffed toy ball or animal) so the child's hands will remain more open and less fisted.

**Objective 4.2: Child Releases Object into Container**

**Position:** Supported sitting
**Materials Needed:** Cubes or small (1 or 2 inches) toys, box, bowl, can, cup
**Prerequisite:** "Child Exchanges Object Hand-to-Hand" (Objective 4.1)

**Figure 8.32**

**Teaching Activities:**
1. Place child in supported sitting in a highchair or at a table. Give her some cubes or other small toys to play with.
2. Place a container such as a box, bowl, can, or cup in front of the child in the midline.
3. Demonstrate putting an object in the container and say, "Put it in. *You* put one in."
4. Steps:
   (1) Child places 1 toy in container.
   (2) Child places 2–3 toys in container.
   (3) Child places 4–5 toys in container.
   (4) Child places 6–7 toys in container.

**Consequences:**
(+) 1. Praise the child and say, "Good. You put it *in!*"
(−) 2. If the child is unable to release an object into the container, hold her arm just below the elbow and guide her hand so it is over the container. Then gently shake the forearm, which will cause the hand to relax and release the object.

**Objective 4.3: Child Stacks Cubes**

**Position:** Supported sitting
**Materials Needed:** 1-inch cubes
**Prerequisite:** "Child Releases Object into Container" (Objective 4.2)
**Teaching Activities:**
1. Place the child in supported sitting in a highchair or at a table. Give him several 1-inch cubes to play with.
2. Build a tower of two or three cubes and say to the child, "See, I built a tower. Now *you* build one!"
3. Steps:
   (1) Child stacks 2 cubes.
   (2) Child stacks 3–4 cubes.
   (3) Child stacks 5–6 cubes.

**Consequences:**
(+) 1. Praise the child for stacking each successive cube.
(−) 2. If the child is unable to stack, guide his arm from the forearm so that the cube is directly over the cube on the table. Then gently shake the forearm to help the hand relax and release the cube. If the child starts throwing the cubes, turn away from him and ignore him for 15–20 seconds. Then return to the activity and begin again. You may wish also to try this activity with larger cubes if they are easier for your child to stack. Do this activity as part of play time.

## Goal 5: Midline Activities

**Objective 5.1: Child Plays with Hands in Midline**

**Position:** Lying on side, on back, on stomach, or in supported sitting
**Materials Needed:** Soft, furry toy
**Teaching Activities:**
1. Place the child *first* in side-lying, which will help to position the shoulders forward and thus encourage bringing the hands together in midline. Put a pillow behind the child's back to keep her from rolling.
2. Facilitate from behind the child by bringing the shoulders forward and helping her to gently rub her hands together.
3. Steps:
   (1) Child plays with hands in midline while side-lying.
   (2) Child plays with hands in midline while in supported sitting.
   (3) Child plays with hands in midline while lying on back.
   (4) Child plays with hands in midline while lying on stomach.

**Consequences:**
(+) 1. Praise the child for playing with her hands and exploring her fingers.
(−) 2. If the child does not play with her hands in midline, give her a soft, furry toy to hold and play with in midline. Gradually give her smaller toys so eventually she will play with her hands as well as the toy. Elastic bracelets with toys attached or interesting gloves may encourage your child to play with her hands in midline position.

### Objective 5.2: Child Bangs Two Objects Together

**Position:** Supported sitting
**Materials Needed:** Cubes, spoons, rattles
**Prerequisite:** "Child Plays with Hands in Midline" (Objective 5.1)
**Teaching Activities:**
1. Place the child in supported sitting. Present cubes, spoons, rattles, or other small toys to each hand (or place them in the child's hands if he is not yet able to reach and grasp them).
2. Steps:
   (1) Child bangs objects together 1–2 times.
   (2) Child bangs objects together 3–4 times.
   (3) Child bangs objects together repeatedly.

**Consequences:**
(+) 1. Praise the child and make a game of banging different objects together in the midline.
(−) 2. If the child does not bang objects together, facilitate this activity by bringing his shoulders forward (stand behind him) and helping him bang objects together repeatedly.

### Objective 5.3: Child Plays Pat-a-Cake in Midline

**Position:** Supported sitting
**Materials Needed:** None
**Teaching Activities:**
1. Sit behind the child with her on your lap and with both of you facing a large mirror.

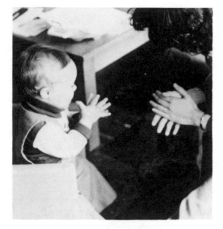

**Figure 8.33**

2. Bring her shoulders forward so that her hands come together and gently facilitate pat-a-cake.
3. Steps:
   (1) Child plays pat-a-cake with adult help.
   (2) Child plays pat-a-cake 1–2 times independently after being helped.
   (3) Child plays pat-a-cake independently and repeatedly.

**Consequences:**
(+) 1. Praise the child and play the pat-a-cake nursery rhyme or song.
(−) 2. If the child does not play pat-a-cake independently, continue to help her by facilitating at the shoulders. If the child's hands remain fisted (as in some children with hypertonia), gently shake out the fists by shaking up and down at the forearms. You may also have to rotate the child's arms inward so the palms are facing one another before helping her to play pat-a-cake.

## Goal 6: Manipulating Objects

### Objective 6.1: Child Waves Object and Turns It Up and Down

**Position:** Supported sitting or lying on back
**Materials Needed:** Ring, spoon, bell, or rattle
**Teaching Activities:**
1. Place child in sitting and give him a ring, spoon, bell, or rattle to play with.
2. Observe whether the child rotates his forearm so that his palm is alternately up and down while grasping and playing with the toy. Therapists refer to this as *pronation* (palm down) and *supination* (palm up). This is an important functional activity that will enable the child to feed himself later on.
3. Steps:
   (1) Child turns object up and down with adult facilitation at the forearm.
   (2) Child turns object up and down independently.

**Consequences:**
(+) 1. Praise the child and make a game of turning different toys up and down, thus encouraging pronation and supination.
(−) 2. If the child is unable to do this activity independently, continue to help him by providing facilitation at the forearm. Using toys that make noise, such as jingle-bells or a rattle, may make this activity more fun.

### Objective 6.2: Child Shakes Objects to Make Noise

**Position:** Supported sitting or lying on back
**Materials Needed:** Bell, rattle, or jingle-bells
**Teaching Activities:**
1. Give the child a bell, rattle, or jingle-bells (or a small sealed container with balls or beads inside).

2. Demonstrate by shaking the bell or rattle gently, saying, "See, it makes a noise!"
3. Steps:
    (1) Child shakes toy with assistance from adult (holding at forearm).
    (2) Child shakes toy independently.
4. Make sure that the child is really shaking the toy to produce the appropriate noise and not just banging the toy against the table (a less mature response).

**Consequences:**

(+) 1. Praise the child and give her time to play with and explore the toy.
(−) 2. If the child persists in banging the toy rather than shaking it to make noise, remove the toy and demonstate with another toy. Place the child in your lap so she does not have a hard surface against which to bang the toy. *Caution:* Some children, especially those with hypertonia, may startle very easily to any new or loud noise. Use a quiet rattle or a small, tinkling bell so as not to produce a startle reflex.

### Objective 6.3: Child Draws with Crayon

**Position:** Supported sitting or prone-lying on a wedge
**Materials Needed:** Large crayon, felt-tip marker
**Prerequisite:** Ability to grasp a crayon with some pronation of the forearm (turning palm down)
**Teaching Activities:**
1. Place a paper in front of the child and give him a large crayon or felt-tip marker during play time.
2. Demonstrate by scribbling or drawing a picture for the child. You can also try to get the child to imitate making horizontal or vertical strokes on the paper. Taping the paper to the table or tray may make it easier for the child.
3. Steps:
    (1) Child scribbles on the paper.
    (2) Child makes a horizontal stroke on the paper (after demonstration).
    (3) Child makes a vertical stroke on the paper (after demonstration).

**Consequences:**

(+) 1. Praise the child for any attempts at scribbling or drawing. Give him various colors to draw with.
(−) 2. For the child who has difficulty holding a crayon, hold his hand with the crayon in it and guide the scribbling or stroking. If there is great difficulty in holding a crayon, try finger-painting—making horizontal and vertical strokes with the finger-paints.

### Objective 6.4: Child Turns Pages of Book

**Position:** Supported sitting, lying on stomach on wedge, or standing in prone
**Materials Needed:** Baby-proof book with thick, cardboard pages
**Teaching Activities:**
1. Give the child a baby-proof book with thick pages. Point to the pictures and get the child's interest in looking at the pictures.

**Figure 8.34**

2. Say, "Let's turn the page and see more pictures!"
3. Help the child turn the pages and practice this activity, guiding her hand.
4. Steps:
   (1) Child turns pages with help.
   (2) Child turns 2–3 pages at once.
   (3) Child turns pages one at a time.

**Consequences:**

(+) 1. Praise the child for turning pages, taking time to look at and talk about the pictures on each page.

(−) 2. If the child has difficulty turning pages, sit her in your lap and provide facilitation at the shoulders to bring them forward while you guide her hands.

**Objective 6.5: Child Places Ring on Peg**

**Position:** Supported sitting, lying on stomach on wedge, or standing in proneboard

**Materials Needed:** Plastic peg with plastic rings; large dowel with rubber rings from canning lids

**Prerequisite:** "Child Releases Object into Container" (Objective 4.2)

**Teaching Activities:**

1. Use commercially made plastic peg with plastic rings or make a peg with base by using a large dowel. Use rubber rings from canning lids or plastic bracelets as rings.
2. Demonstrate putting several rings on the peg. Take them off and say, "Now *you* put the rings on!"
3. Steps:
   (1) Child places 1 ring on peg.
   (2) Child places 2–3 rings on peg.
   (3) Child places 4–5 rings on peg.

**Consequences:**

(+) 1. Praise the child for putting each ring on the peg.

(−) 2. If the child has difficulty placing the ring on the peg, give assistance at the shoulder guiding the hand until it is directly over the peg.

### Objective 6.6: Child Places Peg in Pegboard

**Position:** Supported sitting, supported standing, or prone (stomach-lying) on wedge

**Materials Needed:** Pegs and pegboard

**Prerequisite:** "Child Releases Object into Container" (Objective 4.2)

**Teaching Activities:**

1. Start out with larger pegs (½-inch or 1-inch diameter) and progress to smaller pegs once the child has mastered the large pegs.

2. Demonstrate putting pegs in the pegboard for the child. Then say, "Now *you* put them in!"

3. Steps:
   (1) Child places 1 peg in pegboard.
   (2) Child places 2–3 pegs in pegboard.
   (3) Child places 4–5 pegs in pegboard.
   (4) Child places 6–7 pegs in pegboard.

**Consequences:**

(+) 1. Praise the child for *each* peg that he puts in the pegboard at first, then later praise after he places several pegs.

(−) 2. If the child is unable to put a peg in, facilitate at the shoulder and guide the hand so it is over the pegboard. Help the child pronate the forearm so that the peg is facing down into the hole.

### Objective 6.7: Child Places Pieces in Puzzle

**Position:** Supported sitting or supported standing

**Materials Needed:** Wooden puzzle board with 3–4 wooden shapes (circle, square, triangle)

**Teaching Activities:**

1. Start by using a simple 3- or 4-piece noninterlocking puzzle with large shapes (circle, square, triangle).

2. Take the pieces out and then demonstrate putting them in for the child, saying, "The circle goes in here, the square goes in here."

3. Some wooden puzzles have knobs on the puzzle pieces, making it easier for the child to pick up the pieces and put them in.

4. Steps:
   (1) Child places 1 puzzle piece correctly.
   (2) Child places 2 puzzle pieces correctly.
   (3) Child places 3–4 puzzle pieces correctly.

**Consequences:**

(+) 1. Praise the child after *each* piece is placed correctly. Praise her for trying even if the piece goes in the wrong space.

(−) 2. For the child who has difficulty with this activity, use puzzle pieces with wooden knobs. Guide the child's movements at her shoulders. Putting the puzzle at an angle on a tiltboard may make it easier for some children with fine motor handicaps.

# Oral-Motor Activities

Oral-motor activities are those involving the coordinated use of the muscles around the mouth, the tongue (which is also a muscle), and the jaw. Many young children with motor delay will also have delayed or abnormal oral-motor development. Delayed development in oral-motor control may lead to difficulties in feeding, drinking, talking, and breath control.

The teaching activities in this section will be primarily related to feeding and drinking, since these are often considered prespeech activities. A developmental sequence will be followed for each goal so that the objectives under each goal follow a developmental hierarchy. This is one of the most important areas in which you can work with your child since mealtime is an important socialization time.

Before beginning the teaching activities in this section, please reread Chapter 7 to reacquaint yourself with proper positioning for your child for feeding. Remember that it is important that your child be positioned symmetrically and that his muscle tone is "normalized" before beginning to work on feeding or drinking. Another excellent reference on feeding is the book by Suzanne Evans Morris entitled *Program Guidelines for Children with Feeding Problems*.

Certain foods should always be *avoided* in working with the young child since they may lead to choking; these include peanuts, popcorn, raw carrots and celery, grapes, and hotdogs. If you are unsure whether a certain food would be safe and appropriate for your child, check with your child's physical or occupational therapist first. If your child is bottle-fed, avoid using liquids with a high sugar content, such as sweetened fruit juices. When beginning cup-drinking, use slightly thickened liquids such as eggnog, milkshakes, or thinned yogurt. These make for less dribbling and easier handling. Beginning finger foods should be those which dissolve in the mouth after two or three chews, such as breadsticks, soda crackers, or toast strips. Following is a sequence of liquids and foods, ordered by the ease in which the child can manage them: (1) liquids, (2) strained foods, (3) mashed foods, (4) chopped foods, (5) bite-size food, (6) regular table food, (7) food requiring extensive chewing. When beginning the meal, start with more advanced food since the child will be most hungry then and most motivated. For the very young child, you will probably *not* progress beyond regular table food since even the nonhandicapped young child would not be expected to eat food which required chewing.

Feeding and drinking are important social activities and create nice opportunities to interact with your child. The following activities will encourage positive interactions between you and your child and will lead to greater functional skills for the child.

## Goal 1: Drinking

### Objective 1.1: Child Sucks from Bottle or Breast

**Position:** Lying on lap with both arms forward or sitting in infant seat or adapted chair

**Materials Needed:** Baby bottle

**Teaching Activities:**

1. If you are nursing or bottle-feeding the young infant in your lap, make sure that both of the child's arms are forward (to encourage hands to midline).
2. Present the breast or bottle to the child and watch for coordinated sucking activity in the lips and cheeks.
3. If the child does not suck initially, gently tug on breast or bottle to stimulate this response.

**Consequences:**

(+) 1. Praise the child and stroke his face. Continue feeding until he has finished.

(−) 2. If the child does not suck or has difficulty sucking, try a special ''premie'' nipple (for premature babies), which is designed for babies with weaker sucks. While breast-feeding is very popular because the mother's milk helps to provide immunities to illness, it requires a much stronger and coordinated suck by the infant to take milk from the breast rather than from a bottle. For the child with motor delay, especially the child with hypotonia or hypertonia, breast-feeding may be too difficult because of a weak sucking ability. So it may be preferable, from a nutritional standpoint, to bottle-feed your baby. You may want to use a breast pump and then bottle-feed the baby with your own milk.

**Figure 8.35**

**Objective 1.2: Child Drinks from Cup Held by Adult**

**Position:** Supported sitting
**Materials Needed:** Plastic cup, favorite liquid
**Teaching Activities:**
1.  Present the cup to the child in midline. Use jaw control if necessary (see Chapter 7). A special cutout cup may help you see whether or not the child is getting the liquid to her mouth (see *Fred Sammons Be-OK Self-Help Aids* in Adaptive Equipment Appendix 2).
2.  Place the cup on the child's lower lip just in front of the teeth. Tip the cup gently and slowly so that only a small amount of liquid flows into the mouth. Do *not* tilt the child's head backwards.
3.  Give the child ample time to swallow. Place the cup back on the tray before beginning to work on the next drink.
4.  Steps:
    (1)  Child drinks and swallows 1 ounce of liquid from cup.
    (2)  Child drinks and swallows 2–3 ounces of liquid from cup.
    (3)  Child drinks and swallows 4–5 ounces of liquid from cup.

**Consequences:**
(+) 1.  Praise the child for drinking and reward her with a bite or spoonful of favorite food.
(−) 2.  If the child has difficulty drinking without lots of dribbling, thicken the liquid with tapioca, cornstarch, or gelatin or use thinned yogurt. If the child does not like the "feel" of the cup touching her lip, firmly stroke her lips and gums first to desensitize the oral area. If the child is *very* resistant to using a cup but you want to wean her from the bottle, try spoon-feeding liquids as you would soup or broth.

**Objective 1.3: Child Holds and Drinks from Bottle**

**Position:** Supported sitting, side-lying, or lying on back
**Materials Needed:** Baby bottle (plastic, lightweight)
**Prerequisite:** "Child Sucks from Bottle or Breast" (Objective 1.1)
**Teaching Activities:**
1.  Place the child in side-lying, back-lying, or supported sitting. Side-lying is probably the easiest position to start with for the child.
2.  Start by feeding the child yourself, then place his hands up around the bottle. Say, "You hold on, now!"
3.  Once the child has learned to hold his own bottle in side-lying, progress to back-lying and supported sitting (as in an infant seat).
4.  Steps:
    (1)  Child places hands on bottle but needs adult help to hold bottle.
    (2)  Child holds and drinks from bottle for 5–10 seconds.
    (3)  Child holds and drinks from bottle for 10–20 seconds.
    (4)  Child holds and drinks from bottle for 20–30 seconds.
    (5)  Child holds and drinks from bottle independently until bottle is empty.

**Consequences:**
(+) 1.  Praise the child and encourage him to continue drinking.

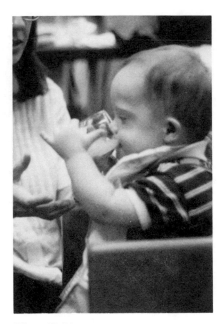

**Figure 8.36**

(−) 2. If the child is unable to hold the bottle himself because of fine motor delays, you may want to skip this activity and just continue to work on semi-independence or independence in cup-drinking (Objectives 1.2 and 1.4).

**Objective 1.4: Child Holds and Drinks from Cup**

**Position:** Supported sitting
**Materials Needed:** Plastic cup, favorite liquid
**Prerequisite:** "Child Drinks from Cup Held by Adult" (Objective 1.2)
**Teaching Activities:**
1. Present the cup to the child in midline, helping her to put both hands on the cup. Start with the cup only about half full. Use a cutout cup so that the cutout portion would be over the child's nose as she drinks.
2. You could also use a two-handled cup or other lightweight plastic tumbler.
3. Steps:
   (1) Child holds and drinks from cup with minimal help/guidance from adult.
   (2) Child holds and drinks 1–2 ounces from cup independently.
   (3) Child holds and drinks 3–4 ounces from cup independently.
   (4) Child holds and drinks 5–6 ounces from cup independently.

**Consequences:**
(+) 1. Praise the child for holding and drinking from the cup herself. Reward each successful swallow with a bite of a favorite food.
(−) 2. If the child is unable to hold and drink from the cup independently, as are some children with severe motor handicaps, you may have to continue working on Objective 1.2 indefinitely. To allow the child *some* choice and control in the feeding situation, let her choose from a variety of liquids. Even the child who is physically dependent on the adult for feeding and drinking should have some choices.

## Goal 2: Eating

**Objective 2.1: Child Removes Food from Spoon**

**Position:** Supported sitting
**Materials Needed:** Plastic or latex-covered spoon with a flat bowl; soft or strained foods
**Teaching Activities:**
1. Present the spoon with a small amount of food to the child in midline. Use jaw-control if needed (see Chapter 7).
2. Place the spoon in the child's mouth and slowly pull it straight out, being careful not to scrape the food off the spoon with the upper teeth (if there *are* any!).

3. You can use your index finger to press down on the upper lip to help the child remove the food if needed.
4. After removing the spoon, give the child time to swallow.
5. Steps:
    (1) Child removes food from one spoonful and swallows within 1 minute.
    (2) Child removes food from two spoonfuls and swallows after each spoonful, within 1 minute.
    (3) Child removes food from three spoonfuls and swallows after each spoonful, within 1 minute.

**Consequences:**
(+) 1. Praise the child for taking the food off the spoon and swallowing it.
(−) 2. If the child has difficulty removing the food from the spoon, use your index finger and thumb to press his lips together to help remove the food. If the child shows a bite reflex when the spoon is in the mouth, gently flex the head forward, bringing his chin toward his chest. This will help relax the jaw muscles and allow you to withdraw the spoon. If your child has a persistent bite reflex, as do some children with hypertonicity, consult your PT or OT to help in managing this.

**Objective 2.2:  Child Munches (Chews Up and Down)**

**Position:** Supported sitting
**Materials Needed:** Finger foods (crackers, breadsticks) or lumpy foods (cottage cheese, scrambled eggs)
**Prerequisite:** "Child Removes Food from Spoon" (Objective 2.1)
**Teaching Activities:**
1. Present a crunchy or lumpy food to the child. If using a cracker or breadstick, present it slightly to one side of the midline for the child to bite off a piece. If presenting a lumpy food, present the spoon to midline.
2. Use jaw control if needed.
3. After the child has taken a bite or a spoonful, remove the finger food or spoon and allow her time to munch the food. Watch for up-and-down movements of the jaw. Be sure the child swallows before presenting more food.
4. Steps:
    (1) Child munches one bite or spoonful in 1 minute.
    (2) Child munches two bites or spoonfuls in 1 minute.
    (3) Child munches three bites or spoonfuls in 1 minute.

**Consequences:**
(+) 1. Praise the child for munching and swallowing.
(−) 2. If the child does not munch, massage your fingers over her jaw on either side to help encourage an up-and-down chewing motion.

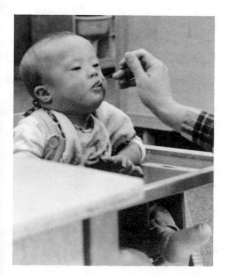

**Figure 8.37**

### Objective 2.3: Child Finger-Feeds

**Position:** Supported sitting
**Materials Needed:** Crackers, pretzels, cookies, or toast strips
**Prerequisite:** "Child Munches (Chews Up and Down)" (Objective 2.2)
**Teaching Activities:**
1. Place the finger food on the child's tray or hand it to him directly.
2. Make sure he bites off a fairly small piece of food initially.
3. Steps:
   (1) Child finger-feeds cracker or breadstick when placed in his hand.
   (2) Child finger-feeds cracker or breadstick independently (when placed on tray).
   (3) Child finger-feeds small foods independently (raisins, Cheerios).

**Consequences:**
(+) 1. Praise the child by saying, "Good, you're eating all by yourself!"
(−) 2. If the child has difficulty bringing the food to his mouth, you can facilitate by guiding him at the shoulder, elbow, or forearm. Direct his hand so the food is presented slightly to one side of the midline of his mouth.

### Objective 2.4: Child Feeds Self with Spoon

**Position:** Supported sitting
**Materials Needed:** Plastic or latex-covered spoon with flat bowl; lumpy or thick, strained foods such as cottage cheese, applesauce, yogurt with fruit; a plastic floor-covering or towel to catch spills
**Prerequisite:** "Child Removes Food from Spoon" (Objective 2.1)
**Teaching Activities:**
1. Place the food in a shallow bowl with edges for scooping. You may wish to use one with suction cups to hold it in place on the tray.
2. Give the child the spoon and encourage her to dip it in the food.
3. Demonstrate by taking a spoonful yourself.
4. Steps:
   (1) Child brings spoonful of food to mouth with assistance at wrist.
   (2) Child brings spoonful of food to mouth with assistance at forearm.
   (3) Child brings spoonful of food to mouth with assistance at elbow.
   (4) Child brings spoonful of food to mouth independently.
5. Be sure the child chews and swallows each mouthful before taking another spoonful.

**Consequences:**
(+) 1. Praise the child by saying, "You're eating all by yourself!"
(−) 2. If the child is unable to hold the spoon by herself, try using a Velcro strap and a built-up spoon handle to enable her to hold the spoon independently. If the child scoops the food but then throws the spoon, ignore this behavior *and* the child for 10–15 seconds. Then pick up your own spoon and demonstrate again before presenting her with her spoon.

Figure 8.38

**Objective 2.5: Child Lateralizes Tongue (Moves Tip of Tongue to Either Side)**

**Position:** Supported sitting
**Materials Needed:** Small pieces of food, such as cheese, raisins
**Teaching Activities:**
1. Place a small piece of soft or sticky food on the outer side of the upper gum underneath the upper lip to one side.
2. Watch the child's tongue movements as he tries to retrieve the food with his tongue.
3. Vary the places in the mouth where you place the food (i.e., to either side or farther back in the mouth near where the molars will be).

**Consequences:**
(+) 1. Praise the child for locating the food with his tongue and eating it.
(−) 2. If the child has difficulty retrieving the food, allow him to taste and chew it first by placing it directly in his mouth. Be sure to use a food he particularly likes.

**Objective 2.6: Child Chews Using Rotary Motions of Jaw**

**Position:** Supported sitting
**Materials Needed:** Chewy or crunchy foods such as chicken or tunafish, cooked vegetables, bananas, crackers, or dried cereals
**Prerequisite:** "Child Munches (Chews Up and Down)" (Objective 2.2)
**Teaching Activities:**
1. Present a chewy or crunchy food to the child.
2. Use jaw control if needed.
3. After the child has taken a bite or spoonful of food, allow her time to chew. Watch for rotary movements of the jaw; the jaw will move from

side to side as well as up and down (as in the earlier munching stage), thus moving in a rotary direction.

**Consequences:**

(+) 1. Praise the child for chewing and eating.

(−) 2. If the child does not use rotary jaw movements, present a very chewy food such as "fruit leather" or orange sections to one side of the mouth. After the child bites off a piece of food, provide jaw control and help to move the jaw in a rotary motion (combination of side-to-side and up-and-down motions).

## Goal 3: Oral Hygiene

### Objective 3.1: Child Cooperates in Toothbrushing

**Position:** Supported sitting

**Materials Needed:** Soft child's toothbrush (Nuk toothbrushing set), cup of water

**Teaching Activities:**

1. Demonstrate to the child by brushing your own teeth first. Let him play with the toothbrush so it doesn't surprise him to have it put into his mouth.

2. Wet the toothbrush in water (you need not use toothpaste; most dentists recommend water only).

3. Use jaw control if necessary (this may be helpful even for a less severely handicapped child).

4. Use gentle, circular massaging motions at the area where the gums join the teeth. Brush in circular motions at the gum level of the upper teeth and then stroke downward across the teeth. Stroke upward for lower teeth (following circular brushing at the gum line).

5. Be sure to brush both outer and inner surfaces of the teeth and tops of the molars.

**Consequences:**

(+) 1. Praise the child for cooperating in toothbrushing.

(−) 2. If the child resists or bites down on the toothbrush, do just a little bit of brushing on outer teeth surfaces for the first time. Gradually, over time, the child should become less sensitive to the toothbrush. Use a very small amount of toothpaste if this increases the child's level of cooperation. *Note:* Toothbrushing is extremely important for children with motor delays! Many children with motor handicaps are more likely to have dental problems, and very early dental hygiene is very important in helping to prevent such problems.

# CHAPTER 9

# Social, Cognitive, and Communication Activities

This chapter presents activities in the areas of social, cognitive, and communication development. These activities also are essential for the child with motor delays. Many of these suggestions can be used during play time with your child. Other references for activity guides are listed in Appendix 3.

**Figure 9.1**

# Social

From birth the baby learns about the world largely through social interactions. Parents can enhance this learning by responding consistently (each time) to the child's social responses and by responding in tune or in rhythm to the child's responses. Furthermore, parents can provide their baby with many social opportunities—visits with family and friends, trips outside the home, play with other children. All of these activities help the child to develop socially and learn more about the world.

## Responsiveness to People

The young baby appears particularly able to interact with people. He enters the world equipped to look at important people in his life, and he also shows early preferences for those important people—namely Mom and Dad.

1. Be responsive to your baby's signals. In the beginning these will be mostly signals of distress. Pick up your baby and attempt to soothe her. When she is in an alert state, talk to her face to face. Smile at her and hold her so that she can see your face. All babies have different personalities—some like to be held closely and cuddled, others prefer not to be. Some babies are very volatile or changeable while others are very quiet, consistent, and placid. Your baby will soon teach you all about her personality. Try to hold your baby so that she is relaxed and be responsive to her cues.

2. Talk to your baby while you are holding him and when you approach. He will soon come to recognize your voice and the voices of other family members.

3. Be attentive to your baby's initiations. When your baby cries, coos, gazes at you, or moves, respond to her. As you interact with your baby, try to make your talking and moving in synchrony or in rhythm with the baby. These interactions are often characterized by a pattern of "exchanges": the baby looks or coos, pauses, the parent looks or coos back, pauses, the baby looks or coos, and so on. Each partner gives the other a chance to respond. Your baby will also signal when she doesn't want to interact anymore. Typical signals may include glancing away, turning away, vomiting or spitting up, crying, fussing, grimacing or frowning, yawning, or arching. Babies use behaviors such as these to indicate that they need a break from the interaction. Be sensitive to these cues, give the baby a break, and interact again when the baby looks at or orients toward you and indicates a willingness to proceed.

4. Encourage your baby to smile and/or laugh. When he does, smile back. Play tickle games, peek-a-boo games, and roughhousing games with the infant who can tolerate the movement. (Discuss these activities first with your child's physical or occupational therapist to make sure they are appropriate for your child.)

5. Call your baby by her name. Talk to her as you are feeding, bathing, dressing her. Name her body parts (e.g., "This is Marie's tummy") and describe what you are doing (e.g., "I'm pulling the shirt over Susan's head").

6. Play with your baby at a mirror. Let the baby pat the image in the mirror. Change your facial expressions and smile and laugh at the baby in the mirror.

7. Play simple games with your baby often. Games such as pat-a-cake and peek-a-boo are always a big hit with babies. So are games that the child can anticipate, like "Tickle, Tickle" and "I'm Going to Get You!"

8. Encourage your baby to imitate your actions and gestures. Usually at around 8 months of age, babies enjoy waving bye-bye and playing pat-a-cake. Try teaching your baby to throw a kiss, "give me five," or imitate any one of many gestures used by your family.

## Social Initiations

Babies soon become very adept at initiating interactions, too. Watch for their initiations and be responsive.

1. Encourage your baby to make a signal or gesture to indicate a want. For example, the baby may raise his arms to indicate that he wants to be picked up or wiggle his fingers to indicate that he wants more.

2. Help your child to start offering or showing toys to others. Say, "Give Mommy the book. Thank you." Show excitement when the child shares his toys, then return the item to the child so that he does not become discouraged.

3. Your baby may also begin to initiate games with you. Favorite games are putting a diaper or cloth over the head to initiate peek-a-boo, or peering around the furniture to initiate hide and seek. Your baby may also place her hands on your hands to get you to play pat-a-cake. Be responsive to all these rich social interactions.

4. Take turns with your baby in play. Splash the water, then let the baby splash. Swing in time to music and let the baby move with you. Initiate peek-a-boo, then give the baby a chance to initiate. Try to take turns in all your activities.

5. Label body parts on the child and others during play. For example, say, "This is Tyrone's head. Can you find your head?" Or say, "Can you find Daddy's ear?" or "Point to Dolly's eyes." Begin with large body parts that the child can easily see, such as the tummy and head. Then move to parts of the face—eyes, ears, hair, nose—and also to the hands, feet, elbows, and shoulders. From there you can get very specific with body parts, such as teeth, cheek, eyebrows, eyelashes, chin. This helps to increase the baby's awareness of himself and can be an enjoyable game to play.

## Play and Relationships with Others

After babies learn how to make social initiations, they begin to play. First they play primarily alone. Then they play next to other children and finally learn to play with others. They also learn to take turns and show affection for others.

1. Play cooperatively with your baby. A good game for teaching a child to take turns and cooperate is playing ball (rolling a ball back and forth). Also introduce a toy and wind it up or move it and give the child a chance to do the same.

2. Set up expectations for your child by describing what you're going to do next. For instance, describe your activities like "I have to go to the store, but I'll be back in a little while. Laura will stay here with you." Or "After you take your nap, you can put on your new T-shirt and we'll go to Grandma's house." This helps the child learn to prepare for the next activity. It also helps teach the child to wait.

3. Motivate your child to play independently for increasingly longer periods of time. Provide lots of objects to manipulate and toy baskets full of objects and toys.

4. Give the baby opportunities to "play" with other children. In the beginning don't expect a lot of cooperation. Babies will just play next to each other and demonstrate little interaction or sharing. Babies, however, seem to prefer other children, such as brothers and sisters, over adults as playmates. These other children may be able to encourage cooperation in play with toys. You can also enhance cooperation by the toys you provide. With children close to the same age, you can either give each child a similar set of toys in order to reduce competition or you can set up cooperative games like pulling each other in a wagon or rocking on the rocking board.

5. Teach your child about other family members by naming them and showing the child pictures of them. Encourage your child to "Go find Grandma or Sister" when that person is named.

6. Be affectionate to your baby. Your baby will learn affection for others by your model. Provide lots of hugs and kisses and cuddles. Also help the child to practice nice behavior with toys he loves (e.g., "Pat your dolly," "Kiss the bunny").

7. Talk about your feelings and label the feelings of others (e.g., "He looks sad"). Encourage your child to comfort other children when they are sad. Collect pictures of people exhibiting different feelings and talk about the pictures (e.g., "The little boy is very happy. His mommy is hugging him" or "She is unhappy because she lost her dolly").

8. Your baby may engage in some beginning pretend play. Toy sets of farm animals, household items, boats, trucks, and dolls are often used for pretend play.

9. Help your child to participate in social activities with other children—nursery songs, see-saw activities, and other playground play, sound-producing musical activities, dancing. In the beginning, adult supervision is needed to monitor the play environment. You will have to set reasonable limits for the children's activities.

10. Encourage pretend play. Provide adult clothes for dress-up, toy telephones, grocery cartons for playing house or store, and dolls or doll sets. Children love to take on different roles, and this provides a good way for them to express their feelings. They also have a lot of fun playing with others.

# Cognitive

Though many children with motor difficulties develop normally in the area of intellectual or cognitive development, even mild motor delays may make it difficult for the child to move around the environment and gather new information. For the child with multiple and severe handicaps, intervention in the area of cognitive development is often needed. The following activities can be used by parents or teachers to assist children in this area. These activities should be used together with activities in the areas of motor, communication, and social development because all areas of development are interrelated and must be coordinated for the young child to develop optimally.

## Sensing

During the first months, the baby gathers information primarily through his senses—sight, sound, touch, taste, smell. Many children with physical disabilities also have sensory impairments such as visual or auditory disorders. Therefore, it is important to consult a specialist in these areas early on so that any problems can be properly diagnosed and treated. If the baby cannot use all his senses, he is being blocked from gathering information. The following activities include all the sensory systems, though most focus on hearing and sight. If your baby has a sensory impairment, say in vision, concentrate on providing information in other sensory areas, such as audition (hearing). However, even though children may be diagnosed as deaf or blind, they usually have some residual vision or hearing. In order to learn to use that vision or hearing functionally, the child's senses must be stimulated or used in that area. Don't be afraid to experiment and determine how much your child can see or hear even if the diagnosis indicates limitations. Use whatever strengths your child has to the fullest!

1. Provide varied sensory experiences to your baby. Talk to your baby. Let her listen to a music box. Present different smells. For example, keep your child close by as you are cooking dinner. Babies also love visual stimulation. Present a mobile, brightly colored pictures, pieces of bright and shiny wrapping paper or cards, patterned sheets, contour shapes—there is no end to visual objects that babies find interesting. Babies especially like bright, shiny, moving objects and objects with definite contour or contrast, such as bull's-eyes or patterned fabric. Babies also like to be touched. Try gently massaging your child with lotions or stroking with a washcloth during bath time. (Some children with physical disabilities find it difficult to be touched. If your child does not like to be touched, consult with your physical or occupational therapist to devise strategies so that your child will learn to accept increasing levels of touch.) Also try rubbing your baby's

body with different types of fabric—cotton, velvet, silk, corduroy, fur. Shift your child's position so that you don't always feed, pick up, or carry from the same side. This will allow your child to look around and become accustomed to different handling techniques and positions.

2. Use visual or auditory stimuli to alert your child or to get your child to focus on an object. For example, present a shiny bell. Ring the bell, wait for the child to look at it, then ring it again when she does!

3. Provide the infant with toys that make sounds when and if the infant moves. Good objects for this activity include mobiles placed within the infant's reach, bells attached to the infant's wrists or ankles, and rattles or chime balls.

4. Usually by 4 to 6 months of age everything goes into the mouth. Provide your infant with toys that are safe to mouth. This is a major way of learning about objects at this age. Place toys and other safe objects in your child's hand. Give her a chance to explore them as best she can.

5. Provide different-textured objects. A clutch ball covered with different kinds of fabric is good for this activity.

6. Tie a balloon gently to your baby's wrist. See how the baby watches the balloon when it moves. Do this activity only when you are present.

## Learning about Objects

At around 4 to 6 months babies begin to notice objects more. They also try new actions—banging, waving, shaking. These beginning random movements eventually become purposeful ways of manipulating objects. Babies now learn about cause-and-effect relationships—they learn that when they do something, something happens.

1. Present an object visually. Give your baby experience following or tracking the object as you move it gradually from side to side or up and down. Make a sound with an object out of your infant's sight. Does the baby turn toward the sound? Give your baby time to react and reach toward objects that are presented.

2. Provide your baby with toys and objects that can be easily manipulated and that have an obvious outcome. Such toys provide *contingent feedback* to the child—the toy does something when the baby makes an action. They help teach the baby valuable lessons about cause-and-effect relationships. Examples include a jack-in-the-box, toy telephone that can be rung, a button that can be pushed to produce a sound, a mechanical wind-up toy. "Busy boxes" are good examples of these kinds of toys, especially those with just one or two activities per side.

3. Show the baby an object and attract her attention. When she looks, cover it up with your hand or with a cloth. Then uncover the object for the baby to see.

4. Give your baby new sensory experiences. Allow him to play in water. Play with a touch-and-feel book. Go for walks outdoors and look at, smell, and touch the trees, grass, flowers. Talk about these objects while the baby is experiencing them. Provide the baby activities in which he can use his fingers—paper to crumple, dials to turn, pudding or dough to squish, holes to poke.

5. Give your child ordinary household objects—bowls, spoons, sponges, a hairbrush, towels—to pat, rub, bang, and wave. Provide floating bath toys. Give the child a set of bells. Encourage your baby to manipulate objects by shaking, squeezing, hitting, and turning them over.

6. Practice hiding objects under cloths (e.g., diapers, napkins, washcloths). Show your baby a favorite toy, then hide it under one of two cloths. You may wish to begin this game by just partially hiding the object and letting the child find it. When the child locates it, let her play with it.

7. Games are particularly important at this point. Play games that encourage a response from the child. Tickle the child, then wait. Does the baby giggle and ask to be tickled again? Blow on a pinwheel; does she ask you to repeat the action? When your baby has a definite way of signaling you, ask the baby to make the signal before you do the activity. For example, some babies raise their hands to be picked up or move back and forth to signal "I want to play horsey."

8. Babies quickly begin to learn about spatial relationships, too. Place an object slightly out of reach, or on top of something, or under something so that the baby must adjust her reach to get the object.

## Knowing about Objects

By about one year, the baby knows all sorts of basic things about objects. She knows about cause-and-effect relationships and about the basic properties and relationships between objects.

1. Give your baby toys and objects that continue to challenge exploration—rings to stack on a peg or dowel, tiny objects (such as a raisin) that require a pincer grasp to pick up, pegs to put in a pegboard, objects to put in a container.

2. Help your child learn about spatial relationships by providing toys that nest (fit inside one another) or stack. Pots and pans are great for this activity!

3. Present your baby with objects that go together—bowl and spoon, comb and brush, socks and shoe, hat and coat. Mix them all up and see if the baby can pair them up correctly.

4. Continue to provide your baby with new objects to manipulate. Help him practice what he's learned and apply it to new objects. For example, if your baby can put blocks into a can, see if he can also place his toys inside a basket.

5. Give your infant toys that can be played with in several ways. Peg people can be placed in their car and then pushed or pulled in the car, for instance. Blocks can be placed in the form ball and then the ball can be rattled around to make noise.

6. Help your child learn the functional use of objects. Give the child a hairbrush and ask her, "What do we do with this?" Does she brush her hair or your hair with the brush? Give her a cup, a Kleenex tissue, a shoe, or a toothbrush and toothpaste and ask her the same question about the object's function. Practice these activities in your daily chores. Also ask your child to choose objects that are needed for a particular activity. For example, before eating, ask the child, "What do we need?" and let her select the cup and bowl and spoon.

7. Help the child learn that objects exist even when they are out of sight (*object permanence*). Play peek-a-boo and hide and seek. Hide a favorite toy behind several barriers and let the child go after it. If your baby can't physically go after the object, play the game by letting him indicate the object's location with his eyes or by pointing.

8. After your infant knows about cause-and-effect relationships, you can help him learn to use one object to go after another. For instance, place a cracker in a pan and tie a string to the pan. Put the pan out of the child's reach. Does the child use the string to pull the pan within reach? Give the baby a dowel or stick to use for moving things toward him which are out of reach. Put a toy on a towel or pillow and observe whether your baby uses the towel or pillow to get the toy.

9. Kitchen cupboards can be safe and fun play environments. If you have the room, set aside a cupboard that belongs just to your infant and let him play with pots and pans, plastic bowls, spoons, measuring cups.

## Problem-Solving

Typically, after a year of age, babies apply their knowledge about objects to new tasks: learning to make fine discriminations among objects, understanding new concepts, understanding size relationships and shape relationships, solving problems. Try the following activities to enhance your child's learning.

1. Design a "feely bag" (a bag that your child can reach into to feel hidden objects). Fill it with familiar toys—toys that are varied in size, texture, and shape. Can your child guess what's in the bag?

2. Give your child a simple puzzle or formboard with noninterlocking pieces. Start with simple shapes such as circles, triangles, squares; then progress to harder ones as your child gets better at the activity.

3. Hide things in lidded boxes and let your child practice finding them. Let your child hide things for you, too!

4. Present your child with two or three common objects such as a book, shoe, and spoon. Then show your child an object identical to one of these,

**Figure 9.2**

such as another book, and ask her to "Find the same." This game can be played throughout the day with various household objects. It allows infants to learn important concepts such as *same* and *different* and also to learn how to match. Allow your child to look at the materials and talk about them when you are playing this learning game.

5.  Ask your child to retrieve something for you. When you're working around the house, have the child bring you an object that you call by name, such as "the cup" or "the newspaper" or "the book."

6.  Play hide and seek with the child. Tell her you are going to hide and then "hide" so that you are still partially visible. Let her find you! Play the game again and again as long as the child is interested and practice hiding in different places. Urge your child to hide, too, so that you can find her!

7.  Encourage your child to imitate your actions or gestures. Nursery rhymes and songs are wonderful ways to teach this behavior. Favorite songs include "The Wheels on the Bus," "Itsy Bitsy Spider," "Twinkle, Twinkle Little Star," and "Going on a Bear Hunt," to name just a few!

8.  Hide an object that makes a distinct sound (e.g., a rattle, a music box, an alarm, a bell) in one of several containers. Have your child close his eyes and then make the object produce a sound. Can your child guess where the sound is coming from? Can he also identify an object by its sound?

9.  Practice matching animal sounds to the animals. Looking at books or playing with pets or visiting a farm or zoo are good occasions for doing this activity.

10. Provide the child with new sensory experiences such as playing in a sandbox or playing with musical instruments. Teach the child to discriminate between different sounds (loud vs. soft) and visual traits (tall vs. short).

11. Give the child practice ordering objects of different sizes or characteristics. Line up three or four objects according to different characteristics—short to tall, fat to thin, large to small. Discuss the characteristics with your child and let her have a try at ordering. This will be very hard in the beginning; for the older infant it is an introductory activity to more difficult sorting tasks.

12. Show the child objects and pictures of the object and help the child match them to one another. To do this activity, place several pictures on a table or floor (e.g., pictures of a dog, cup, pencil). Hand the child an object, such as a toy dog, and ask the child to find the same.

13. Read lots of stories to your infant. Make a family scrapbook with your family photos, photos of your pet, photos of places you go. Encourage your child to point to family members or places when asked and allow your child to talk about the pictures. "Reading" stories together is a wonderful learning activity.

14. Provide your child with matching activities. For example, collect different swatches of cloth in different kinds of textures. Mix them up and see whether the child can match the same textures to one another—velvet to velvet, corduroy to corduroy, burlap to burlap.

15. Other matching and sorting activities are fun, too. Give the infant colored chips (e.g., poker chips), then make a design with the chips and see if your child can match your design. You can also use chips or similar objects for sorting activities. Give your child two plastic containers and ask him to put the red chips in one container and the white chips in the other. Give enthusiastic praise for the child's attempts and successes.

16. Other sorting activities include sorting by shape and sorting by function. For example, ask the child to put all the circles in one pile and the triangles in another. Or ask the child to put all the objects we use to eat with in one place and all the objects we wear in another.

17. Children can also begin to learn about classes of objects at this point. Provide the child with pictures (or objects) of different classes of items, such as food, animals, furniture, toys, clothes. Ask the child to sort them into "things that go together." There is no end to the sorting games that you can develop for your child.

# Communication

Communication involves several different processes. To communicate we must have a way to express ourselves (*expressive language*), and we must also have a knowledge of the world and understand what is being communicated to us (*receptive language*). We typically use speech or gestures to express ourselves. However, many children with motor delays have problems with expressive language because of the effect of the physical impairment on the oral-motor area. Thus, a number of exercises and suggestions were provided in the division on motor programs to assist you in normalizing tone in your child's body and oral-motor area and in facilitating more normal oral-motor movements. If your child has problems speaking, we also suggest that you work closely with a communication specialist (e.g., speech and language clinician or pathologist) who has had experience with young children with motor and language delays. The activities and suggestions provided here will assist you, but a thorough assessment of your child's individual needs will be necessary and desirable.

The activities in this section will provide you with general teaching ideas that you can use to increase your child's sound-making ability and understanding of the world around her. In order to communicate, your baby must have a knowledge about the world so that she has something to say. Moreover, she must learn how to say it, and she must have the motivation to communicate. You will notice that many of the activities are similar to those listed under the social and cognitive sections; all areas of development are so interrelated that overlap exists in the suggestions. Capitalize on this overlap when you are working with your baby. Don't just focus on one area of development; rather, try to do activities that combine goals. Communication, in particular, involves all areas of development—cognitive (knowledge of objects and environment), social (reason for communicating), and motor (way to use the motor systems for expression).

**Figure 9.3**

## Making Sounds

The young baby is, of course, limited in his means of communicating. Communication involves primarily crying and then making sounds. However, very early on, babies learn to make effective use of these cries and sounds to "train" their parents to respond. Here are some suggestions for the early months to enhance your baby's communication techniques.

1. Encourage your baby to make sounds—particularly vowel sounds. Talk to your baby face to face and make vowel sounds and smile. Vary your facial expression and the pitch of your voice. Don't be shy about sounding silly; research has shown that the way adults talk to babies is very different from the way adults talk to other adults. Your variations in pitch and facial expressions are likely to make the baby more interested in what you are saying than if you were to talk as if you were reciting your grocery list! Active movement is often effective in eliciting sounds from the baby. Follow the movement suggestions listed in the chapter on motor activities.

2. Respond to your baby's cries and sounds immediately and consistently. It is only through your consistent responsiveness that the baby will learn that her sounds and cries can be used to convey messages to you about her wants and needs. Observe your baby closely so that you can determine when certain cries or sounds are used to indicate special needs, such as "I am hungry." If your baby is unable to make sounds, watch closely for physical movements such as body orientation or finger movements that may convey specific messages.

3. Talk to your baby often face to face. Also talk to your baby as you are doing your daily activities. Describe what you are doing even though the baby is too young to understand your specific words. Sing songs or nursery rhymes to your baby.

4. Babies typically start to vocalize in chains, which is referred to as babbling. Babbling may sound like "ba-ba-ba" or "ma-ma-ma" and so on. Make babbling sounds to your infant. Imitate these sounds when your baby makes them.

5. Babies also soon begin to combine sounds—like "ah-ga" or "ga-goo." Imitate your baby when he vocalizes and show excitement over his talking!

6. Take turns with your baby while you are "conversing." Make a sound you have heard your baby make, then wait while looking at the baby. If the baby makes a sound, imitate the sound. If she does not make a sound, smile at her while she watches you and repeat your sound again. When your infant vocalizes spontaneously, smile and stroke her and repeat her sound. Always remember to give your baby time to initiate or respond—be careful not to bombard her with noises or sounds. Try to interact with a fine-tuned synchrony or rhythm, just as if you were dancing or talking with a friend. Practice taking turns making sounds during all activities with your baby—diapering, feeding, bathing, and playing.

## Understanding and Using Sounds

By the end of the first year, the baby develops the ability to understand simple and familiar words. She also learns to use specific sounds or beginning words such as "da-da" and "ma-ma."

1. Use specific labels for the baby and for other family members so that the baby comes to learn his name and the names of others in the family. Also consistently label familiar objects or activities, such as "bottle," "go," "Teddy," "doggie." Soon your infant will learn to associate that label with the object or activity.

2. Introduce new sounds and labels to the child. For example, when the infant is finished eating or playing, say "All done." Or when the infant falls or drops something, say "Oh-oh." Practice environmental sounds like "vroomm" for car sounds, "zzzz" for razor sounds, and so on.

3. Imitate the infant's sounds, words, and actions. Imitate smacking, clapping, playing, kissing, etc.

4. Encourage the baby to identify familiar people, pictures, and objects. Frequently give him practice by making requests such as "Go find Daddy" or "Bring Daddy the book." Reading stories provides many opportunities for this activity—you can ask the baby to find animals, people, or actions going on in the pictures.

5. When something occurs naturally in the environment, point to it, explain it, and provide a sound when possible. For example, when an airplane flies by overhead, point to the plane and say, "Look, it's an airplane—zoom!"

6. Give your infant practice following simple commands, such as "Go get your Teddy," "Shake the rattle," "Clap your hands."

7. Ask your baby simple questions like "Where's the doggie?" or "Find Mommy's shoe" or "Where is Daddy's nose?"

8. Begin to pair labels for objects with action words. Some common phrases are "eat cracker," "go car," "push truck," "love (hug) babydoll." Use these commands and see if the infant knows the appropriate action to take.

9. Label body parts. Usually it is easier to start to label body parts on a doll or on the parent since the child can see the part of the body being discussed. Point to your eye and say, "Eye. Mommy's eye. Can you point to Mommy's eye?" If the child points, reward the child with praise and smiles.

10. Encourage the child to communicate through nonverbal signals as well as verbal ones. The child may shake her head to indicate "no," make her hands into a "spider" to indicate a wish to play "Itsy Bitsy Spider," or point to his diapers to indicate that he is wet or soiled. When the baby uses these nonverbal means of communicating, respond to the action and verbally label the action (e.g., "Do you want to play 'Itsy Bitsy Spider?'" or "Are you wet?"). Also label the baby's facial expression—a powerful

means of nonverbal communication (e.g., "Are you mad?" or "You seem sad."). These nonverbal signals may be particularly important for the child with motor delays who has difficulty speaking.

## Using Words and Understanding New Concepts

After the first birthday the child typically begins to add new words to her vocabulary and then phrases. She also becomes increasingly capable of understanding new concepts and labels.

1. Sing songs and nursery rhymes and encourage the child to sing and move to the rhyme of the verse. This is a good setting in which to introduce new sounds and actions for the child to imitate.

2. Introduce new sounds and words and urge your baby to imitate you. Use sounds that you have not yet heard your baby make and use them in words that represent familiar items or actions to the child. For example, if your baby does not use the "p" sound, help him try to say words like "puppy" and "peek."

3. Make a list of your child's words and meaningful sounds. Be aware of other objects, people, or actions that the child can learn to say and provide a good language model of that label. Read to your child frequently. Talk about what you are doing all the time. Describe and explain events and objects to the child.

4. Help your child combine words into phrases. Beginning phrases often include combinations such as the following:

    | | |
    |---|---|
    | person + action | "Mommy go" |
    | action + object | "push car" |
    | "more" + object | "more milk" |
    | person + object | "doggie food" |
    | action + person | "hug dolly" |
    | object + action | "car go" |
    | negation | "no eat" |
    | greeting | "Hi, Auntie" |
    | location | "Nana house" |

5. Help the child identify and show his possessions to others. Encourage him to go find various items upon request and then label them. For example, "Go find your book. Show your book to Granddad."

6. Introduce and label time concepts. For example, when you are getting ready to eat, say "It is dinner time." Likewise label bath time, bedtime, time to go to the store, time to go pick up Mommy or Daddy, and so on.

7. Imitate your baby's actions—patting her cheek, tapping her feet. Introduce new actions and see if your baby can imitate you.

8. Provide new books for your baby. Books about animals and babies are always favorites. Read simple stories to your child. Continue to ask the child to point to pictures and label pictures.

9. Provide new materials and toys, particularly toys that require an action—like Dapper Dan, which has zippers, buttons, and snaps. Ask your child to perform an action such as zipping, and then ask your child to label what he's doing.

10. Use your child's name when you are calling her, dressing her, playing with her. Label her possessions (e.g., Lauren's coat, Sarah's truck). In play, point to her and say, "Who is this?" When she's looking in a mirror, ask her who she sees (e.g., "Who is that? Is that Kate?").

11. Help your child identify body parts on himself. Label body parts when he is dressing, feeding, bathing. Use a mirror for these activities. Songs can be useful, too, such as "Heads, Shoulders, Knees, and Toes."

12. Describe events to your child. For example, when you are at the supermarket, describe what is happening—"Look, the man dropped the boxes" or "Oh! The baby is mad. He is crying."

13. Use dolls and puppets for telling stories and reading stories or describing events. Let your child use the puppet, too, to tell you a story!

14. Ask your child to follow directions that have two components. For example, you might say, "Throw the paper in the trash basket, then close the door to the cupboard" or "Teddy is tired. Give him a hug, then put him to bed."

15. Encourage the child to talk about himself and also expand the child's phrases. If, for example, he says something like "Aric yogurt," expand the phrase and say, "Yes, Aric is hungry and wants some yogurt." Also urge the child to talk about his experiences. For example, if the child says, "Brett go car," you could say, "Oh! Brett got to go for a ride in the car with Daddy. Did you have fun?" You'll find many opportunities throughout the day to practice this communication activity.

# References

Adelson, E., & Fraiberg, S. (1974). Gross motor development in infants blind from birth. *Child Development*, *45*, 114–126.

Appleton, A., Clifton, R., & Goldberg, S. (1975). The development of behavioral competence in infancy. In F. Horowitz (Ed.), *Review of child development research* (Vol. 4) (pp. 101–186). Chicago: University of Chicago Press.

Baldwin, V. L., Fredericks, H. D., & Brodsky, G. (1973). *Isn't it time he outgrew this? or A training program for parents of retarded children*. Springfield, IL: Charles C Thomas.

Bayley, N. (1969). *Bayley scales of infant development*. San Antonio: The Psychological Corporation.

Bobath, K., & Bobath, B. (1972). Cerebral palsy. In P. H. Pearson & C. E. Williams (Eds.), *Physical therapy services in the developmental disabilities* (pp. 31–185). Springfield, IL: Charles C Thomas.

Bell, R. Q. (1968). A reinterpretation of the direct effects of studies of socialization. *Psychological Review*, *75*, 81–95.

Bleck, E. E. & Nagel, D. A. (Eds.). (1982). *Physically handicapped children: A medical atlas for teachers* (2nd ed.). New York: Grune & Stratton.

Butler, C., Okamoto, G. O., & McKay, T. (1983). Powered mobility for very young disabled children. *Developmental Medicine and Child Neurology*, *25*, 472–474.

Campbell, P. H., Green, K. M., & Carlson, L. M. (1977). Approximating the norm through environmental and child-centered prosthetics and adaptive equipment. In E. Sontag (Ed.), *Educational programming for the severely and profoundly handicapped* (pp. 300–320). Reston, VA: Council for Exceptional Children.

Connor, F. P., Williamson, G. G., & Siepp, J. M. (1978). *Program guide for infants and toddlers with neuromotor and other developmental disabilities*. New York: Teachers College Press.

Finnie, N. R. (1975). *Handling the young cerebral palsied child at home* (2nd ed.). New York: E. P. Dutton.

Fraiberg, S. (1977). *Insights from the blind*. New York: Basic Books.

Frankenburg, W. K., & Dodds, J. D. (1969). *Denver Developmental Screening Test*. Denver, CO: University of Colorado Medical Center.

Garland, C., Stone, N. W., Swanson, J., & Woodruff, G. (1981). *Early intervention for children with special needs and their families*. Monmouth, OR: Western States Technical Assistance Resource (WESTAR).

Hanson, M. J. (1977). *Teaching your Down's syndrome infant: A guide for parents*. Austin, TX: PRO-ED.

Hanson, M. J. (1984). Effects of early intervention. In M. J. Hanson (Ed.), *Atypical infant development* (pp. 385–406). Austin, TX: PRO-ED.

Harris, S. R. (1981). Effects of neurodevelopmental therapy on motor performances in infants with Down's syndrome. *Developmental Medicine and Child Neurology*, *23*, 477–483.

Holm, V. A., Harthun-Smith, L., & Tada, W. L. (1983). Infant walkers and cerebral palsy. *American Journal of Diseases of Children*, *137*, 1189–1190.

Knobloch, H., & Pasamanick, B. (Eds.). (1974). *Gesell & Amatruda's developmental diagnosis* (3rd ed.). New York: Harper & Row.

Lewis, M., & Rosenblum, L. A. (Eds.). (1974). *The effect of the infant on its caregiver*. New York: John Wiley & Sons.

Morris, S. E. (1977). *Program guidelines for children with feeding problems*. Edison, NJ: Childcraft Education.

Mueller, H. A. (1975). Feeding. In N. R. Finnie, *Handling the young cerebral palsied child at home* (pp. 113–132). New York: E. P. Dutton.

Mueller, H. A. (1972). Facilitating feeding and pre-speech. In P. H. Pearson & C. E. Williams (Eds.), *Physical therapy services in the developmental disabilities* (pp. 283–310). Springfield, IL: Charles C Thomas.

Saunders, R., & Koplik, K. (1975). A multi-purpose data sheet for recording and graphing in the classroom. *AAESPH Review, 1*, 1–8.

Seligman, I. (1975). *Helplessness: On depression, death, and development*. San Francisco: Freeman.

Sewell Early Education Development Program (SEED). Prepared by J. Herst, S. Wolfe, G. Jorgensen, & S. Pallan. (1976). *SEED Development Profiles* (Rev.). Denver, CO: Sewell Rehabilitation Center.

Sherrod, K., Vietze, P., & Friedman, S. (1978). *Infancy*. Monterey, CA: Brooks/Cole.

Stockmeyer, S. A. (1972). A sensorimotor approach to treatment. In P. H. Pearson & C. E. Williams (Eds.), *Physical therapy services in the developmental disabilities* (pp. 186–222). Springfield, IL: Charles C Thomas.

Stone, J. L., Smith, H. T., & Murphy, L. B. (Eds.). (1973). *The competent infant*. New York: Basic Books.

# Glossary

**abduction** (away from midline). Movement away from the midline of the body or a body part, as in raising the arms to the side and away from the body, spreading the legs, or spreading the fingers or toes.

**abnormal patterns of movement**. Forms of movement which are associated with brain damage and which are not observable at any stage of a normal full-term infant's motor development.

**adaptive equipment**. Devices used to position or to teach special skills.

**adduction** (to the midline). Movement to the midline of the body or body part or the anatomical position of closing the fingers or toes or bringing the arms close to the trunk.

**alignment**. To bring into a straight line.

**alternate strategy**. A strategy for teaching a skill in a way that is different from the typical teaching strategy.

**ambulation**. Walking.

**anomaly**. Marked difference from normal structure.

**antigravity posture**. A position, such as sitting or standing, which requires that the child be able to support himself against the force of gravity.

**approximately**. Close to.

**articulation** (in speech). The ability to speak clearly and distinctly.

**aspiration**. Inhalation of foreign substances (such as fluid or dust) into the lungs.

**assessment**. Observations or tests to determine a child's abilities.

**asymmetry**. One side of the body different from the other.

**ataxic**. One type of classification of cerebral palsy where balance and fine motor functions such as coordination are impaired.

**athetoid movement** (or athetosis). Uncontrolled and continuous movement associated with cerebral palsy (and other movement disorders) where involuntary writhing movements occur, particularly in the hands and feet.

**atrophy**. Wasting of the muscles, typically from disuse.

**attend**. To look at.

**atypical**. Unusual or different.

**auditory**. Pertaining to sound.

**automatic movement**. A type of movement which is performed without thinking or conscious control and which aligns body parts or restores and maintains balance.

**balance**. Stability of the body against gravity; equilibrium.

**baseline**. A measure of initial performance on a particular task.

**behavior**. Any action of a person.

**bilateral**. Involving two sides of the body, as in use of both hands together when holding a toy.

**bolster**. A long, narrow, rounded pillow or cushion. A pillow rolled over and tied makes a good bolster. Ideal size is 6-12 inches in diameter.

**cerebral palsy**. A disorder of posture and movement which results from damage to the brain and which produces atypical postural tone and unusual ways of moving.

**chorea**. Involuntary jerky movements.

**clonus**. A repetitive tremor of spastic muscles after those muscles have been stretched or after pressure (such as in weight bearing).

**co-contraction**. Contraction of muscle groups on both sides of the body part (trunk, legs, arms) which enable the child to assume and maintain antigravity postures, such as sitting or standing.

**command**. An order; a direction.

**communication devices**. Equipment that enables a child to express needs, desires, and ideas to other people through pointing or using various electronic switches.

**compensatory movement**. An atypical movement pattern used to compensate for the inability to perform a normal movement; may produce abnormal muscle tone.

**congenital**. Occurring at or around birth.

165

**consecutive**. Following in regular order.

**consequation**. Anything that follows a behavior (response). Examples: ''Good boy'' or ''no'' following your child's reach. A hug following your husband's/wife's compliment.

**consistency** (of muscle). The softness or firmness of the muscle tissue when you press it with your fingers or thumb.

**contracture**. Permanent shortening of muscles or tendons which produces limited range of motion at the involved joints.

**coordination**. The process in which muscles or parts of the body work together to produce smooth movements.

**corner chair**. A piece of adaptive equipment that can be used to seat the child and is shaped in a 90° angle.

**crawl**. Movement forward, with child's stomach on floor. Child moves legs in alternate way (moves one, then the other).

**creep**. Movement forward on hands and knees, stomach up, in quadruped. Child moves one hand and opposite knee, then other hand and opposite knee, and so on.

**criterion**. A definition of the behavior the child is to do. A criterion should be stated in a very specific way so you can decide whether or not your child does the behavior. This decision allows you to see whether your teaching is changing the child's behavior. Example: the child has to walk five steps in a row without help.

**cruise**. To walk sideways holding onto furniture or other supports. Example: child walks around coffee table and couch, stepping sideways and hanging on to furniture.

**cue**. Something you do to get the baby to behave or respond in a certain way. Cues can be verbal or physical. Verbal cues: ''Come here, Tommy'' or ''Put it here, Mary.'' Physical cues: touching child behind the knee to get child to lift leg and take a step or guiding child's hand to lift spoon to mouth.

**data**. Information you collect or gather about your child's behavior. Recording and reading data can help you decide whether your teaching programs are working.

**deformity**. Permanent change in the joints of the body which can only be altered through surgical intervention and which results from imbalance in muscle action (as in cerebral palsy or meningomyelocele).

**depression** (lowering). Movement that produces a lowering of a particular area; the opposite of *elevation*. The movement most typically occurs to return the elevated part to the anatomical position (returning the scapula to normal alignment) or can occur as an isolated movement as in mandibular (or jaw) depression, which opens the jaw.

**developmental milestone**. A behavior normally seen in most children at a particular time.

**diagnosis**. The determination of a condition through examination and consideration of the symptoms.

**diplegia**. A type of cerebral palsy where the muscles in the legs are more involved than those in the arms.

**dislocation** (of a joint). Complete separation or displacement of the bones that form a joint. In hip dislocation, the hip bone (femur) is pulled out of its socket (acetabulum) in the pelvis.

**distal**. Farthest from the body trunk, toward the hands and feet.

**Down syndrome**. Cluster of characteristics due to chromosomal disorder of the 21st chromosome pair, usually associated with some degree of mental retardation.

**dysarthria**. Faulty speech articulation.

**elevation** (raising). Movement that produces a raising of a particular area such as scapular elevation or raising (shrugging) the shoulders or mandibular elevation (closing the jaw). The term *elevation* is always used in combination with the name of the bone being moved (scapular) or, more generally, the body area being moved (shoulder elevation or jaw elevation).

**elongation** (muscle elongation). Increase in the length of the muscle.

**environment**. Everything around you; your surroundings—animals, people, weather conditions, all things.

**equilibrium reactions**. Automatic patterns of body movements that enable restoration and maintenance of balance against gravity.

**etiology**. Cause of disease or disorder.

**expressive language**. Any form of communication that allows expression of thoughts and ideas (usually speech).

**extension** (straightening). Movement that causes an increase in the angle between two adjoining bones, such as straightening the knee or elbow.

**extremity.** A body limb, such as the arm (upper extremity) or leg (lower extremity).

**facilitation.** Techniques that make it possible to move; physical techniques where guidance is specifically provided at key points (shoulders, head, hips/ pelvis) to normalize tone and promote more normal forms of movement.

**fine motor.** Small muscle movements; use of hands and fingers.

**fixate.** To look at or stare at; to focus eyes on something.

**flaccid.** Lacking force; weakness (as in muscles).

**flexion** (bending). Movement that decreases the angle between two adjoining parts, such as bending the elbow to bring the forearm toward the upper arm.

**floppy.** Hypotonic, or with low muscle tone.

**fluctuating tone.** Changing from one degree of tension to another (i.e., from low to high tone).

**form.** Way in which the various parts of a movement pattern are arranged in skill sequences (i.e., walking and crawling are two different forms of mobility).

**gesture.** A physical movement or motion (e.g., child raises hands to be picked up, mother moves her hand toward her to motion for the child to come to her).

**gradually.** Little by little.

**gravity.** A force that tends to draw all bodies toward the center of the earth.

**gross motor.** Large muscle movements like walking, sitting, crawling.

**habit** (habitual pattern). Compensatory patterns of movement that have been strengthened through nonsystematic (intermittent) reinforcement and practice.

**handling techniques.** Methods of holding or moving children with motor delay.

**head control.** Ability to bring head in a straight, upright position when tilted in any direction. Mouth should be in a horizontal (lateral) position, parallel to floor.

**hemiplegia.** A type of cerebral palsy where half of the body (arm, leg, and trunk on same side) is primarily involved.

**high tone.** Hypertonia or increased tone.

**hydrocephalus.** Accumulation of spinal fluid in the brain which results in an abnormally large head.

**hyperextensibility.** Extreme flexibility of joints due to loose or lax ligaments; ''double-jointedness''; a characteristic of many children with hypotonia or athetoid cerebral palsy.

**hyperextension.** Movement that increases the angle between two adjoining parts *past* a straight position (180°).

**hypertonia.** Increased tension in the muscles that results in limited range of motion of the joints.

**hypotonia.** Decreased tension in the muscles that results in excessive range of motion and inability to move against gravity.

**ignore.** To pay no attention to.

**imitate.** To copy; to do as someone else does.

**independent(ly).** Without assistance or support. Criterion used in teaching programs to encourage child to do something with no additional help.

**inhibition.** Physical guidance techniques provided at postural proximal key points (shoulders, head, hips/ pelvis) to decrease tone and eliminate atypical patterns of movement.

**insult.** Injury.

**intervention.** Treatment.

**inverted.** Upside down.

**involuntary movements.** Accidental or unintentional movements that are not performed by choice.

**joint.** The place where two or more bones of the skeleton are joined. In the hip joint, the hip bone (femur) is joined with the pelvis and held in place by ligaments.

**joint compression.** A therapy technique in which pressure is applied to bring the joint spaces closer together. Joint compresson down through the shoulders and into the pelvis brings the vertebrae (bones that form the spine) closer together. Also known as *joint approximation*.

**key points of control.** The parts of the body nearest the center of the body; the head, neck, shoulder girdle, and hips. These key points are used in handling and positioning the child with motor delay.

**ligament.** A thick band of tissue that connects bone to bone to help form the joint.

**low tone.** A term often used in place of hypotonia to indicate decreased tension in the muscles.

**maintain.** To hold or keep in place.

**manipulation**. Use of the hands and fingers in relation to objects, including such actions as holding, pointing, pounding, releasing.

**meningomyelocele**. Developmental disability present at birth in which there is an opening in the spine through which part of the spinal cord and its covering protrude.

**microcephaly**. Abnormal smallness of head usually associated with mental retardation.

**midline**. The middle of the body from top to bottom; an imaginary line drawn from the top middle of the head, over the nose, and down the middle of the body.

**mobility**. Capability to move or to be moved (i.e., movement of a body muscle or body part or movement of the whole body from one place to another).

**motivate**. To encourage, to make the child want to do something.

**movement patterns**. Organization of components of muscle action required to produce various forms of total movement that result in a change of position of the body as a whole or of an extremity (arms or legs).

**muscle strength**. Amount of power of the muscle fibers in relation to contraction of the muscles under varying conditions of resistance; typically rated as good, poor, fair, trace.

**muscle tone**. Degree of tension in the muscles at rest or under conditions of movement.

**muscle weakness**. Decreased power of the muscle fibers in relation to various conditions of gravity and with ratings of fair or trace.

**myelomeningocele**. (same as meningomyelocele)

**neurodevelopmental treatment (NDT)**. A form of treatment of children and adults with disturbances in posture and movement that relies on facilitation and inhibition techniques used when handling and when teaching movement skills.

**normalized tone**. Postural (muscle) tone that has been made more normal through use of procedures to alter tone.

**object manipulation**. To handle objects or things; refers to the way children move, touch, and play with objects or things.

**objective** (goal). The aim of a teaching activity (e.g., to teach a child to walk without help).

**observe**. To watch.

**occupational therapist**. Professional trained to work with fine motor activities, self-help skills, visual-motor activities, and activities of daily living.

**occupational therapy**. A method of treatment that helps the individual function as normally as possible. With children, occupational therapy typically emphasizes the improvement of movement in play and daily living.

**option**. A choice; another way.

**oral-motor coordination**. Interaction of the muscles of the neck, lips, tongue, cheeks, and jaw to produce smooth movement in eating and phonation.

**orthopedic conditions/problems**. Specific problems that involve the bones, joints, and muscles of the body and that include deformities such as scoliosis (spine), hip/shoulder dislocations, or muscle contractures.

**parallel**. Similar or corresponding to another object.

**parallel play**. Playing alongside but not with other children.

**pathological**. Due to or involving abnormality.

**patterns of movement**. The combination of various muscle contractions in order to move a body part in space or to accomplish a particular objective.

**pelvis**. A bone that forms the hips; the area of the body below the trunk and above the legs.

**perform**. To act; to do.

**phonation**. The production of sounds.

**physical guidance**. A training (or teaching) procedure in which the required movement is produced by physical manipulation by another person.

**physical therapist**. Professional trained to work with gross motor activities, mobility, and ambulation.

**physical therapy**. A method of treatment that helps the individual perform movement as normally as possible.

**pivot**. The first way that an infant moves when in prone (on the stomach); by shifting weight on the arms, the infant moves in a semicircle on her stomach.

**positioning**. Ways of placing an individual that will help to normalize postural tone and facilitate normal patterns of movement; may involve the use of adaptive equipment.

**postural fixation**. Co-contraction of specific muscle groups to provide a stable base for movement that can result in normal stability or compensatory stability with atypical postural tone.

**postural tone.** The degree of tension in the muscles with the body at rest and when actively moving; the degree of tension in the muscles with the body at rest and under various conditions of environmental stimulation.

**prerequisite.** Something required or needed before going on to something else. Used in teaching programs to show that certain programs or activities should be done or the child should have certain skills or behaviors before teaching a new program or activity.

**present** (verb). To show or to offer. Used in teaching programs to direct teacher to show something visually to the child or give something to the child.

**primitive patterns/movements.** Patterns of movement that are present in motor development of a normal full-term infant but prolonged past the typical time of disappearance or integration in the child with motor delay.

**probes.** Trials done with the child without using teaching cues or reinforcement. Used to get an idea of what the child can already do before teaching a particular behavior or step.

**procedure.** The way to do something.

**prompt.** See **cue**.

**pronation.** Movement that rotates the forearm so that the palms are down; the opposite of supination. Pronation is a downward rotation of the forearm.

**prone board.** A piece of adaptive equipment on which the child is placed in a supportive standing position with support provided on the frontal surface of the body (i.e., prone stander).

**proprioceptive.** Relating to sensations produced in the joint spaces and muscle tendons of the body.

**proximal.** Situated nearest the center of the body (i.e., closest to the trunk).

**punish.** To follow a behavior with a consequence which weakens that behavior or makes it less likely to occur again. A **punisher** is a consequence which does this (e.g., yelling "no," slapping).

**quadriplegia.** Involving all four body segments (i.e., arms and legs), as well as the trunk.

**quadruped.** The hands-and-knees position, as used in creeping on all-fours.

**range of motion.** The amount of motion present in each joint of the body under conditions of passive movement of the body part (passive ROM) or of active movement produced by the individual (active ROM).

**receptive language.** Understanding what is being communicated or expressed by others verbally or through gestures or symbols.

**recommend.** Suggest, advise.

**reflex.** Stereotypic posture or movement that occurs in response to specific stimuli and is outside of conscious control.

**regurgitation.** The return of partially digested food to the mouth from the stomach.

**reinforce.** To follow a behavior with a consequence that strengthens that behavior or makes it more likely to occur again. A **reinforcer** is one of these consequences (e.g., praise, touches, favorite activities, money, food). **Reinforcement** is the use of this procedure of presenting a positive consequence after a desired behavior has occurred. It should be used immediately after the desired behavior has occurred and only if the behavior is the desired one.

**resistance.** A force to hinder or prevent movement; a therapy technique used to increase muscle tone or muscle strength.

**respiration.** Breathing; the process by which an organism supplies its cells with oxygen and relieves them of carbon dioxide.

**respiration/phonation.** Coordination of the respiratory mechanism and oral-motor coordination to produce speech sounds.

**respiratory distress syndrome.** Lung condition found in premature babies due to immature lung development which requires ventilation to enable the baby to breathe.

**response.** Any action (behavior) of a person. A correct response occurs when child does what you want her to do.

**retrolental fibroplasia.** Visual disorder of particular risk to premature infants.

**righting reactions.** Subconsciously controlled movements that right the body in space and/or the body parts in relation to each other (e.g., head righting, body righting).

**rigid.** A condition of increased postural tone (hypertonus) that prevents any movement at all and in which the individual's body is very stiff and difficult to move by another person.

**rotation.** Movement of the head, trunk, or limb about its axis.

**sequence.** An order of steps; a series.

**shaping.** A procedure used to teach new behaviors. The child is reinforced for behaviors that are closer and closer to the final goal of desired behaviors. For example, the child gets food (reinforcer) at first for merely grasping spoon. Later, child must grasp spoon and move it toward mouth 1 inch before food is given. Later he has to grasp spoon and bring it up 2 inches toward mouth before being reinforced. Finally the child must grasp spoon and bring it to the mouth without help to get the food.

**side-lying.** A position in which the individual is placed on a supporting surface on either the right or left side.

**spasticity.** Increased muscle tone (associated with presence of a stretch reflex) or stiffness; hypertonia.

**specified.** As described or defined. Used in teaching programs to refer to teaching steps that have been described in detail. For example, "Child must lift head as specified for 10 seconds" refers to the step describing how the child must lift head.

**stability.** The contraction of muscles to hold the body against gravity and/or to hold the joints in place to allow movement at other joints.

**startle reflex.** Jerking movements of the body or blinking of the eyes as a result of a loud sound or sudden movement. Some children with hypertonia have exaggerated or hyperactive startle reflexes.

**stiff.** Used to describe spasticity or increased postural tone (hypertonus), which relates to the difficulty in moving the body as a whole or any body part.

**straddle.** To sit on top of something, a leg on either side.

**strategy.** A method or technique; a plan or action used to do something. Used in this manual to refer to specific methods of teaching.

**subluxation.** An incomplete or partial dislocation of a joint.

**supination.** Movement of the forearm such that the palm is facing up.

**symmetrical.** Sameness between two sides compared in size, posture, color, or other variables.

**syndrome.** Set of symptoms occurring together.

**tactile defensiveness.** Extreme sensitivity to touch.

**task analysis.** The process of breaking a behavior into its smaller parts and sequencing the steps needed to perform the behavior.

**tightness** (muscle tightness). Decreased elasticity in a muscle or group of muscles which produces limited range of active movement but which can be stretched to full length passively.

**time-out.** A period in which the child is removed from all opportunities to get reinforcement.

**torso.** Trunk.

**transporter chair.** A piece of adaptive seating equipment that can be used as a car seat to transport a child safely.

**trial.** A try, a test, an attempt. Used in teaching to refer to *each* time the cues and materials are presented to the child to teach a particular behavior. Usually what the child does (correct or incorrect response) is recorded after each trial.

**trunk.** The body, not including the head, the arms, and the legs.

**trunk control.** Ability to bring the body into a straight, upright position when tilted in any direction.

**variety.** Having different forms or kinds.

**vary.** To change.

**vertebrae.** The bones that form the spinal column or spine.

**vestibular.** Relating to sensations produced in the semicircular canals of the ear, which affect balance and posture.

**visual.** Having to do with sight or seeing. Used in teaching programs to refer to use of eyes.

**voluntary movements.** Movements produced under the conscious control of the individual.

**wedge.** A piece of adaptive equipment, like a pillow, that is used to help position the individual in proper body alignment.

**weight-shifting.** Shifting weight off one body part to another. In order to pivot in prone, for example, the infant must shift weight off of one arm (or elbow) and then move that arm while bearing weight on the opposite arm. Weight-shifting in standing allows the child to cruise around furniture and later to walk.

# Developmental Milestones

This section contains charts of developmental milestones* or skills—those skills typically accomplished by children at a particular time. The milestones included here are ones that usually apply to children from birth to 2 years. For presentation purposes these milestones have been separated into four areas of development: Gross Motor (large muscle movements; e.g., walking), Fine Motor (use of hands and fingers), Communication (talking and understanding), and Social and Self-Help (response to self and others and feeding, dressing, and toileting). Under each area, milestones are further subdivided or grouped according to category. For example, under Gross Motor, all skills demonstrated by the young child which relate to being able to sit independently are diagrammed on a chart for "Sitting."

The developmental milestone charts are provided to show the types of skills that are learned by young children during their first 2 years. Each skill is represented on the chart by a diamond that outlines the age range in months during which most children acquire a particular skill (read up and down). The diamond shapes show that there is a wide age span for which children demonstrate any developmental milestone. The age span for the skills listed on the charts is represented by the "tails" of the diamond. The age at which the majority of children perform each skill is shown by the thickest part of the diamond. As an example, refer to the chart for "Standing." The "tails" of the diamond show that most children stand without support between 9 and 16 months

of age. However, the majority of young children (represented by the thickest part of the diamond) demonstrate this skill at around 11 months of age.

Many children with motor delay or impairment will not learn to stand at 11 or 12 months of age and may not be able to stand without support by 16 months of age. The motor delay may also prevent the child from demonstrating other milestones (such as those in areas of Communication and Social/Self-Help) in the same way that the skills are described on the charts or within the typical age ranges diagrammed by the diamonds. You can see that a great deal of motor coordination is required to perform skills listed in each of these developmental areas. For instance, the sixth skill in the Feeding category (under Social/Self-Help) is the child's ability to hold a bottle without help. Many children with basic motor problems are unable to move their arms to the middle of their bodies in a position to hold the bottle. Other children with motor problems may be able to get their hands into position but may not be able to grasp. Inability to perform this milestone may not mean that the child is deficient in Social/Self-Help, but simply indicates that the motor problem which the child has is preventing him from performing an item which, on these developmental milestone charts, is classified as Social/Self-Help. The important point is to know that the motor problem is preventing the child from performing the item; the child should not be further labelled as being "delayed socially" as well.

The information presented in this section can be used as an information source on normal development across the various behavioral areas. Some children will grow and develop according to the milestones and sequences shown in these charts; other children will do so differently. Training activities for each child must be individualized. Physical and occupational therapists working with your child can help you identify the goals

---

*Information on developmental milestones or norms is taken from the following sources: *Bayley Scales of Infant Development* (Bayley, 1969), *Denver Developmental Screening Test* (Frankenburg & Dodds, 1969), *Gesell Developmental Scale* (Knobloch & Pasamanick, 1974), and *SEED Developmental Profiles* (Sewell Early Education Development Program [SEED], 1976).

for your child. These charts on normal development are provided merely as a guide. The information gives you a general indication of developmental skills typically demonstrated by young children so that you will be familiar with the many and varied activities performed by young children. If you wish to keep a record of the age at which your child achieves these milestones, lists of milestones and spaces for recording are provided in ''Baby's Record.''

# Gross Motor

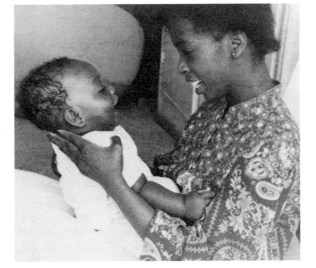

## Head Control

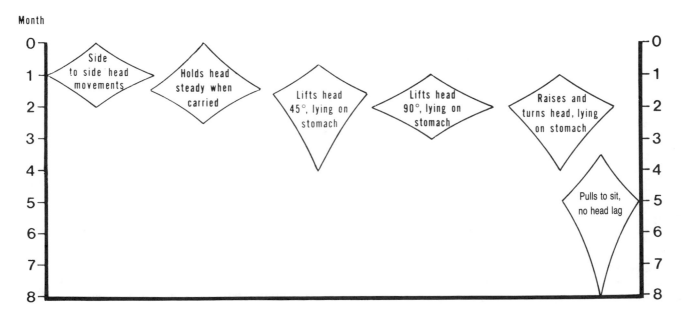

# Sitting

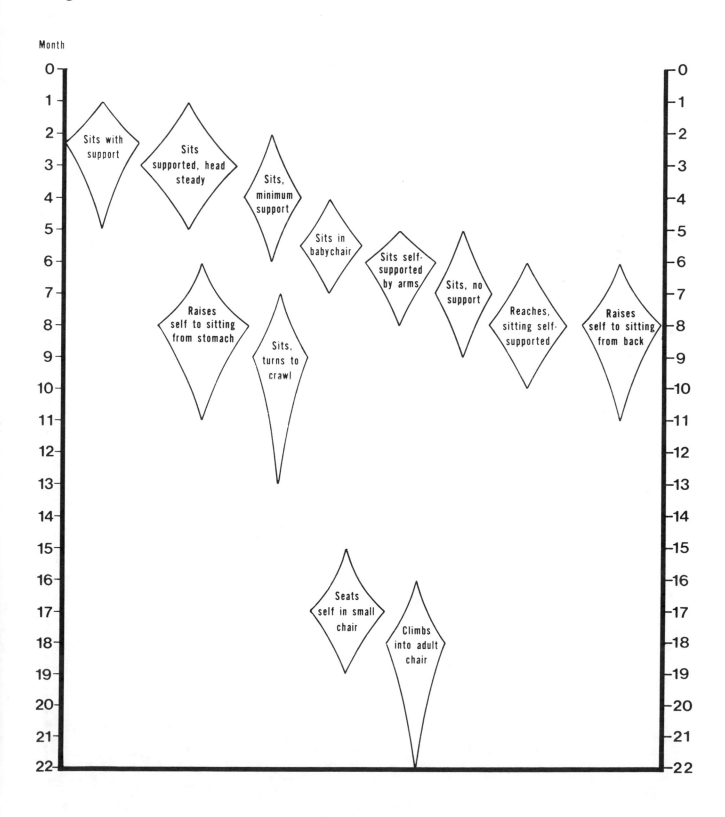

Month

**Rolling**

**Crawling**

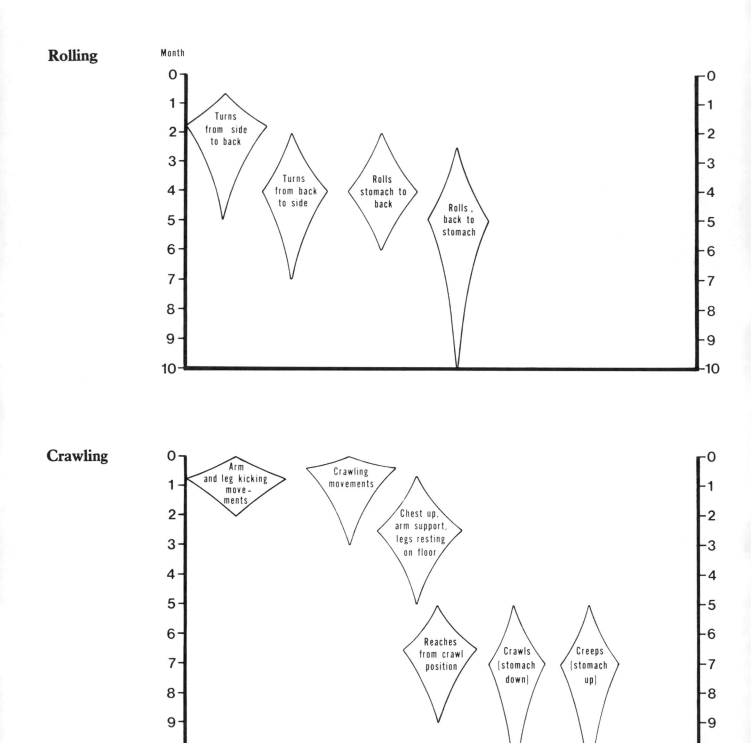

# Standing

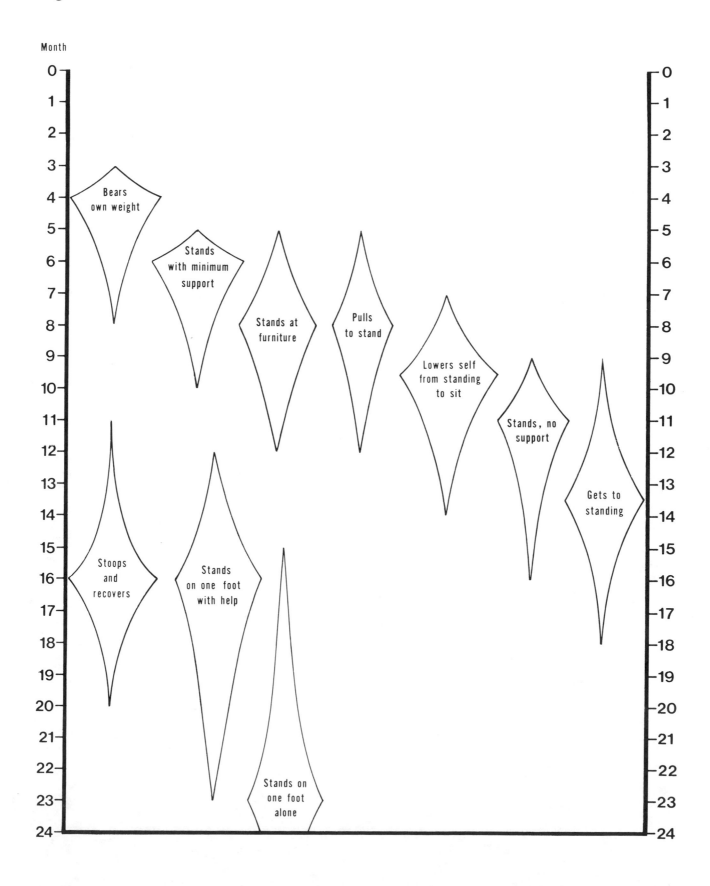

# Walking

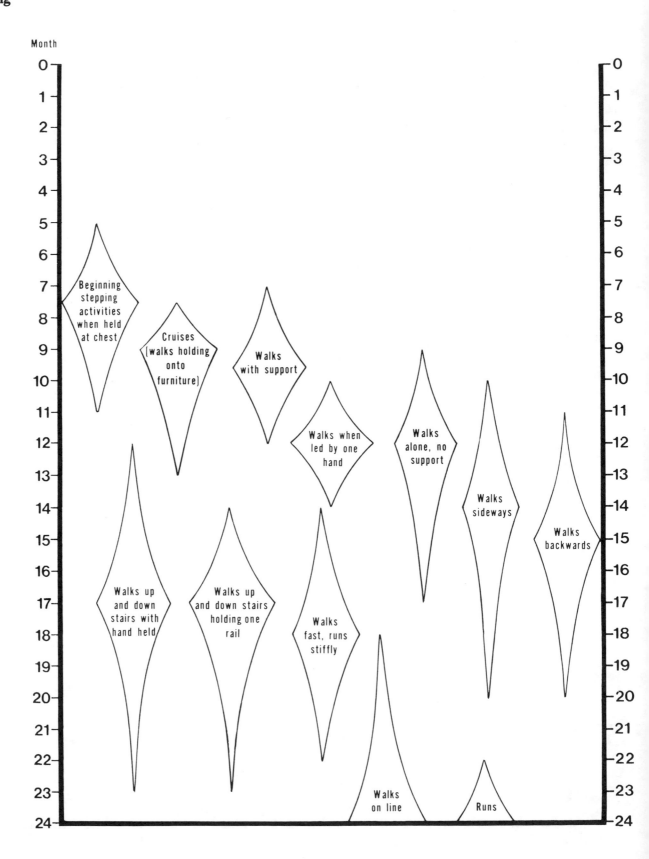

# Kicking and Jumping

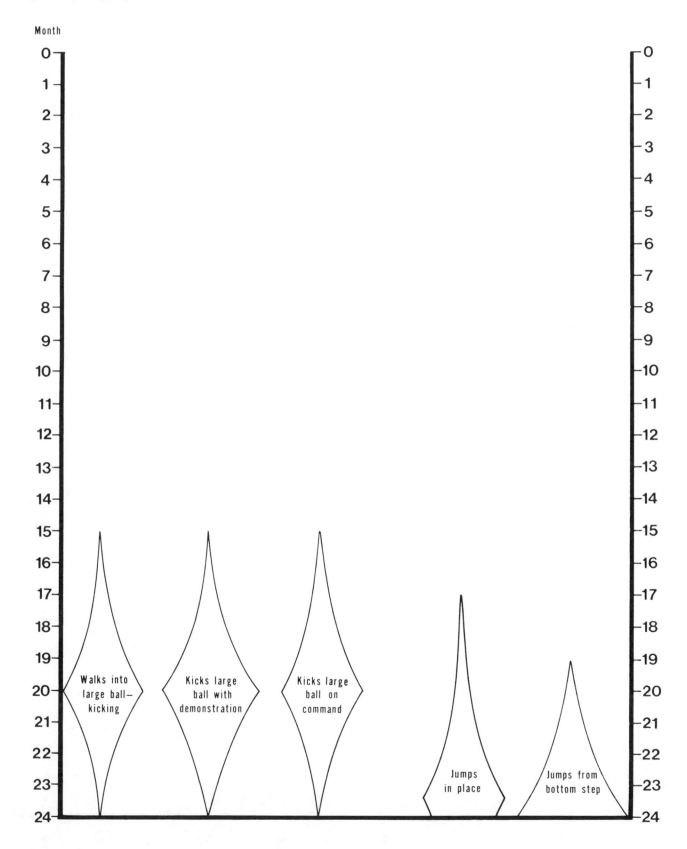

**Throwing**

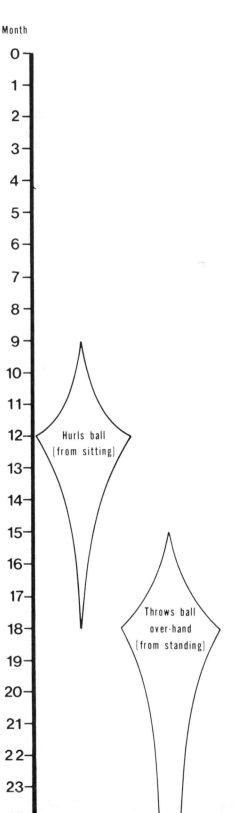

# Fine Motor

## Visual

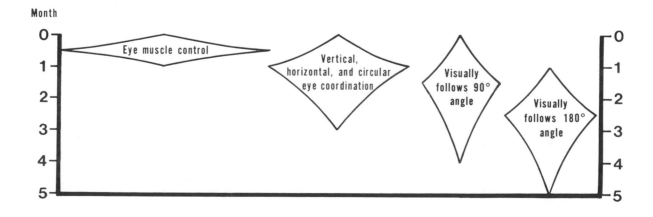

Month

Eye muscle control

Vertical, horizontal, and circular eye coordination

Visually follows 90° angle

Visually follows 180° angle

**Grasping**

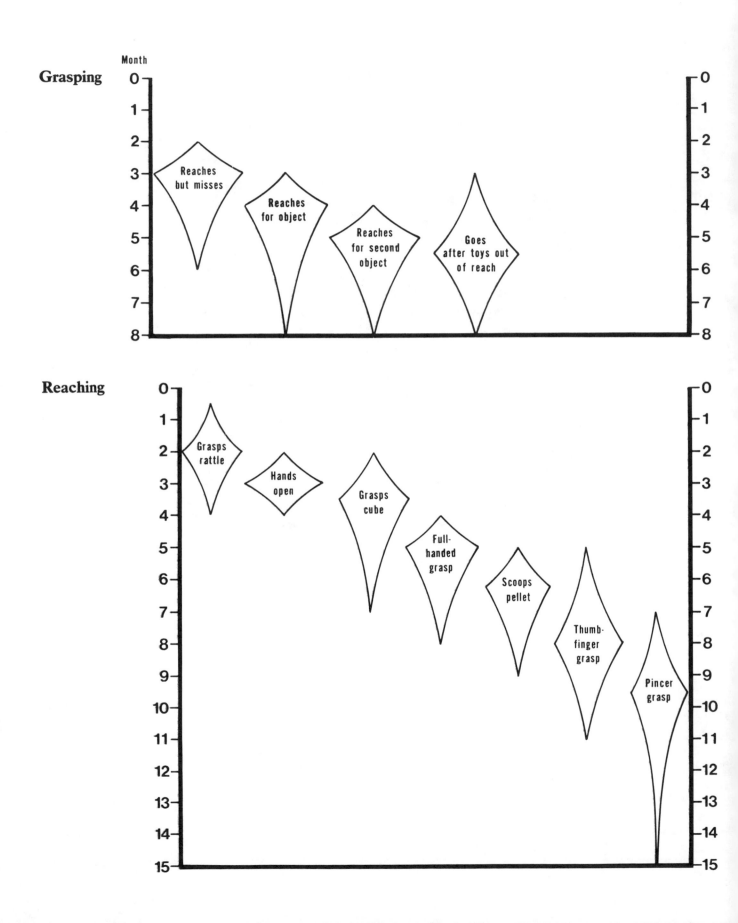

**Reaching**

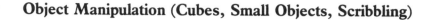

# Object Manipulation (Cubes, Small Objects, Scribbling)

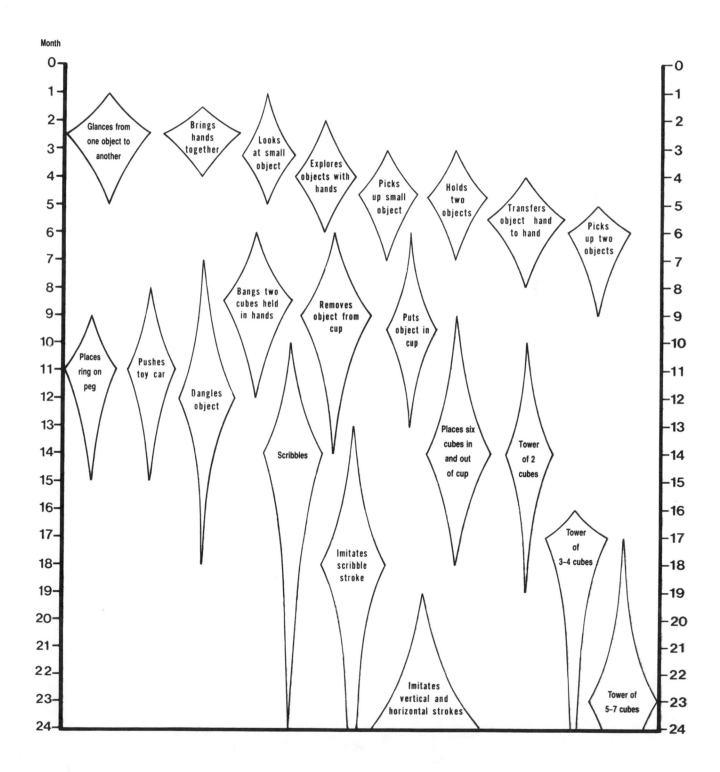

## Object Manipulation (Puzzles, Peg and Pellets, Pages in Books)

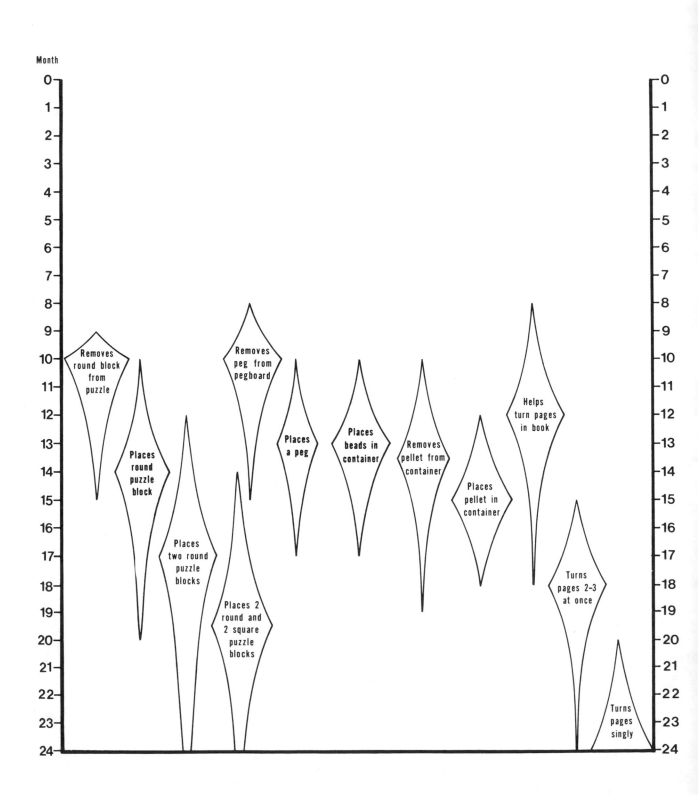

# Problem-Solving

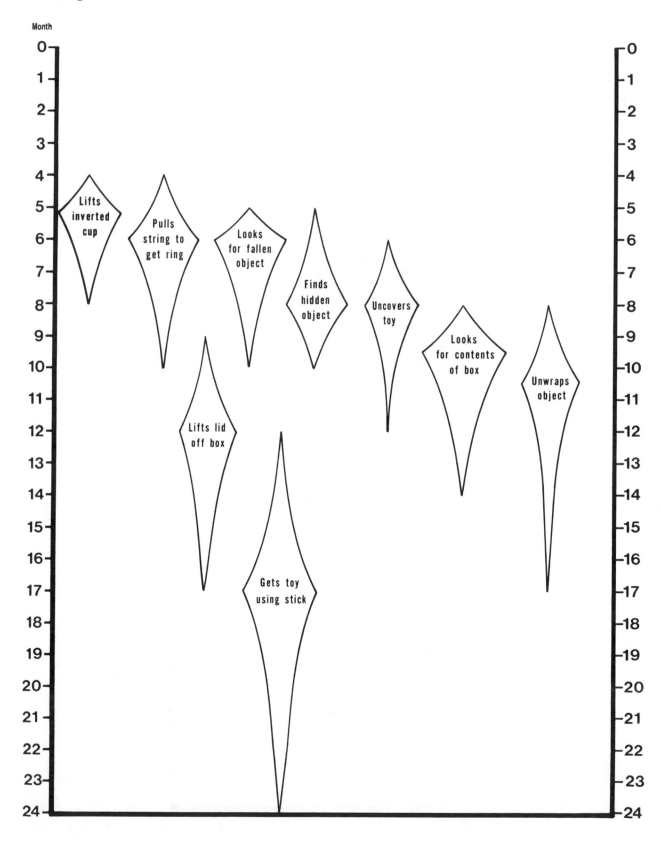

# Communication—Speech and Language

**Early Auditory**

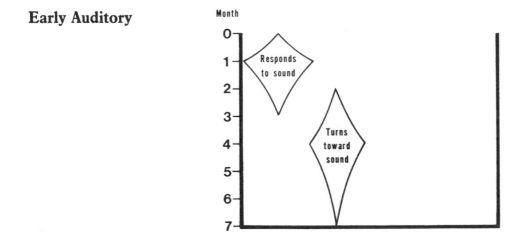

## Expressive Language

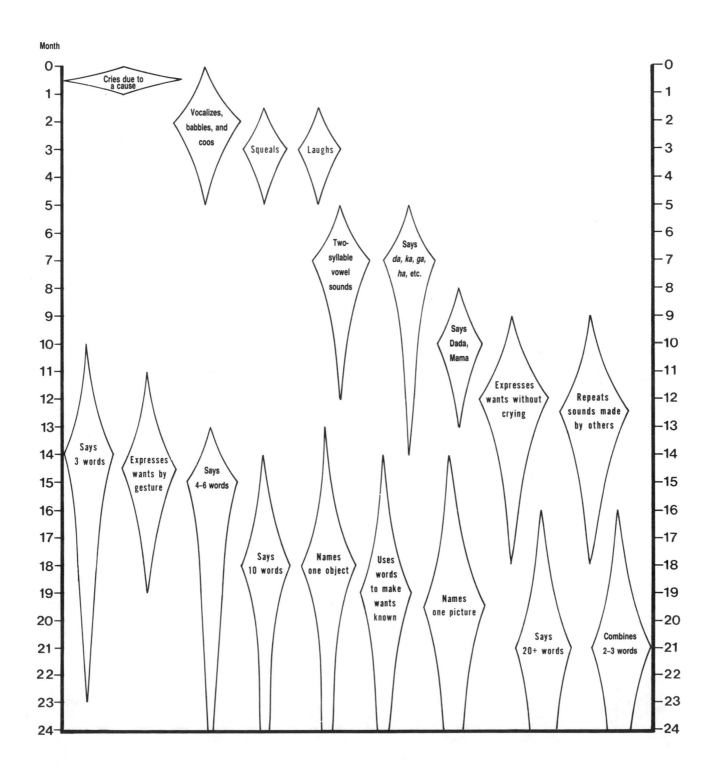

## Receptive Language

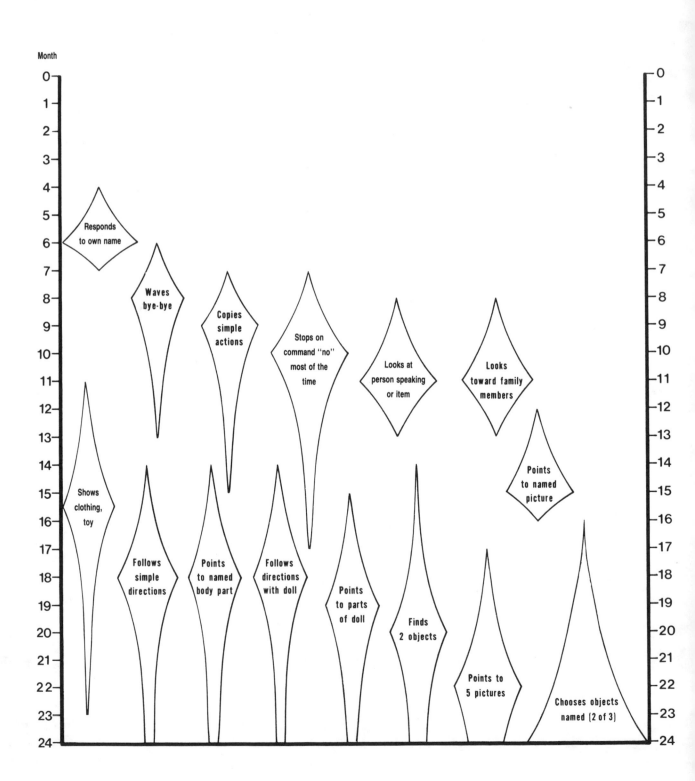

# Social and Self-Help

**Social—Self/Others**

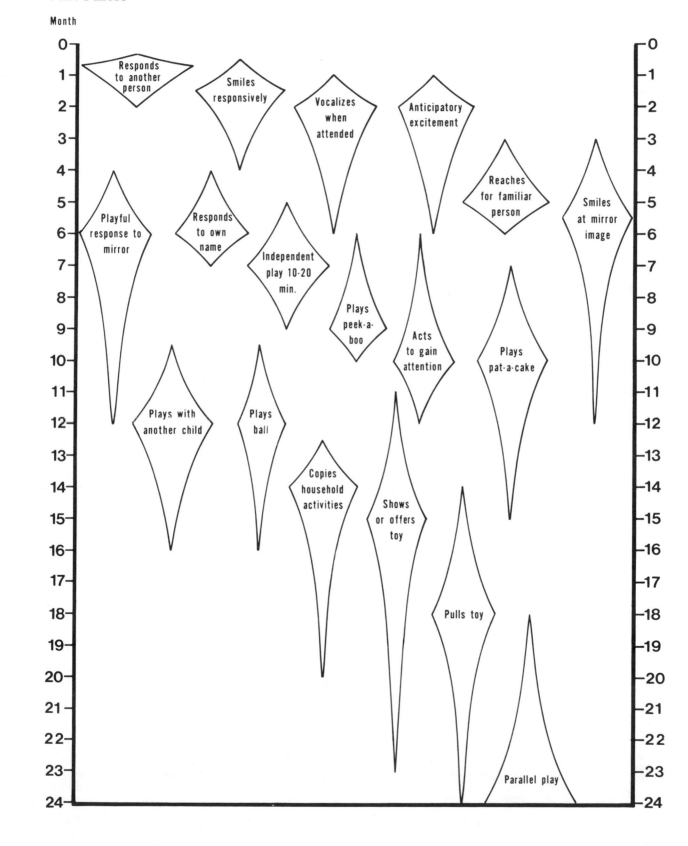

## Feeding

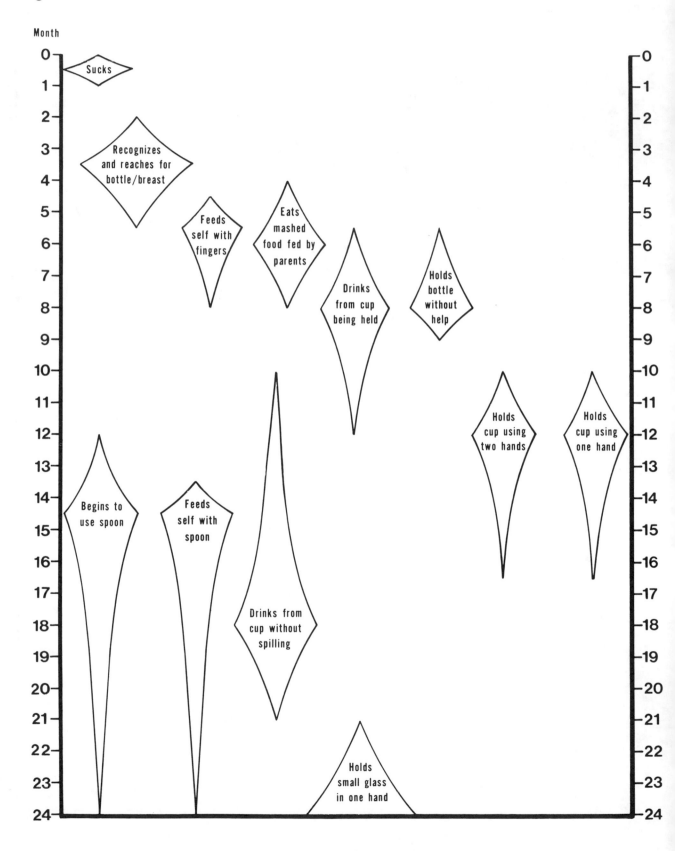

# Dressing and Toileting

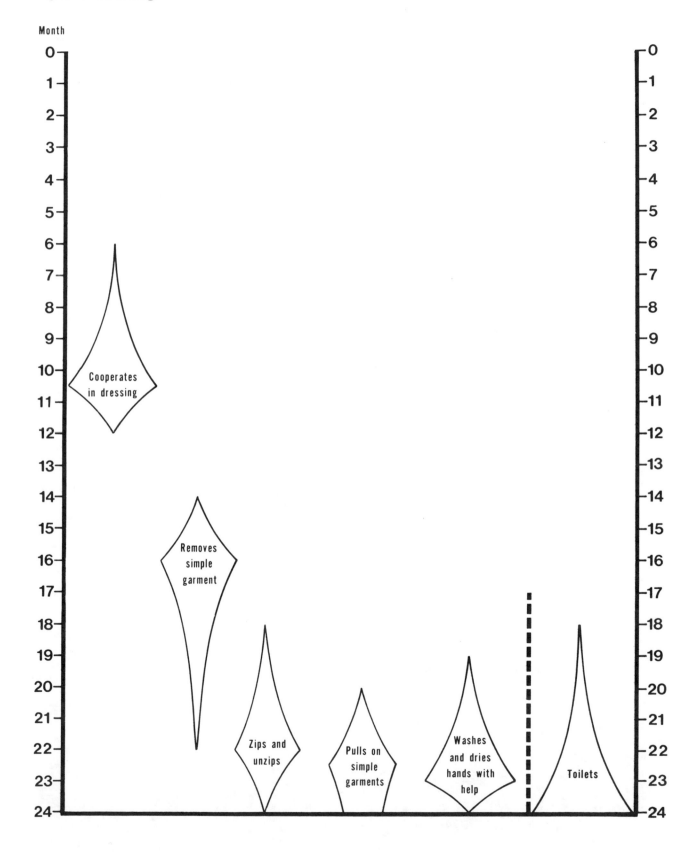

Month

# Motor Development Resources

## Commercial Resources for Adaptive Equipment

The following list includes the major distributors of equipment in the United States. Catalogs are available from each company. The list is not comprehensive, and you may locate equipment through a source not listed here. In addition, local companies that sell health or medical equipment and products are not listed here but can be excellent resources for equipment.

### Achievement Products for Children
P.O. Box 547
Mineola, New York 11501

Transportation: Mobility buggy with insert; trunk jackets
Chairs: Corner floor chairs/trays; pony chairs; wooden toddler chairs/trays
Other Positioning Aids: Wedges with straps; standing boards
Self-Care: Feeding, bathing, and toileting aids/devices
Mobility Aids: Child crawler

### Adaptive Equipment Company
175 Parker Court
Chardon, Ohio 44204

Chairs: Bolster chair/tray; corner chair
Other Positioning Aids: Adaptive harness; standing table; prone board
Mobility Aids: Prone scooter

### Adaptive Therapeutic Systems
683 Boston Post Road
Madison, Connecticut 06443

Transportation: E-Z Rider transporter chair; harnesses
Chairs: Mancino Learning Center
Other Positioning Aids: Prone board
Self-Care: Pulley feeder; self-feeding kit
Adaptive Play and Learning Equipment: Enabler head pointer system; table writer
Communication Aids: Enabler head pointer system; electronic communication boards

### Childcraft Education Corporation
20 Kilmer Road
Edison, New Jersey 08817

Adaptive Play and Learning Equipment: Wooden swing; mirrors; infant-preschool toys
Mobility Aids: Wooden push wagon; Irish mail cart

### Community Playthings
Rifton Line for the Handicapped
Rifton, New York 12471

Chairs: Floor corner chairs/trays; toddler/preschool adaptive chairs/trays
Other Positioning Aids: Side-lyer; standing boards; prone boards
Adaptive Play and Learning Equipment: Adjustable easel/tables
Mobility Aids: Kiddie car; tricycles with attachments; scooters

**Danmar Products, Inc.**
2390 Winewood
Ann Arbor, Michigan 48103

Adaptive Play and Learning Equipment: Swim aids (head floats, swim rings, rafts)

**Equipment Shop**
P.O. Box 33
Bedford, Massachusetts 01730

Chairs: Tripp Trapp chair; corner floor chairs/trays
Other Positioning Aids: Standing boards; seat belts
Mobility Aids: Scooter boards; tricycle adaptations

**Everest & Jennings, Inc.**
3233 E. Mission Oaks Blvd.
Camarillo, California 93010

Transportation: Wheelchairs
Self-Care: Parker chair (for bathing)
Mobility Aids: Powered wheelchairs (for young children)

**Fred Sammons**
Be OK Self-Help Aids
Box 32
Brookfield, Illinois 60513

Self-Care: Devices for feeding, dressing, grooming
Mobility Aids: Deluxe scooter board

**GENAC, Inc.**
2220 Norwood Avenue
Boulder, Colorado 80302

Transportation: Pogon Buggy; stroller chairs

**J. A. Preston, Inc.**
71 Fifth Avenue
New York, New York 10003

Transportation: Mainstreamer transporter chair; stroller insert
Chairs: Wheelchairs; corner chair/tray; floor sitter; hammock chair
Other Positioning Aids: Wedges; bolsters; feeder seat; side-lyer; standing tables; standing boards; prone boards

Self-Care: Adaptive equipment for feeding, bathing, toileting, dressing, grooming
Adaptive Play and Learning Equipment: Specialized materials for play and learning; head pointer
Communication Aids: Head pointer; electronic communication boards
Mobility Aids: Scooters; Mustang scooters; walkers

**Kaye's Kids**
Division of Kay Products, Inc.
1010 E. Pettigrew Street
Durham, North Carolina 27701–4299

Transportation: Seat inserts for strollers
Chairs: Bolster chair/tray; corner chairs/tray
Other Positioning Aids: Prone board
Self-Care: Prone support potty with table top
Adaptive Play and Learning Equipment: Selected toys for children with handicaps
Self-Care: Nuk toothbrush trainer set; feeding spoons; Deluxe Baby Sitter (sitting ring to support child in bathtub)

**Maddak, Inc.**
Pequannock, New Jersey 07440

Adaptive Chairs: Corner seat
Other Positioning Aids: Prone stander; foam wedges (7" and 12")
Self-Care: Maddak child bath seat; scooper plate
Adaptive Communication Aids: Sensory switches for children

**Motor Development Corporation**
P.O. Box 4054
Downey, California 90241

Adaptive Chairs: Corner chairs; tray floor chairs; roll or bolster chairs
Other Positioning Aids: Prone board; standing table; standing frame; body alignment wedge
Self-Care: Posture commode chair; trainer commode; Parker Chair (bathing chair)
Mobility Aids: Padded scooter; Lo-Boy trike; hand-propelled trike; Halpern Wheeler (caster cart)

**Mulholland and Associates**
1563 Los Angeles Avenue
Ventura, California 93003

Transportation: Wheelchairs; transport chairs
Other Positioning Aids: Prone standers

**Ortho-Kinetics, Inc.**
P.O. Box 436
Waukesha, Wisconsin 53187

Transportation: Travel wheelchairs
Adaptive Chairs: Corner chairs; bolster chairs
Other Positioning Aids: Prone standers

**Safety Travel Chairs**
147 Eady Court
Alyria, Ohio 44035

Transportation: Safety Travel Chairs

## Special Clothing

Some children with severe motor handicaps are very difficult to dress because of their motor impairments. Appropriately designed clothes are often hard to find. Other children with mild motor handicaps may have difficulty dressing themselves with traditionally tailored clothes. Many shoes, sneakers, and other types of clothing now have Velcro fasteners, which makes dressing somewhat easier but does not solve all the problems. Listed below is the name and address of a clothing manufacturer for children and adults with special needs. One of the founders of the organization was the mother of a child with cerebral palsy; her daughter wanted to become more independent in dressing herself. All clothes in the catalog will be custom-made for each individual child. To receive a catalog, send $1.00 to:

**On the Rise**
Clothing for Special People with Special Needs
2282 Four Oaks Grange Road
Eugene, Oregon 97404
503–687–0119

## Manuals and Books Describing Adaptive Equipment

Many plans for fabricating adaptive equipment devices have been passed on from person to person through workshops or inquiries. Some of these plans can be obtained by contacting local agencies serving children with motor impairments. The manuals and books included in the list below, in some cases, provide the actual plans. If specific plans are not included, usually helpful illustrations will guide you in construction of many of these pieces of adaptive equipment.

Connor, F., Williamson, G., & Siepp, J. (1978). *Program guide for infants and toddlers with neuromotor and other developmental disabilities*. New York: Teachers College Press.

Guidelines and illustrations are provided for each piece of equipment listed below, along with full instructions for building several but not all pieces of equipment described in the book.

Chairs: Corner chairs; pelvic-tilt chair; sawhorse chair
Other Positioning Aids: Prone board; side-lyer
Adaptive Play and Learning Materials: Peg handle grips

Finnie, N. (1975). *Handling the young cerebral palsied child at home*. New York: Dutton.

Plans are provided for only a few pieces of equipment. However, all designs are well-enough illustrated to allow for easy copying.

Chairs: Box chair; barrel chair; sawhorse chair; hammock chair
Other Positioning Aids: Hammocks; wedges; prone boards
Adaptive Play and Learning Materials: Many suggestions for toy modifications
Mobility Aids: Scooter; tricycle; chair walker

Fraser, B. A., Galka, G., & Hensinger, R. N. (1980). *Gross motor management of severely multiply impaired students*, Vol. 1. Austin, TX: PRO-ED.

This book includes a comprehensive section on commercially available adaptive equipment. However, some of the equipment may be built at home by following the illustrations. While much of the equipment described may be inappropriate for young children or for children with mild motor handicaps, the illustrations provide examples of the varied types of equipment designed to assist individuals with motor impairments.

Golbin, A. (Ed.). (1977). *Cerebral palsy and communication: What parents can do*. Washington, DC: Job

Development Laboratory, George Washington University

This manual provides good guidelines on positioning for speech acquisition as well as full explanation of alternate communication modes (communication boards, books, devices) appropriate for children with severe motor disorders.

Communication Aids: Head pointer; manual communication boards; simple electronic communication boards

High, E. C. (1977). *A resource guide to habilitative techniques and aids for cerebral palsied persons of all ages.* Washington, DC: Job Development Laboratory, George Washington University.

This manual is a reference for both home-constructed and commercial materials. Very few plans are provided, but illustrations of equipment are clearly drawn and easy to follow.

Transportation: Transporter chairs; car seats
Chairs: Various wheelchairs; corner chairs; other chairs
Other Positioning Aids: Prone boards; standing boards
Self-Care Skills: Equipment for feeding, dressing, toileting, bathing, and grooming

Robinault, I. P. (1973). *Functional aids for the multiply handicapped.* New York: Harper & Row.

Many new developments in adaptive equipment have occurred since this book was written. However, instructions for building and guidelines for using some types of adaptive equipment are still current. The book includes equipment for both children and adults and gives examples of equipment for which better designs are now available. Be sure and check with your child's therapist or teacher before constructing items pictured in this book.

Transportation: Trunk support; car seat
Chairs: Corner chairs; inserts for large chairs
Other Positioning Aids: Standing board
Self-Care: Feeding and bathing equipment; toilet chairs
Communication Aids: Communication boards; head pointers; typewriter adaptations

## Home-Constructed Electronic Devices

Some children with movement difficulties have so many problems with movement that manipulation and play skills are not possible without assistive devices. The following guides provide plans for constructing simple electronic devices to help your child activate a toy or to play by herself. Other devices have been constructed to teach specific skills, such as head control. Your therapist can help you decide which devices might benefit your child. This is a recently developed area of adaptive equipment, so be sure to check for other resources besides those mentioned in this section.

Accrino, S. P. *Equipment development manual for active stimulation activities.* Warwick, RI: Trudeau-Zambarano Active Stimulation Program.

Burkhart, L. J. (1980). *Homemade battery-powered toys and educational devices for severely handicapped children.* (Available from Linda Burkhart, 8503 Rhode Island Avenue, College Park, MD 20740.)

Burkhart, L. J. (1982). *More homemade battery devices for severely handicapped children with suggested activities.* (Available from Linda Burkhart, 8503 Rhode Island Avenue, College Park, MD 20740.)

Campbell, P. H., Bricker, W. A., Simmons, T., & Esposito, L. (1981). *Electronic aids for teaching the severely motorically impaired student.* Akron, OH: Children's Hospital Medical Center.

Shein, G. F. (1980, November). *Instructions for constructing a large area flap switch to allow disabled children to control battery-operated toys.* Ontario, Canada: Rehabilitation Engineering Department, Ontario Crippled Children's Centre, 350 Rumsey Road, Toronto, Ontario, M4G 1R8.

## Readings in Motor Development

Apgar, V., and Beck, J. (1973). *Is my baby alright?* New York: Trident Press.

Information presented in this book covers most of the medical problems related to motor impairment and other disorders in infancy and early childhood in fairly easy-to-read terminology.

Bigge, J. L. (1982). *Teaching individuals with physical and multiple disabilities* (2nd ed.). Columbus, OH: Merrill.

This is a book for teachers and other professionals who work with individuals (of all ages) with physical and multiple disabilities. Task analysis provides the major framework of this book. Focused more toward the school-aged and older individual with disabilities, it contains chapters on alternative communication devices, importance of recreation and leisure education, and independence in home and community.

Bleck, E. E., & Nagel, D. A. (1982). *Physically handicapped children: A medical atlas for teachers* (2nd ed.). New York: Grune & Stratton.

This well-illustrated book includes chapters on each of the major handicapping conditions that result in movement disorders as well as information on the visual and auditory systems. There is also an excellent chapter about parents' experiences as well as a reference list of literature for parents and professionals.

Bly, L. (1983). *The components of normal movement during the first year of life and abnormal motor development*. Birmingham, AL: Pittenger and Associates Pathway Press. (Available from Neurodevelopmental Treatment Association, P.O. Box 14613, Chicago, IL 60614.)

This is a monograph written primarily for use by physical and occupational therapists. The first section describes the components of normal movement that occur in the normally developing infant during the first year. The second section discusses abnormal movement problems, such as those found in children with cerebral palsy.

Brinson, C. L. (Ed.). (1982). *The helping hand: A manual describing methods for handling the young child with cerebral palsy*. Charlottesville, VA: Children's Rehabilitation Center, University of Virginia. (To order a copy, send a check for $2.00 to National Clearing House of Rehabilitative Material, Attention: Jean Hudder, 115 Old USDA Building, Oklahoma State University, Stillwater, OK 74078.)

Written by a developmental pediatrician, a PT, an OT, and two speech therapists, this is an excellent manual for parents of young children with cerebral palsy. It addresses common concerns of parents such as "How will my other children adapt to our new child with CP?" and "What should I know about dental care for my child?" Daily concerns of carrying, toileting, dressing, feeding, and bathing are addressed with large, easy-to-understand text and illustrations.

Connor, F. P., Williamson, G. W., & Siepp, J. M. (1978). *Program guide for infants and toddlers with neuromotor and other developmental disabilities*. New York: Teachers College Press.

Chapters on normal/abnormal motor development and on nutritional and health considerations as well as the appendix on adaptive equipment may be particularly helpful for parents. However, this book was written for professional use, and all terminology may not be familiar to parents.

Doyle, P., Goodman, J., Grotsky, J., & Mann, L. (1979). *Helping the severely handicapped child: A guide for parents and teachers*. New York: Thomas Y. Crowell.

This book provides basic information for parents of children with severe physical handicaps and mental retardation. The book is easy-to-read and covers topics such as positioning, feeding, dressing, toileting, adaptive equipment, financial planning, educational rights, and resources.

Finnie, N. H. (1975). *Handling the young cerebral palsied child at home*. New York: Dutton.

This book provides parents with suggestions for managing children with cerebral palsy. Suggestions for feeding, dressing, play, and movement are illustrated for children with various forms of cerebral palsy. Diagrams for making adaptive equipment are also included. Much of the information presented is also helpful to parents of children with handicaps other than cerebral palsy.

Fraser, B. A., Galka, G., & Hensinger, R. N. (1980). *Gross motor management of severely multiply impaired students* (Vols. I–II). Austin, TX: PRO-ED.

Both of these volumes are geared toward medical professionals but have excellent photographs and manufacturer information for many types of adaptive equipment and mobility aids. *Volume I: Evaluation Guide* describes a medical/therapeutic team approach to the evaluation of students with severe, multiple impairments. *Volume II: Curriculum Model* offers therapists a comprehensive, time-saving method of planning individualized gross motor programs for students with handicaps.

Fraser, B. A., & Hensinger, R. N. (1983). *Managing physical handicaps: A practical guide for parents, care providers, and educators.* Baltimore: Brookes.

This book is intended as a practical guide for people who are involved on a day-to-day basis with children and young adults having serious physical handicaps. The focus is on management of physical handicaps, particularly those experienced by students with physical impairments who attend special education programs (age range 3–20 years).

Freeman, R. D., Carbin, C. F., & Boese, R. J. (1981). *Can't your child hear?* Austin, TX: PRO-ED.

This practical guide for parents explores alternative approaches to communication for children with hearing impairments. The authors recommend a Total Communication approach. This book also answers common questions that parents ask about raising a child with hearing impairments.

Golbin, A. (Ed.). (1977). *Cerebral palsy and communication: What parents can do.* Washington, DC: Job Development Laboratory, Division of Rehabilitation Medicine, George Washington University. (Available from 2300 I Street N.W., Room 420, Washington, DC 20037.)

This easy-to-read book provides parents with complete explanations of the effects of cerebral palsy on speech, positioning for speech, feeding therapy, and breathing and speech. Furthermore, it discusses normal development, communication for the child with cerebral palsy and hearing impairment, and alternatives to speech (nonverbal communication).

Hanson, M. J. (1986). *Teaching the infant with Down syndrome.* Austin, TX: PRO-ED.

This clearly written guide for parents and professionals involved in teaching young infants with Down syndrome offers a comprehensive, concise, and optimistic

approach. It presents developmentally sequenced tasks and activities to help realize the child's maximum potential.

Jan, J. E., Ziegler, R. G., & Erba, G. (1983). *Does your child have epilepsy?* Austin, TX: PRO-ED.

This book offers comprehensive and practical information for parents on what they should know about their child's epilepsy. It emphasizes the psychological impact of epilepsy on the child and discusses basic facts that families often wish to know.

Levitt, S. (Ed.). (1984). *Paediatric developmental therapy.* Oxford: Blackwell Scientific Publications.

This book, edited by a British physical therapist, is directed at physical, occupational, and speech therapists in its approach. A breadth of practical suggestions and treatment strategies is included for children with cerebral palsy, spina bifida or myelomeningocele, muscular dystrophy, osteogenesis imperfecta, and severe multiple handicaps. Authors who have contributed chapters to this book include physical, occupational, and speech therapists as well as psychologists. This is a fairly basic text for students in any of the "therapies" who are interested in specializing in the treatment of children with developmental disabilities.

Morris, S. E. (1977). *Program guidelines for children with feeding problems.* Edison, NJ: Childcraft Education.

This manual provides guidelines for parents and teachers in the management of 11 specific feeding problems commonly found among young children with handicaps. Examples of the feeding problems include drooling, chewing problems, and behavior problems during feeding. The book offers a problem-oriented approach to uncovering the feeding problems and then deciding how best to manage them.

Scott, E. P., Jan, J. E., & Freeman, R. D. (1985). *Can't your child see?* (2nd ed.). Austin, TX: PRO-ED.

This book offers parents optimistic, practical guidelines for raising young children with visual impairments. It deals with the impact that a severe visual impairment can have on child development and gives suggestions in an easy-to-read style for helping children achieve their full potential.

Schleichkorn, J. (1983). *Coping with cerebral palsy.* Austin, TX: PRO-ED.

This book provides parents with answers to more than 200 questions often asked about cerebral palsy. Discussion is presented in a highly readable, jargon-free manner.

Sontag, E., Smith, J., & Certo, N. (1977). *Educational programming for the severely and profoundly handicapped.* Reston, VA: Council for Exceptional Children.

This book is basically a text for teachers. However, several chapters on adaptive equipment, early childhood programming, and self-care training make the book a valuable resource for parents as well as professionals.

# Child Development Resources

## Readings in Child Development

Brazelton, T. B. (1969). *Infants and mothers*. New York: Dell.

This easy-to-read book explores the differences in development among babies. The development of three normal babies (an active baby, a quiet baby, and an average baby) from birth to 12 months is described.

Caplan, F. (1973). *The first twelve months of life*. New York: Grosset & Dunlap.

Caplan, F., & Caplan, F. (1977). *The second twelve months of life*. New York: Grosset & Dunlap.

These books provide a month-by-month account of a typical baby's development. Monthly growth charts and many photographs are included.

Fraiberg, S. H. (1959). *The magic years*. New York: Charles Scribner's Sons.

This book discusses typical problems that occur at each stage of development over the first 5 years of age.

Leach, P. (1983). *Babyhood* (2nd ed.). New York: Alfred A. Knopf.

How the baby develops—physically, emotionally, mentally—from birth to 2 years is described in this comprehensive book that summarizes research material used by professional experts.

Leach, P. (1977). *Your baby and child from birth to age five*. New York: Alfred A. Knopf.

This book is a comprehensive guide to child care and development from birth to 5 years. It addresses issues of feeding, dressing, eliminating, teething, sleeping, and bathing. It also describes early development.

McCall, R. B. (1979). *Infants*. New York: Vintage.

This little paperback book summarizes much of the research on infant development with particular emphasis on mental, language, and emotional development.

## Readings in Behavior Management

Becker, W. C. (1971). *Parents are teachers*. Champaign, IL: Research Press.

Patterson, G. R. (1971). *Families*. Champaign, IL: Research Press.

Patterson, G. R. (1976). *Living with children*. Champaign, IL: Research Press.

These small paperbacks are all written for parents and provide easy-to-read descriptions of strategies for effectively teaching children and managing children's behavior. They include techniques for reducing unwanted behaviors (e.g., time-out) and techniques for increasing desirable behaviors.

Deibert, A. N., & Harmon, A. J. (1973). *New tools for changing behavior*. Champaign, IL: Research Press.

Krumboltz, J. D., & Krumboltz, H. B. (1972). *Changing children's behavior*. Englewood Cliffs, NJ: Prentice-Hall.

These paperbacks provide a comprehensive discussion of behavior management strategies.

## Program and Activity Guides for Parents

Burtt, K. G., & Kalkstein, K. (1981). *Smart toys for babies from birth to two*. New York: Harper Colophon.

This paperback describes easy-to-make toys that parents can use to teach their infants.

Cunningham, C., & Sloper, P. (1978). *Helping your exceptional baby*. New York: Pantheon.

This handbook presents a discussion of problems faced when parenting a child with disabilities. It provides a series of activities, exercises, and games that parents can use with their children.

Fewell, R. R., & Vadasy, P. F. (1983). *Learning through play*. Hingham, MA: Teaching Resources.

This resource manual for teachers and parents provides a discussion of early learning as well as activities to stimulate learning for the child from birth to 3 years.

Goldberg, S. (1981). *Teaching with toys*. Ann Arbor: University of Michigan Press.

This book gives ideas for providing infants and toddlers with an enriching home environment. It explains easy-to-make toys that are both fun to use and educational.

Gordon, I. J. (1970). *Baby learning through baby play: A parent's guide for the first two years*. New York: St. Martin's Press.

Gordon, I., Guinagh, B., & Jester, J. E. (1972). *Child learning through child play: Learning activities for two- and three-year-olds*. New York: St. Martin's Press.

Enjoyable play activities for parents and their infants are

described in these two inexpensive and easy-to-read paperback books.

Moyer, I. D. (1985). *Responding to infants*. Minneapolis, MN: T. S. Denison.

This manual lists activity ideas for parents or teachers to use in working with infants from 6 to 30 months. Suggestions for making certain toys and materials are provided.

Painter, G. (1971). *Teach your baby*. New York: Simon & Schuster.

This book provides descriptions of developmental activities, games, and materials parents can use in working with their young children.

Sparling, J., & Lewis, I. (1979). *Learningames for the first three years*. New York: Berkley.

One hundred illustrated adult-child games are presented in this easy-to-use paperback.

## Child Development Magazines, Newsletters and Play Materials

The Growing Child and The Growing Parent
Dunn & Hargitt, Inc.
22 North Second Street
Lafayette, Indiana 47902
(317) 423–2626

This monthly newsletter presents developmental tasks and recommends appropriate playthings for the child each month. *The Growing Parent* assists parents in coping with parenthood.

Infant Development Program
Johnson & Johnson
6 Commercial Street
Hicksville, New Jersey 11801

The program includes the *Infant Development Guidebook* and a series of play materials, all developed by a team of learning specialists, pediatricians, and child psychologists.

The Exceptional Parent
Psy-Ed Corporation
605 Commonwealth Avenue
Boston, Massachusetts 02115
(617) 482–0480

This magazine provides articles on topics of interest to parents of handicapped children, information about new developments in products and services, programs designed to help handicapped children, and articles written by parents of handicapped children. Many parents appreciate the wide range of advertisers in this magazine and the resource information on a variety of topics.

# Parent and Professional Resources

## Parent and Professional Organizations

Some of the organizations listed below have been established by parents, indicated by an asterisk (*), or for parents of children with different types of motor delay. These organizations frequently have local chapters that can be located by looking in your local phone directory, by asking your child's physician, or by inquiring at the hospital or center where your child receives services.

Other organizations listed below have largely been developed by professionals. However, many of these organizations provide services and information for parents of children with handicaps, encourage parent participation in local, state, and national meetings, and welcome parent participation in policy development and on advisory and other types of boards. Many have special membership rates for parents of children with handicaps.

American Academy for Cerebral Palsy and Developmental Medicine
2315 Westwood Avenue, P.O. Box 11083
Richmond, VA 23230
804–355–0147

A multidisciplinary scientific society founded in 1948 to foster professional education, research, and interest in the problems associated with cerebral palsy and other developmental disabilities. Provides free information to laypersons.

American Association on Mental Deficiency
5201 Connecticut Avenue N.W.
Washington, DC 20015
202–686–5400

Professional organization that sets standards for services, conducts public education, and provides information to professionals.

American Council of the Blind
1211 Connecticut Avenue N.W.
Washington, DC 20036

Organization primarily made up of blind persons. Provides educational services, consumer education services, financial and professional assistance in legal cases, and general information.

American Foundation for the Blind, Inc.
15 W. 16th Street
New York, NY 10011
212–924–0420

Carries on research; provides information and advice on improving services to blind persons.

American Occupational Therapy Association (AOTA)
1383 Piccard Drive
Rockville, MD 20850
301–948–9626

An organization of occupational therapists working with individuals of all ages who have various motor and psychiatric disabilities. However, the national office will respond to parent requests for basic information about the policy and practice of occupational therapy.

American Physical Therapy Association (APTA)
1111 N. Fairfax Street
Alexandria, VA 22314
703–684–2782

An organization of physical therapists who are involved with all aspects of physical restoration. The national office will respond to parent requests for basic information about the policy and practice of physical therapy.

American Speech, Hearing, and Language Association
   (ASHA)
10801 Rockville Pike
Rockville, MD 20852
301–897–5700

The professional organization for speech pathologists and audiologists. Like the associations representing physical and occupational therapists, this organization is made up of certified speech therapists and audiologists but will respond to parent requests for information about speech and hearing therapy.

*Association for Persons with Severe Handicaps
7010 Roosevelt Way N.E.
Seattle, WA 98115
206–523–8446

Publishes a newsletter that includes a column for parents written by parents of children with severe handicaps. Parents are encouraged to attend both local chapter and national meetings and are represented in all aspects of the organization. A limited number of publications are available.

*Council for Exceptional Children
1920 Association Drive
Reston, VA 22091
703–620–3660

Consists of a variety of professionals involved in educating children with learning exceptionalities. CEC is divided into many divisions, including divisions for early childhood education and for children with physical disabilities. The organization largely consists of professionals working with exceptional children but publishes many materials of interest to parents of children with motor delay. This group responds to requests for information and welcomes parents of handicapped children at local, state, and national meetings.

Dental Guidance Council for Cerebral Palsy
122 E. 23rd Street
New York, NY 10010
212–677–7400

Services include information on dentists who treat persons with handicaps.

*Down Syndrome Congress
1640 W. Roosevelt Road
Room 156-E
Chicago, IL 60608

Membership Committee
P.O. Box 1527
Brownwood, TX 76801
312–226–0416

Founded by parents of children with Down syndrome. Some local chapters have been organized in various parts of the country. The congress sponsors an annual national meeting and publishes a newsletter with information pertaining to children with Down syndrome.

Down Syndrome—Papers and Abstracts for Professionals
P.O. Box 620
2525 Belmont Road N.W.
Washington, DC 20008

Subscription:
10404 Leslie Court
Silver Springs, MD 20902

Publishes quarterly newsletters on Down syndrome for parents and professionals who are members. The purpose of the newsletter is to review and analyze recent professional literature pertaining to Down syndrome.

Epilepsy Foundation of America
1828 L Street N.W., Suite 405
Washington, DC 20036
202–293–2930

Sponsors a wide variety of programs and activities for people with epilepsy. Local chapters throughout the United States provide direct services as well as information.

Muscular Dystrophy Association
810 Seventh Avenue
New York, NY 10019
212–586–0808

Specifically centered around children and adults with muscular dystrophy and other neuromuscular disorders, this organization has local chapters that distribute equipment and sponsor free medical clinics for treatment of these disorders. Several publications are available from the national office.

*National Association for Retarded Citizens (NARC)
2501 Avenue J, P.O. Box 6109
Arlington, TX 76011
817–261–4961

Established originally by parents of handicapped children. This organizaton now has numerous local chapters, sponsors many educational and interdisciplinary programs for handicapped children (largely preschoolers and adults), and has a number of publications available for purchase. The focus of the organization is on children with developmental delay or disabilities. Parents are welcome participants on both the local and national level.

National Association of the Deaf
814 Thayer Avenue
Silver Springs, MD 20910

An organization of deaf individuals. Most of the information on research, communication, legislation, education, and rehabilitation is free.

National Association of the Physically Handicapped
76 Elm Street
London, OH 43140
614–852–1664

An association dedicated to doing all things necessary to improve the social, economic, and physical welfare of physically handicapped persons. Supports legislation and provides programs not readily available elsewhere.

*National Easter Seal Society for Crippled Children and
    Adults
2023 West Ogden Avenue
Chicago, IL 60612
312–243–8400

This organization has many local chapters that sponsor infant, toddler, and preschool programs for children with motor delay or handicaps. In addition, many useful publications are available from the national office.

National Foundation–March of Dimes
1275 Mamaroneck Avenue
White Plains, NY 10605
914–428–7100

Emphasis on treatment of children with birth defects. This organization spends most of its funds on research to prevent various types of birth defects. Distributes publications which explain congenital problems.

*Spina Bifida Association of America
343 South Dearborn, Room 317
Chicago, IL 60604
312–662–1562

Founded by parents. The many local chapters across the country frequently have their own names (such as ''Myelomeningocele Mothers''); contact the national organization for the names of affiliated organizations located in your area. The association sponsors an annual meeting and has regular newsletters as well as many publications of interest to parents of children with spina bifida/myelomeningocele.

*United Cerebral Palsy Associations, Inc. (UCPA)
66 East 34th Street
New York, NY 10016
212–481–6300

Sponsors an annual national meeting, supports research to prevent cerebral palsy and to study the cause of this motor problem, and supports activities of local and state affiliates. Many local UCP organizations provide services for young handicapped children and for adults, as well as sponsor training courses for parents of cerebral palsied and developmentally delayed children. Information about cerebral palsy can be obtained both from the national and local organizations.

## Advocacy Groups, Services and Agencies

American Association of University-Affiliated Programs
8605 Cameron Street
Silver Springs, MD 20910
301–588–8252

An association comprised of approximately 50 university-affiliated training facilities whose goal is to train professionals in the evaluation and management of children with handicaps.

Children's Defense Fund
1520 North Hampshire Avenue N.W.
Washington, DC 20036
202–483–1470

Publishes a regular newsletter concerning issues/rights of children. Several pamphlets are available for parents explaining federal legislation and providing names and addresses for state and local assistance. This group lobbies for legislation to benefit handicapped children and maintains a staff to refer parents with questions to appropriate resources.

*Closer Look*
National Information Center for the Handicapped
Box 1492
Washington, DC 20013

A regular newsletter that describes programming and other services available for children with handicaps. In addition, parents can obtain sources of local assistance and direction in obtaining services from this group. Write and ask to be placed on the mailing list.

Handicapped Children's Early Education Program
(HCEEP)
Office of Special Education (OSE)
Donohue Bldg., Room 3117
400 Maryland Avenue S.W.
Washington, DC 20202

A program maintained by the federal government to provide funds for development of programs to serve infants and preschoolers with handicaps. Funds are competitively awarded to agencies, schools, and universities that submit proposals describing innovative programming for young children with handicaps. Parents can obtain a list of all HCEEP projects and can secure information by writing to projects directly or visiting one of the programs. Many projects have developed materials for parents that are available at limited or no charge. In addition, OSE will provide parents with information about services, early childhood programs, and state agencies that might offer services for their children.

National Center for Law and the Handicapped
P.O. Box 477

University of Notre Dame
Notre Dame, IN 46556
219–283–4536

Publishes a newsletter on legal issues and interpretation of national laws relating to the care, education, and training of individuals with a variety of handicapping conditions. Contacting this organization can be helpful when parents need assistance in obtaining legal representation or require specific information about the variety of laws pertaining to the rights of persons with handicaps.

National Institute of Child Health and Human
Development
National Institutes of Health
Public Health Service
Department of Health and Human Services
Bethesda, MD 20014
301–496–5133

One of the National Institutes of Health. NICHHD supports research and training relating to maternal and child health, provides information, and refers individuals to other agencies when needed.

National Institute of Handicapped Research (NIHR)
Office of Special Education and Rehabilitative Services
U.S. Department of Education
Washington, DC 20202
202–732–1134

Created in 1978 by Public Law 95–602, the Rehabilitation, Comprehensive Services, and Developmental Disabilities Amendments of the 1973 Rehabilitation Act. NIHR provides leadership and support for a national and international program of comprehensive and coordinated research regarding the rehabilitation of individuals with handicaps. Another goal is the dissemination of information concerning developments in rehabilitation procedures and methods and devices which can improve the lives of persons with disabilities.

Office of Human Development Services
Department of Health and Human Services
309F Hubert H. Humphrey Building
200 Independence Avenue S.W.
Washington, DC 20201
202–245–7246

Administers a variety of programs for which individuals with handicaps may be eligible. These include Head Start, Social Security, and Medicaid. The Administration on Developmental Disabilities is also part of this office, as is the Child Health Bureau. Listings of local resources, qualification guidelines, and other information related to the treatment of children with handicaps are provided by this office.

President's Committee on Mental Retardation
Regional Office Building (ROB) 3
7th and D Streets S.W.
Washington, DC 20201
202–245–7520

Includes representatives from throughout the country who have recognized expertise in the field of handicapping conditions and particularly in mental retardation. The committee makes recommendations for development of programs to serve persons with handicaps. Reports and other information are regularly published.

# *Baby's Record*

Baby's First
Photograph
here

# Birth and Growth Record

Baby's Name _____

Date of Birth _____

Place of Birth _____

Hospital _____

Doctors' _____
Names _____

Color of Hair _____

Color of Eyes _____

| | Weight | Height |
|---|---|---|
| Birth | _____ | _____ |
| 1 month | _____ | _____ |
| 2 months | _____ | _____ |
| 3 months | _____ | _____ |
| 4 months | _____ | _____ |
| 5 months | _____ | _____ |
| 6 months | _____ | _____ |
| 12 months | _____ | _____ |
| 18 months | _____ | _____ |
| 24 months | _____ | _____ |

# Medical Record

**Immunizations**

Diphtheria (DPT)
    Series _____
Whooping Cough (DPT)
    Series _____
Tetanus (DPT)
    Series _____
Polio
    Series _____
    Series _____
    Series _____

**Date**

Booster _____

Booster _____

Booster _____

Booster _____

**Date**

Mumps _____
Measles _____
Rubella _____
Smallpox _____
Others: _____
    _____

**Tests:**
    Tuberculin: _____
    Others: _____
    _____

# Record of Illnesses

| Description | Date | Doctor | Treatment |
|---|---|---|---|
| | | | |
| | | | |
| | | | |
| | | | |
| | | | |
| | | | |
| | | | |
| | | | |
| | | | |
| | | | |
| | | | |

# Dental Record

## Months

| | Midpoint | Range |
|---|---|---|
| Central Incisors | 9.6 | 6–12 |
| Lateral Incisors | 12.4 | 7–18 |
| Cuspids | 18.3 | 11–24 |
| First Molar | 15.7 | 10–20 |
| Second Molar | 26.2 | 13–31 |
| | | |
| Second Molar | 26 | 13–31 |
| First Molar | 15.1 | 10–20 |
| Cuspids | 18.2 | 11–24 |
| Lateral Incisors | 7.8 | 7–15 |
| Central Incisors | 11.5 | 5–11 |

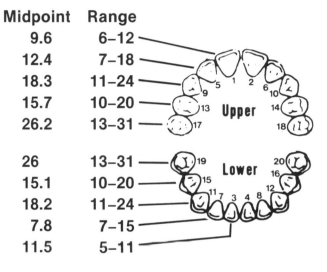

**Upper**       Date

| | | | |
|---|---|---|---|
| Central Incisor | 1 _____ | 2 _____ |
| Lateral Incisor | 5 _____ | 6 _____ |
| Cuspid | 9 _____ | 10 _____ |
| First Molar | 13 _____ | 14 _____ |
| Second Molar | 17 _____ | 18 _____ |

**Lower**

| | | | |
|---|---|---|---|
| Central Incisor | 3 _____ | 4 _____ |
| Lateral Incisor | 7 _____ | 8 _____ |
| Cuspid | 11 _____ | 12 _____ |
| First Molar | 15 _____ | 16 _____ |
| Second Molar | 19 _____ | 20 _____ |

# Baby's Favorites

**Toys:** _____

_____

_____

_____

**Foods:** _____

_____

_____

_____

**Activities and games:** _____

_____

_____

_____

**Stories and songs:** _____

_____

_____

_____

**People and playmates:** _____

_____

_____

_____

**Pets:** _____

_____

_____

_____

**Other:** _____

_____

_____

_____

On the following pages record the date on which your child achieves the particular developmental milestone listed. These milestones correspond with the graphs in Appendix 1.

# Developmental Milestones

## Gross Motor

### Head Control                                          Date
Side-to-side head movements ....................... _____
Holds head steady when carried .................... _____
Lifts head 45°, lying on stomach................... _____
Lifts head 90°, lying on stomach................... _____
Raises and turns head, lying on stomach ............ _____
Pulls to sit, no head lag........................... _____

### Sitting
Sits with support ................................. _____
Sits supported, head steady........................ _____
Sits with minimum support......................... _____
Sits in babychair ................................. _____
Sits self-supported by arms and hands ............. _____
Sits, no support .................................. _____
Reaches, sitting self-supported .................... _____
Raises self to sitting from back.................... _____
Raises self to sitting from stomach ................ _____
Sits, turns to crawl............................... _____
Seats self in small chair .......................... _____
Climbs into adult chair ........................... _____

### Rolling
Turns from side to back ........................... _____
Turns from back to side ........................... _____
Rolls, stomach to back ............................ _____
Rolls, back to stomach ............................ _____

### Crawling
Arm and leg kicking movements .................... _____
Crawling movements............................... _____
Chest up, arm support, legs resting on floor ........ _____
Reaches from crawl position ....................... _____
Crawls (stomach down)............................ _____
Crawls (stomach up) .............................. _____
Creeps up and down stairs......................... _____

## Standing
Bears own weight . . . . . . . . . . . . . . . . . . . . . . . . . . . . . . . . . . . . . . . . _____
Stands with minimum support . . . . . . . . . . . . . . . . . . . . . . . . . . . _____
Stands at furniture . . . . . . . . . . . . . . . . . . . . . . . . . . . . . . . . . . . . . . _____
Pulls to stand . . . . . . . . . . . . . . . . . . . . . . . . . . . . . . . . . . . . . . . . . . . _____
Lowers self from standing to sit . . . . . . . . . . . . . . . . . . . . . . . _____
Stands, no support . . . . . . . . . . . . . . . . . . . . . . . . . . . . . . . . . . . . . . _____
Gets to standing . . . . . . . . . . . . . . . . . . . . . . . . . . . . . . . . . . . . . . . . _____
Stoops and recovers . . . . . . . . . . . . . . . . . . . . . . . . . . . . . . . . . . . _____
Stands on one foot with help . . . . . . . . . . . . . . . . . . . . . . . . . . . _____
Stands on one foot alone . . . . . . . . . . . . . . . . . . . . . . . . . . . . . . . _____

## Walking
Beginning stepping activities when held at chest . . . . . . . . _____
Cruises (walks holding onto furniture) . . . . . . . . . . . . . . . . . _____
Walks with support . . . . . . . . . . . . . . . . . . . . . . . . . . . . . . . . . . . . . _____
Walks when led by one hand . . . . . . . . . . . . . . . . . . . . . . . . . . . _____
Walks alone, no support . . . . . . . . . . . . . . . . . . . . . . . . . . . . . . . . _____
Walks sideways . . . . . . . . . . . . . . . . . . . . . . . . . . . . . . . . . . . . . . . . _____
Walks backwards . . . . . . . . . . . . . . . . . . . . . . . . . . . . . . . . . . . . . . _____
Walks up and down stairs with hand held . . . . . . . . . . . . . . _____
Walks up and down stairs, holding one rail . . . . . . . . . . . . . _____
Walks fast, runs stiffly . . . . . . . . . . . . . . . . . . . . . . . . . . . . . . . . . _____
Walks on line . . . . . . . . . . . . . . . . . . . . . . . . . . . . . . . . . . . . . . . . . . _____
Runs . . . . . . . . . . . . . . . . . . . . . . . . . . . . . . . . . . . . . . . . . . . . . . . . . . _____

## Kicking and Jumping
Walks into large ball — kicking . . . . . . . . . . . . . . . . . . . . . . . . . _____
Kicks large all with demonstration . . . . . . . . . . . . . . . . . . . . . _____
Kicks large ball on command . . . . . . . . . . . . . . . . . . . . . . . . . . _____
Jumps in place . . . . . . . . . . . . . . . . . . . . . . . . . . . . . . . . . . . . . . . . _____
Jumps from bottom step . . . . . . . . . . . . . . . . . . . . . . . . . . . . . . . _____

## Throwing
Hurls ball (from sitting) . . . . . . . . . . . . . . . . . . . . . . . . . . . . . . . . _____
Throws ball overhand (from standing) . . . . . . . . . . . . . . . . . . _____

## Fine Motor

### Visual                                                    Date
Eye muscle control ........................................ _____
Vertical, horizontal, and circular eye coordination ........ _____
Visually follows, 90° angle ............................... _____
Visually follows, 180° angle .............................. _____

### Reaching
Reaches but misses........................................ _____
Reaches for object ....................................... _____
Reaches for second object ................................ _____
Goes after toys out of reach ............................. _____

### Grasping
Grasps rattle ............................................ _____
Hands open .............................................. _____
Grasps cube ............................................. _____
Full-handed grasp ....................................... _____
Scoops pellet ........................................... _____
Thumb-finger grasp ...................................... _____
Pincer grasp ............................................ _____

### Object Manipulation (cubes, small objects, scribbling)
Glances from one object to another ...................... _____
Brings hands together .................................... _____
Looks at small object .................................... _____
Explores object with hands ............................... _____
Picks up small object .................................... _____
Holds two objects ....................................... _____
Transfers object hand-to-hand ........................... _____
Picks up two objects .................................... _____
Bangs two cubes held in hands........................... _____
Removes object from cup ................................. _____
Puts object in cup ...................................... _____
Puts cubes in cup ....................................... _____
Tower of two cubes ...................................... _____
Tower of 3–4 cubes ...................................... _____
Tower of 5–7 cubes ...................................... _____
Places ring on peg ...................................... _____
Pushes toy car .......................................... _____
Dangles object .......................................... _____
Scribbles ............................................... _____
Imitates scribble stroke.................................. _____
Imitates vertical and horizontal stroke ................... _____

## Object Manipulation (puzzles, pegs and pellets, pages in books)

Removes round block from puzzle...................... _____

Places round puzzle block ........................... _____

Places two round puzzle blocks....................... _____

Places two round and square puzzle blocks ............ _____

Removes peg from pegboard .......................... _____

Places a peg ...................................... _____

Places beads in container .......................... _____

Removes pellet from container ....................... _____

Places pellet in container .......................... _____

Helps turn pages in book ........................... _____

Turns pages, 2–3 at once .......................... _____

Turns pages singly................................. _____

## Problem-Solving

Lifts inverted cup ................................. _____

Pulls string to get ring............................. _____

Looks for fallen object ............................. _____

Finds hidden object ................................ _____

Uncovers toy ..................................... _____

Looks for contents of box........................... _____

Unwraps object.................................... _____

Lifts lid off box .................................. _____

Gets toy using stick................................ _____

## Communication/Speech and Language

### Early Auditory                                          Date
Responds to sound .................................. _____
Turns toward sound .................................. _____

### Expressive Language
Cries due to a cause ................................ _____
Vocalizes, babbles, coos............................ _____
Squeals ............................................. _____
Laughs .............................................. _____
Two-syllable vowel sounds .......................... _____
Says *da, ka, ga, ba*, etc. ......................... _____
Says *Dada, Mama* .................................. _____
Expresses wants without crying ..................... _____
Repeats sounds made by others ..................... _____
Says three words .................................... _____
Expresses wants by gesture......................... _____
Says 4–6 words...................................... _____
Says ten words ...................................... _____
Names one object .................................... _____
Uses words to make wants known ................... _____
Names one picture................................... _____
Says 20+ words ...................................... _____
Combines 2–3 words ................................. _____

### Receptive Language
Responds to own name............................... _____
Waves bye-bye ...................................... _____
Copies simple actions ............................... _____
Stops on command "no" most of time ................ _____
Looks at person speaking and/or item ............... _____
Looks toward family members ....................... _____
Points to named picture ............................. _____
Shows clothing or toy ............................... _____
Follows simple directions............................ _____
Points to named body part .......................... _____
Follows directions with doll ......................... _____
Points to parts of doll .............................. _____
Finds two objects.................................... _____
Points to five pictures .............................. _____
Chooses objects named (two of three) ............... _____

## Social and Self-Help

### Social — Self/Others                                           Date
Responds to another person . . . . . . . . . . . . . . . . . . . . . . . . . . . _____
Smiles responsively . . . . . . . . . . . . . . . . . . . . . . . . . . . . . . . . . . . _____
Vocalizes when attended . . . . . . . . . . . . . . . . . . . . . . . . . . . . . . _____
Anticipatory excitement . . . . . . . . . . . . . . . . . . . . . . . . . . . . . . . _____
Reaches for familiar person . . . . . . . . . . . . . . . . . . . . . . . . . . . _____
Smiles at mirror image . . . . . . . . . . . . . . . . . . . . . . . . . . . . . . . . _____
Playful response to mirror . . . . . . . . . . . . . . . . . . . . . . . . . . . . . _____
Responds to own name . . . . . . . . . . . . . . . . . . . . . . . . . . . . . . . . _____
Independent play 10–20 minutes . . . . . . . . . . . . . . . . . . . . . . _____
Plays peek-a-boo . . . . . . . . . . . . . . . . . . . . . . . . . . . . . . . . . . . . . _____
Acts to gain attention . . . . . . . . . . . . . . . . . . . . . . . . . . . . . . . . . _____
Plays pat-a-cake . . . . . . . . . . . . . . . . . . . . . . . . . . . . . . . . . . . . . _____
Plays with another child . . . . . . . . . . . . . . . . . . . . . . . . . . . . . . . _____
Plays ball . . . . . . . . . . . . . . . . . . . . . . . . . . . . . . . . . . . . . . . . . . . _____
Copies household activities . . . . . . . . . . . . . . . . . . . . . . . . . . . _____
Shows or offers toy . . . . . . . . . . . . . . . . . . . . . . . . . . . . . . . . . . . _____
Pulls toy . . . . . . . . . . . . . . . . . . . . . . . . . . . . . . . . . . . . . . . . . . . . _____
Parallel play . . . . . . . . . . . . . . . . . . . . . . . . . . . . . . . . . . . . . . . . _____

### Feeding
Sucks from bottle/breast . . . . . . . . . . . . . . . . . . . . . . . . . . . . . . _____
Recognizes and reaches for bottle/breast . . . . . . . . . . . . . . _____
Feeds self with fingers . . . . . . . . . . . . . . . . . . . . . . . . . . . . . . . _____
Eats mashed food fed by parents . . . . . . . . . . . . . . . . . . . . . _____
Drinks from cup being held . . . . . . . . . . . . . . . . . . . . . . . . . . . _____
Holds bottle without help . . . . . . . . . . . . . . . . . . . . . . . . . . . . . _____
Holds cup using two hands . . . . . . . . . . . . . . . . . . . . . . . . . . . _____
Holds cup using one hand . . . . . . . . . . . . . . . . . . . . . . . . . . . . _____
Begins to use spoon . . . . . . . . . . . . . . . . . . . . . . . . . . . . . . . . . _____
Feeds self with spoon . . . . . . . . . . . . . . . . . . . . . . . . . . . . . . . . _____
Drinks from cup without spilling . . . . . . . . . . . . . . . . . . . . . . . _____
Holds small glass in one hand . . . . . . . . . . . . . . . . . . . . . . . . _____

### Dressing and Toileting
Cooperates in dressing . . . . . . . . . . . . . . . . . . . . . . . . . . . . . . _____
Removes simple garments . . . . . . . . . . . . . . . . . . . . . . . . . . . _____
Zips and unzips . . . . . . . . . . . . . . . . . . . . . . . . . . . . . . . . . . . . . _____
Pulls on simple garment . . . . . . . . . . . . . . . . . . . . . . . . . . . . . _____
Washes and dries hands with help . . . . . . . . . . . . . . . . . . . . _____
Toilets . . . . . . . . . . . . . . . . . . . . . . . . . . . . . . . . . . . . . . . . . . . . . _____

# Notes

# Notes

# Notes

## About the Author

Dr. Marci Hanson is professor of Early Childhood Special Education at San Francisco State University, where she coordinates the master's and doctoral degree training programs. She is also program director of an early intervention program that serves families and children with disabilities from birth to three years of age. Dr. Hanson is involved actively in research and service activities for young children with special needs and their families.

Dr. Susan Harris is associate professor and program coordinator of physical therapy educational programs at the University of Wisconsin at Madison. Formerly, she was physical therapy department head at the Clinical Training Unit of the Child Development and Mental Retardation Center at the University of Washington. Dr. Harris is an active researcher, clinician, and consultant for high risk infants and young children with motor delays.